"Fascinating and beautifully written. . . . Rea[...] [...] to learn that early twentieth-century African-American leaders such as Booker T. Washington lobbied the U.S. government to send African American soldiers to Liberia to orchestrate the conquest of indigenous communities."

—TIM STAPLETON, professor of history at the University of Calgary and author of *A Military History of Africa*

"An important book for anyone working in security sector reform in Liberia or elsewhere."

—COL. SUE ANN SANDUSKY, U.S. Army (Ret.) and former U.S. Defense attaché to Liberia, Democratic Republic of Congo, Côte d'Ivoire, and Nigeria

"The author chronicles America's shifting foreign policy and Americo-Liberian intransigence in maintaining its dominion over native tribes through the military support of the U.S. In the process he recounts tribal rebellion, the slave trade, the involvement of the struggling country in World Wars I and II, the rise of corporate power, civil war, and Liberia's rebirth as a true democracy."

—FLOYD R. THOMAS JR., curator emeritus of the National Afro-American Museum and Cultural Center

"A brilliant, comprehensive historical analysis of African American military officers and the impact of their roles in Liberia amid the complex, multidimensional U.S./Liberia relationship."

—RENOTTA L. YOUNG, Charles Young family member

"A seminal contribution to military history, presenting the exemplary qualities of leadership, professionalism, and resilience that have relevance today. This book is worth reading by historians and history buffs alike."

—FOMBAH SIRLEAF, director of Liberia National Security Agency

AFRICAN AMERICAN OFFICERS IN LIBERIA

AFRICAN AMERICAN OFFICERS IN LIBERIA

A Pestiferous Rotation, 1910–1942

BRIAN G. SHELLUM

Potomac Books

An imprint of the University of Nebraska Press

For my mother
Harriet V. (Hedner) Shellum
1919–2014
An army officer's wife

Contents

Illustrations

Preface

African American Officers in Liberia tells the story of the first American military training mission undertaken in Africa. Between 1910 and 1942, seventeen African American officers trained, reorganized, and commanded the Liberian Frontier Force to defend Liberia. Few know about this American military operation in Liberia, an early example of the security force assistance undertaken regularly in Africa today known as Train, Advise, Assist, and Equip. This stability mission in Liberia was a unique component of American dollar diplomacy and enabled the minority Americo-Liberian regime to survive a perilous period in its history.

I focus on the African American officers themselves, so do not expect a comprehensive history of Liberia nor a complete survey of diplomatic relations between the United States and Liberia. I include some Liberian history and review portions of the diplomatic dealings between Monrovia and Washington DC, but only to set the context of the U.S. military involvement there in the first half of the twentieth century.

Liberia, a sovereign nation since 1847, is an anomaly when compared to other African countries. While the rest share a history of occupation and exploitation by white foreign powers, only Liberia was settled by blacks. Liberia's colonial era began in the early nineteenth century with the arrival of former American slaves sent by the American Colonial Society. It continued into the early twentieth century to be settled by free African Americans seeking a better life. Absent this connection, there would have been no U.S. involvement in Liberia.

From the beginning, the colonizing newcomers, who called themselves Americo-Liberians, discriminated against the much larger indigenous African population. Tension between settlers and locals created social unrest and conflict. From the landing of the first colonists in Monrovia in 1820, the U.S. Navy protected the immigrants against attacks by local ethnic groups. Hostilities between the Americo-Liberians and the indigenous people continued into the early twentieth century, presenting challenges to the African American officers serving in Liberia.

The main existential threat to Liberia came from the white colonial powers that hemmed the country on three sides. From the founding of the republic in 1847 to the first decade of the twentieth century, Liberia lost nearly half of its original territory to England and France. During the European "Scramble for Africa" starting in the 1880s, Liberia came under increasing pressure from these countries to protect its territory but lacked the resources and troops to adequately secure its borders. If not for the intervention of the United States in the first decade of the twentieth century, Liberia would have been partitioned by its colonial neighbors.

What was it like for African American officers to fight for the survival of Liberia in the early years of the twentieth century? That was precisely the mission of Benjamin O. Davis, Charles Young, John E. Green, and fourteen other African American officers who trained and commanded the Liberian Frontier Force from 1910 to 1942. These black American officers signed on to a complex and risky enterprise financed by Washington yet directed by the Liberian government. Essentially, the United States extended its newfound imperial reach and dollar diplomacy to cover Liberia, defending an Americo-Liberian colonial government against encroachment and partition by Britain and France. At the same time, the Americo-Liberian minority who ruled in Monrovia employed the African American officers to subjugate the indigenous people living in the hinterland, the word generally used by Americo-Liberians for the tribal areas inland from the coastal settlements.

These African American officers carried out this challenging mission for an American government that did not treat them as equal citizens at home. In the first decades of the twentieth century, the United States was a place where southern blacks were systematically disenfranchised by Jim Crow laws and frequently lynched by the Ku Klux Klan. Even in a U.S. Army offering opportunities to black soldiers and noncommissioned officers, institutional racism persisted and a clear color line prevailed. These former U.S. Army servicemen performed their duties as instruments of imperialism for a country ambivalent about having them serve under arms at home.

Learning about the officers who advised and led the Liberian Frontier Force in West Africa is a challenge for historians because there is scant record of their reports in the State and War Department files at the National Archives. It is more difficult to uncover details of what they thought of their mission and of how the Americo-Liberians and the indigenous groups perceived them. Aside from Charles Young, most of the officers never wrote detailed accounts of their lives and experiences in Liberia, so we are left with only general comments from letters and reports. Nevertheless, this book examines the lives, experiences, and frustrations of these African American officers and measures their success.

My narrative includes acts of violence perpetrated against the indigenous inhabitants of Liberia during this period, mainly by Americo-Liberians. I have attempted to describe these events as accurately as I can; the reader should not mistake my attitude as casual or inflammatory. A historian is charged with recounting the objective facts and making an impartial analysis. Moreover, blacks in the United States lived their daily lives amid terrible brutalities during this era. The NAACP reported that nearly one hundred blacks were lynched in 1917 and 1918. In 1917, while Lieutenant Colonel Charles Young was leading the black troopers of the Ninth Cavalry in the pursuit of Pancho Villa in Mexico, he collected money from his men to send to the NAACP's antilynching fund.

The African American officers served in Liberia amid primitive living conditions, widespread diseases, and lack of adequate medical care. I coined the phrase *pestiferous rotation*, which a reader later recommended I use in the title, to reflect the pestilential training cycle to which these soldiers exposed themselves by volunteering for the mission. Their sacrifice cannot be understated.

The primary audience for this book is the reader interested in the service of African American soldiers in the first decades of the twentieth century. Much has been written about the Buffalo Soldiers in the post–Civil War era who played a prominent role in the Indian Wars in the West and the Spanish-American War at the turn of the century. Much less is known about the service of black regular soldiers and volunteers in the first quarter of the twentieth century. Almost nothing has been written about their important role in preserving the independence of Liberia.

Other audiences for this story are historians and academics engaged in the study of the U.S. Army in the early twentieth century. Benjamin Davis, John Green, and Charles Young served in a Regular Army that was making the transition from a western frontier force to a modern military. The black regular regiments comprised approximately 10 percent of the line strength of the army at the turn of the century. Young and his fellow officers were key figures in this transitional period, and their experiences contributed to the transformation of what historian Edward C. Coffman called the "Old Army."

Policy historians will be interested in details of this chronicle because the U.S. State Department played such a preeminent role in Liberia. Beside Haiti, Liberia was the only place where black officials served as U.S. consul generals and heads of missions. In Monrovia the consul general, vice consul general, and staff were almost all African American, as were the assigned military attachés. Therefore, black American officials formulated and implemented U.S. policy in Monrovia, which was quite extraordinary for the time.

Scholars, teachers, and students of African American and African history will be especially interested in these important black military trailblazers. Very little is known about Davis, Green, and Young beyond the basic outline of their lives and military records. Even less is known about the former enlisted soldiers and volunteer officers who led and fought with the Liberian Frontier Force. This is the first detailed account of their experiences.

Beyond a doctoral dissertation and a handful of scholarly articles, no book has been written solely on the military experiences of the African American officers who led and advised the Liberian Frontier Force from 1910 to 1942. My second book on Charles Young, *Black Officer in a Buffalo Soldier Regiment: The Military Career of Charles Young*, published in 2010 by the University of Nebraska Press, discusses his experiences in Liberia briefly in two chapters. David Kilroy's book *For Race and Country: The Life and Career of Charles Young*, released by Praeger in 2003, covers Young's Liberian military service in little detail. Marvin Fletcher's *America's First Black General: Benjamin O. Davis, Sr., 1880–1970*, published by the University Press of Kansas in 1989, devotes a small portion of a single chapter to Davis's tour in Liberia.

Timothy Rainey's "Buffalo Soldiers in Africa: The Liberian Frontier Force and the United States Army, 1912–1927," a doctoral dissertation submitted to Johns Hopkins University in 2001, is the best single source for information on the topic to date. Though Rainey does an excellent job of framing the narrative, one hundred pages does not offer adequate space for the detail this story deserves, and the paper is available to a limited audience. Further, Rainey did not have access to the papers of Charles Young at Wilberforce, a rich source of information on the subject.

When I mention the story of black American officers in Liberia in circles of well-informed military historians, even those who specialize in African American history, I get quizzical looks followed by astonished interest. Other people with no expertise in history are surprised and want to hear more. *African American Officers in Liberia* responds to that need.

Acknowledgments

I owe a great deal of gratitude to my wife, Paula, for offering me the time and encouragement to complete this book. She has ever been my chief advocate and supporter along the way. I am also grateful to my daughter, Kara, and son, Greg, who cheered me on from a distance.

In addition to the National Archives and Records Administration (NARA), one other institution provided the majority of the research materials for this book. Floyd Thomas, Chuck Wash, and the National Afro-American Museum and Cultural Center (NAAMCC) in Wilberforce, Ohio, have been my chief sources of original research materials and advice. Floyd Thomas was the first person I contacted when I began my research on Charles Young in 1996, and I have been back to consult with him many times since. Chuck Wash, the current director of the NAAMCC, has made great strides in making the materials at the center accessible and has always made me feel welcome. The NAAMCC possesses the most important original source documents, letters, and photos from the U.S. military effort in Liberia between 1910 and 1942. Much of this material came into the possession of Jill and Malina Coleman in the 1970s when Young's household items went to auction before the sale of his house in Wilberforce, Ohio. I spent countless hours at Jill and Malina's house copying and scanning Young's letters and documents and later convinced them to donate the bulk of the collection to the NAAMCC.

I was fortunate to have a group of dedicated readers who worked over my various drafts. Tom Phillips, coauthor of *The Black Regulars: 1866–1898*, spent more time than any other of my readers and reviewed each chapter of my first draft to offer detailed comments and suggestions. He also picked out a line in my fourth chapter about John Green and convinced me to use it in the title. I have already mentioned Floyd Thomas, who reviewed all my drafts and gave me wonderful suggestions and endless encouragement along the way. My sister, Rolynn Anderson, spent countless hours over the years reviewing the drafts of my books and offering advice. As a former English teacher she also recommended ways to improve my structure and organization. Laura Harrington, a cultural anthropologist, reviewed my introductory chapter on Liberia. Marvin Fletcher, author of *America's First Black General: Benjamin O. Davis, Sr., 1880–1970*, reviewed my chapter on Davis. Martha Hoverson, who has written about Buffalo Soldiers in Hawaii, reviewed my chapter on Young's first tour in Liberia. Mark Benbow, former resident historian at the Woodrow Wilson House, reviewed the same chapter with respect to policy changes by the Wilson administration. Anthony Powell, a historian and owner of Portraits in Black, reviewed my chapter on John E. Green in Liberia. Mary Williams, a historian retired from Fort Davis National Park, reviewed my chapter on Charles Young's second tour in Liberia.

In the peer review process undertaken by the University of Nebraska Press, four readers who specialize in African American history worked over my drafts and provided me with important and insightful comments. The final product is a much better book because of their time and effort. I thank them all for their contributions and fine work. Col. Sue Ann Sandusky, U.S. Army, retired, a former defense attaché who served in Monrovia recently, also reviewed the entire final draft and gave me some outstanding comments. Finally, I thank a group of Liberians who reviewed my draft in its final stages: Fombah Sirleaf, H. Boima Fahnbulleh Jr., Edward Sharpe, and Col. Prince C. Johnson III.

In addition to those already mentioned, I would like to thank the following organizations for their support: the Charles Young Buffalo Soldiers National Monument, Ninth and Tenth (Horse) Cavalry Association, West Point Association of Graduates, West Point Library Special Collections, Ohio Historical Connection, Ripley Museum, John Parker House, Kentucky Gateway Museum, and Nebraska State Historical Society. Other individuals who assisted and encouraged me along the way include Dean Alexander, Paul Berg, Brandon Billips, John Birzneiks, Charles Blatcher III, Tom Buecker, Ed Colchado, Peter Cozzens, Roger Cunningham, Clarence Davenport, Cheryl Dawson, Ward Eldridge, Joe Fitzharris, Buddy Gallenstein, Alison Gibson, Jerry Gore, John W. Green, Karen Green, Bill Gwaltney, Greg Haitz, Bob Hendrikson, Shelton Johnson, Joy Kinard, Axel Krigsman, Justine Lai, Burt Logan, Bill McCurtis, Bennie McRae Jr., John Morlock, John Motley, George Palmer, Robert Parker, Rik Penn, Marcus Pearl, Jim Potter, Tim Rainey, Jim Rawlings, Ed Roach, Keith Rountree, Dennis Russell, Krewasky Salter, Shelley Smith, Tim Stapleton, Scott Stephenson, Reggie Tiller, Mirlin Toomer, Gregory Urwin, Curtis Utz, John Vinson, John Votaw, Guy Washington, Sandra Washington, Houston Wedlock, Jonathon Winkler, Karen Winn, Lawrence Young, and Renotta Young.

Chronology

1863	President Abraham Lincoln issues the Emancipation Proclamation, declaring slaves in the rebellious states free
1865	The Thirteenth Amendment abolishes slavery in the U.S.
1875	U.S. dispatches USS *Alaska* to mediate Grebo rebellion after a series of defeats by the Americo-Liberians
1884–85	Berlin Conference regulates African colonization
1898	U.S. defeats Spain in Spanish-American War and occupies Cuba, Guam, Puerto Rico, and the Philippines
	U.S. annexes Hawaii
	London creates the British West African Frontier Force
1899	U.S. Senate ratifies Treaty of Paris, ending the war and annexing Guam, Puerto Rico, and the Philippines
	Philippine War begins when Filipinos resist U.S. rule
1902	U.S. defeats insurgents in the Philippine War
1904	U.S. takes control of the Panama Canal Zone
	Arthur Barclay elected president of Liberia
1906	London and Monrovia sign British loan agreement
1907	Paris and Monrovia sign Binger-Johnson Treaty, ceding two thousand square miles of Liberia to France
1908	Liberia sends a delegation to U.S. seeking economic and political assistance
	Monrovia creates the Liberian Frontier Force (LFF) in accordance with French and British agreements
1909	Monrovia appoints British officers to lead the LFF
	Monrovia expels British officers after LFF mutiny
	President Taft sends a U.S. Commission "to investigate the interests of the United States and

its citizens in the Republic of Liberia" to examine the situation and the possibility of assistance

1910   President Taft sends commission findings to Congress, recommending a loan agreement and military assistance for Liberia

War Department sends Lt. Benjamin O. Davis as military attaché to Monrovia to examine the mission

Grebo groups rebel around Cape Palmas

1911   LFF mutinies and demands back pay

Germany completes transatlantic cable from Liberia to Brazil

Lieutenant Davis asks to be recalled due to health issues and Liberian intransigence

Booker T. Washington asks Capt. Charles Young to undertake the mission in Liberia as military attaché

1912   Daniel E. Howard elected president of Liberia

Capt. Charles Young arrives in Monrovia with Maj. Wilson Ballard, Capt. Arthur Browne, and Capt. Richard Newton

Major Ballard assumes command of LFF

Major Ballard assists Anglo-Liberian Boundary Commission

Captain Browne arrests Liberian officials accused of killing Kissi chiefs

Major Ballard defeats Kru revolt at River Cess

Germans demand international commission on German merchants' property losses during Kru revolt

Major Young leads mission to rescue Captain Browne from rebellious Gio and Mano groups

Loan agreement of 1912 finalized and takes effect

1913	Major Young departs on sick leave in the U.S. due to blackwater fever and gunshot wound
	Monrovia does not renew Captain Browne's contract; Browne departs Liberia
	Major Young recruits Capt. Eldridge Hawkins from the consulate staff to replace Browne
	Gbandi and Kissi communities rebel in the north
	Kru communities rebel at River Cess
1914	Lt. Joseph Martin and Lt. William York arrive after Major Young's request for new officers
	Captain Newton dies of pulmonary tuberculosis
	World War I begins
1915	Major Ballard, Captain Hawkins, and Lieutenant Martin resign and depart Liberia
	William York promoted to major and assumes command of LFF
	Kru rebellion begins in the southeast
	USS *Chester* arrives in Monrovia to support Liberians in suppressing the Krus
	Major Young departs at the end of his tour in Liberia
1916	NAACP presents Major Young the Spingarn Medal for his achievements in Liberia
	First Lt. John Green arrives in Monrovia as military attaché
	United States sends weapons and ammunition for the LFF to use against the Krus
	Capt. James Gillespie and Capt. William Rountree arrive in Liberia
	American officers and LFF defeat Kru rebellion
	Liberia proffers court-martial charges against Major York for embezzlement of funds

1917	Captain Gillespie resigns and departs Liberia
	Major York settles out of court, resigns, and stays in Liberia as civilian
	LFF mutinies and demands back pay
	United States demands reforms in Liberian government's expenditures on LFF
	Gio and Mano communities rebel in the interior
	Maj. John Anderson arrives to take command of the LFF
	Liberia declares war on Germany
1918	Captain Rountree resigns and departs Liberia
	German submarine shells Monrovia
	World War I ends
1919	Grebo communities rebel near Cape Palmas
	Gola and Gbandi communities rebel in the north
1920	Charles D. B. King elected president of Liberia
	Col. Charles Young arrives in Monrovia with Capt. Henry Atwood, Capt. William Nabors, and Capt. Allen Bean
	Marcus Garvey and UNIA develop plan to resettle black Americans in Liberia
1921	President of Liberia sails to Washington DC to lobby for $5 million loan agreement
	Liberia rejects Marcus Garvey and UNIA plans to use Liberia as springboard for the Back-to-Africa movement
1922	U.S. Senate rejects Liberian $5 million loan agreement
	Colonel Young dies during intelligence mission in Nigeria
	War Department decides not replace Young as military attaché

Captain Atwood and Captain Bean resign and depart Liberia

Major Anderson departs on sick leave to the U.S.

Captain Nabors assumes command of the LFF

1923   Liberia promotes Nabors to major in command of the LFF

Major Nabors departs on sick leave in the U.S.

Capt. Moody Staten arrives in Liberia

1924   Harvey Firestone begins negotiations for loan and rubber production in Liberia

1925   Liberia promotes Staten to major in command of the LFF

Capt. Hansen Outley arrives in Liberia

1927   Firestone and Monrovia sign agreement for loan and rubber production

Major Staten resigns and departs Liberia

Monrovia turns over command of LFF to Liberian officer

1930   U.S. State Department recalls Captain Outley to make way for new nominations under the Firestone Agreement

Maj. George Lewis, a white officer, arrives in Liberia as an adviser under the Firestone Agreement

League of Nations commission investigates charges of forced labor and slavery in Liberia

President King resigns as a result of the UN commission findings

President Edwin Barclay sworn in as president of Liberia

U.S. refuses to recognize the Barclay government

1931   President Barclay reelected as president of Liberia

	President Barclay asks for League of Nations assistance
	Kru rebellion begins in the southeast
1932	Major Lewis resigns and departs Liberia
1934	President Barclay announces extensive political and economic reforms and asks for Western assistance
1935	U.S. and UK recognize Barclay government
1936	Kru rebellion ends
	Capt. William Nabors arrives in Liberia as adviser under the Firestone Agreement
1942	Capt. William Nabors departs Liberia
1944	William Tubman elected president of Liberia
	Liberia declares war on Germany
1956	LFF renamed Armed Forces of Liberia
1971	William R. Tolbert Jr. elected president of Liberia
1980	Coup by Samuel Doe ends 133 years of Americo-Liberian rule after assassination of President Tolbert
1986	Samuel Doe elected president of Liberia
1989	Charles Taylor and a group of fighters enter Liberia from Ivory Coast, triggering civil war
1990	Fighters led by Prince Y. Johnson kill Samuel Doe
1989–97	First Civil War in Liberia
1997	Charles Taylor elected president of Liberia
1997–2003	Second Civil War in Liberia
2004	United Nations begins rebuilding Liberian Armed Forces
2005	Ellen Johnson Sirleaf elected president of Liberia
2010	United States hands operational control of Armed Forces of Liberia to the government in Monrovia
2011	Ellen Johnson Sirleaf reelected as president of Liberia
2014	Nigerian officers turn over command of Armed Forces of Liberia to Liberian officers

AFRICAN AMERICAN OFFICERS IN LIBERIA

1

Liberia

Black Colony

My first impulse would be to free all the slaves and send
them to Liberia, to their own native land.

—ABRAHAM LINCOLN, 1854

L iberia is unique in Africa. While the rest of the continent
shares a history of conquest and occupation by white European powers, Liberia's colonizing minority was wholly black.
Paradoxically, the majority population of indigenous Liberians
was also black, differing from their masters only in the genealogy
of their birth and darkness of their skin.[1]

Liberia occupied a little bend on the west coast of Africa, wedged
between the French colonies of the Ivory Coast to the east and
Guinea to the north, and the British colony of Sierra Leone to
the west. Bounded by 350 miles of coastline and a jagged interior
frontier, the republic enclosed an area of about forty-one thousand square miles, a territory roughly the size of the U.S. state of
Ohio. The country was abutted in the south by the Atlantic Ocean
and a uniform band of coastal plain, remarkably free of the fever-
laden mangrove swamps and marshy lagoons that characterize the
regions to the east and west of Liberia. This littoral plain adjoined
an increasingly hilly belt, backed by a grassy savannah, leading to
the highest mountains in West Africa.[2]

Before the arrival of colonists from the United States, Liberian
territory was home to about 750,000 inhabitants comprising six-

teen indigenous ethnic groups of the Niger-Congo family. These groups further subdivided into four ethnic clusters based on cultural and linguistic similarities: the Kwa (Bassa, Belle, Dey, Grebo, Krahn, and Kru); Mende-Fu (Gbandi, Gio/Dan, Kpelle, Loma, Mano/Ma, and Mende); Mende-Tan (Mandingo and Vai); and Mel (Gola and Kissi). In the early part of the eighteenth century, these ethnic groups lived surrounded in an area yet unclaimed by the European powers of Great Britain and France.[3]

Liberia's colonial era began in 1822 with the arrival of former American slaves and free blacks sent by the American Colonial Society (ACS). The ACS formed in 1817 to send free African Americans to Africa as an alternative to emancipation in the United States. The ACS was an unlikely coalition of evangelicals who supported abolition and slaveholders who did not want free blacks living in the South. The society sent more than thirteen thousand emigrants to Liberia between 1820 and 1867. Blacks from the Caribbean and Africans captured by the U.S. Navy from American-bound slave ships later joined the initial American settlers. The colonists called themselves Americo-Liberians.[4]

The U.S. Navy played a significant role in establishing Liberia in its formative years and later provided military muscle to support the Americo-Liberians against the indigenous inhabitants. USS *Cyane*, commanded by Capt. Edward Trenchard with Lt. Matthew Perry second in command, escorted the brig *Elizabeth* with the first thirty families to the west coast of Africa in 1820. The colonists put ashore temporarily on fever-ridden Sherbro Island off the British colony of Sierra Leone, where many died of disease.[5]

Lt. Robert Stockton, commander of USS *Alligator*, rescued the surviving original colonists in 1822. He negotiated with the local Dey communities to purchase land on Cape Mesurado to establish a settlement, which later became the Liberian capital, Monrovia. Stockton negotiated a purchase price of about $300 worth of goods, backed by the threat of a pistol to the head of the local Dey king, Peter. The settlers named the new capital in honor of U.S. President James Monroe, an early supporter of colonization.[6]

Soon after the departure of the navy, the colonists made enemies of the Deys by trying to evangelize them and suppress the local slave trade. The final straw came when the Americo-Liberians prevented the Deys from plundering a British schooner that ran aground near Cape Mesurado, a prerogative customarily enjoyed by the locals. The settlers protected the crew and helped refloat the ship, and the grateful captain rewarded them with a bronze cannon complete with ammunition. In October 1822 several hundred Dey fighters responded to this affront by attacking the colonists, who desperately repulsed the attack with the help of the bronze cannon.[7]

This was merely the opening salvo of a long and bloody conflict between the local inhabitants and the colonizing Americo-Liberians, who were often assisted in their struggle by the U.S. Navy. From 1820 to 1861, the U.S. Navy Africa Squadron patrolled the coast of West Africa, freeing more than six thousand Africans from slave ships and transporting them to Liberia. The squadron was a prominent presence on the Liberian coast in these early years, teaching the indigenous people tangible lessons with gunpowder. The U.S. Navy insured the survival of the Liberian republic during its most vulnerable time in the second half of the nineteenth century. Realizing a strong Liberia was the best defense against the British-allied Krus and other groups, the American Bluejackets always sided with the Americo-Liberians in settling disputes.[8]

In one early example of U.S. Navy intervention, Commodore Matthew Perry arrived in 1843 on the southeastern Liberian coast to punish the Greboes for attacks on American shipping and assist the colonists in conflict with the local indigenous groups. He settled the matter between the settlers and the Greboes, and after investigating the murder of a crewmember from an American schooner, arrested the responsible chief, tried him, and had him killed when he tried to escape. Perry then helped the Americo-Liberians burn the offending village to the ground. In 1854 USS *John Adams* sailed into Cape Palmas to help the Liberian colonists drive two thousand Grebo people from land the settlers claimed. This was gunboat diplomacy in its most direct and effective form.[9]

Missionaries played a major role in the settlement of Liberia, working hand in glove with both the Americo-Liberians and the U.S. Navy. Hundreds of black and white missionaries sailed to West Africa over the years. In 1873, after the steamer USS *Plymouth* fired a salute to the French flag on the Gaboon River, an American missionary exclaimed, "Fire again captain; every gun converts a heathen." From the beginning, the missionaries and Americo-Liberian settlers considered it their Christian duty to replace the "barbaric" religions and customs of the indigenous people with their "superior" Western values and Christianity. Moreover, conversion to Christianity and cultural assimilation was the only way the local ethnic people could move up the ladder to Americo-Liberian society and citizenship.[10]

With the coastal ethnic groups cowed by the U.S. Navy, the chief threat to the Americo-Liberians came from the European colonial powers that hemmed the country on three sides. From the founding of the republic in 1847 to the first decade of the twentieth century, Monrovia lost 44 percent of its land area and 150 miles of coastline to England and France. During the European "Scramble for Africa" in the 1880s, the Americo-Liberians came under increasing pressure to safeguard their territory but lacked the resources or troops to adequately protect their borders. The Berlin Conference of 1885 introduced the principle of "effective occupation," which obligated colonial powers in Africa to establish administration and maintain order in their colonies to retain lands they claimed. When Monrovia failed to do this, it ceded substantial coastal areas to the neighboring British colony of Sierra Leone, and large littoral and vast interior areas to the French Ivory Coast and French Guinea (see Fig. 1).[11]

While Great Britain and France carved away at Liberia's borders, Germany dominated its economy by establishing trading centers on the coastline and investing heavily in the colony, aggressively defending these interests, often to the detriment of Monrovia. Germany, a latecomer to the scramble for African colonies, controlled about two-thirds of Liberia's exports. The German cruiser SMS *Panther* visited the Liberian coast frequently—whenever a German ship was threatened or a German citizen mistreated by the locals. Liberia found itself defenseless against this gunboat diplomacy after its two small armed cutters sank by accident in 1900, and it possessed no real navy.[12]

The presence of vital cable stations in Liberia also complicated relations with the European powers. Germany and France situated strategically important wireless and cable relay stations in Monrovia, enabling communications in Africa and across the Atlantic to South America. Germany laid a transatlantic cable from Liberia across the ocean to Brazil between 1896 and 1911, which connected to a cable that ran north through the Canary Islands, the Azores, and Spain to Germany. This military and commercial communication node proved vital to Germany and provided direct contact with its far-flung colonies in Africa and economic interests in the southern hemisphere. Great Britain made plans to block or cut this secure German communication line in time of crisis and did so during World War I.[13]

Further confounding relations with Britain, France, and Germany was Monrovia's inability to control many of the ethnic groups in the interior of Liberia. The border ethnic communities crossed from Liberian territory into French and British colonies to raid for slaves and booty. Monrovia never possessed the soldiers necessary to subdue the major indigenous groups, so the colonists reluctantly adopted indirect rule, treaties, and incentives to extend a tenuous authority over most parts of Liberia, a practice used by colonial powers throughout Africa. Some of the more powerful ethnic groups resisted; Greboes rebelled in the late 1800s, and Krus revolted in the early 1900s. The French and British used some of these upheavals as excuses to occupy and annex territory. Other disturbances served as the pretext for a German warship's shakedown of the defenseless government in Monrovia for reparations.[14]

In the first decade of the nineteenth century, Liberian territory embraced scattered coastal colonies of Americo-Liberians and sixteen major ethnic groups, including the Bassa, Belle, Dey, Grebo, Krahn, Kru, Gbandi, Gio/Dan, Kpelle, Loma, Mano/Ma, Mende, Mandingo, Vai, Gola, and Kissi. The Americo-Liberians exploited the historical animosities and feuds between groups to gain political and military advantage. The settlers also took advantage of the geographic divide between the coastal ethnic communities that came into earlier and more frequent contact with Americo-Liberians and Europeans and the interior groups, which they considered less developed and more warlike.[15]

The powerful Kwa-speaking ethnic communities in southeast-ern Liberia, often collectively referred to as the Krus, were skilled mariners and traders in demand for service on British merchant and fighting ships. The Greboes comprised the other major Kwa-speaking group in the south, centered on Grand Cess and Cape Palmas, and were also renowned seamen, merchants, and migrant workers. The coastal Krus, Greboes, Bassas, and Deys had an easier time assimilating than the interior groups because of their histori-cal contacts and sustained interactions with the Americo-Liberians. But they also came into more frequent conflict with Monrovia, often with the support of British or French colonial officials.[16]

Americo-Liberians, numbering roughly 15,000 of the total pop-ulation of approximately 750,000 in the early 1900s, struggled from the beginning to control an indigenous population scattered across 41,000 square miles of virtually uncharted territory. Unlike the colonial white powers in Africa, Monrovia had no resources to draw on from the colonizing country, and it had no developed economy or professional military. Though the U.S. Navy patrolled Liberian shores and private American support fueled Monrovia's feeble economy, the United States did not consider it a colony.[17]

Complicating the conflicts between the Americo-Liberians and the indigenous inhabitants was the fact that the territory of most of the ethnic groups in Liberia extended into the neighboring French and British colonies. Refugees of revolts in Liberia could seek sanc-tuary with their cousins in neighboring colonies. Further muddling matters was the reality that ethnic groups were neither cohesive nor united. When one ethnic community rebelled against Americo-Liberian rule, another from the same group might not participate in the resistance. Frequently, a community fought alongside gov-ernment troops to gain some advantage over its neighbor from the same ethnic group.[18]

Unlike their Monrovian overlords, the indigenous groups spoke their own languages, lived in village communities ruled by a chief or village elder, held land communally, and practiced animism or Islam. Apart from the color of their skin, the Americo-Liberian set-tlers differed little from the white British colonists in Africa, par-ticularly in the way they governed the ethnic communities. The settlers considered themselves superior to the indigenous peoples in religion, culture, and technology. Many of the local groups, for their part, considered the Americo-Liberian colonists as little more than liberated slaves and disdained their permissive attitude toward sexual behavior and their lack of ethnic connections.[19]

The ruling Americo-Liberian elite was far from a cohesive and unified minority. There were four distinct orders in the hierarchical caste system of Liberian society, partly based on skin color. At the apex stood the educated Americo-Liberian elite, mainly light-complexioned people of mixed black and white ancestry descended from the original colonists or from later Caribbean immigrants. Darker-skinned Americo-Liberians who worked as small farmers and laborers occupied the second rung of society. Third came the former slaves, or recaptives, who had been rescued from slave ships by the U.S. Navy, of darker complexion still. At the very bottom stood the indigenous groups who had occupied Liberia before the arrival of the colonists.[20]

The four-tiered hierarchy was far from rigid, however, with several ways an indigenous person or repatriated slave moved up to earn Liberian citizenship. From the time of Liberia's establishment, the American Colonial Society encouraged an apprenticeship scheme in which Monrovia placed both recaptured slaves and the children of indigenous groups with settler families to be educated, evangelized, and taught a skill or trade. Once the recaptive adults completed their training, the government awarded them citizenship and settled them in so-called Congo towns adjacent to Americo-Liberian settlements. The recaptives were called Congos because of the presumed origin of most enslaved people in that period. In time the indigenous people of Liberia used the term Congos interchangeably for both the Americo-Liberians and the recaptive slaves, assuming most of both groups originated from the Congo River basin.[21]

The apprenticeship program for recaptive children differed from that of adults. The Liberian government placed recaptive children with Americo-Liberian families to be trained and attend school at least one month each year per the law. Monrovia paid a stipend to the Liberian families to care for and feed the children until they reached the age of twenty-one for boys and eighteen for girls. In addition to receiving the stipend, the host families often saw the system as one that provided free labor in exchange for room and board. Occasionally, Americo-Liberian families boasted of having recaptives working in their plantations and homes, a haunting echo of their former lives in the American South.[22]

The Liberian government later adopted a ward scheme as a means of assimilating indigenous people into Americo-Liberian society and granting them citizenship. Like the apprentice system for recaptive children, the ward system placed indigenous children with settler families to be educated, learn a trade, and convert to Christianity. At the completion of the period at the age of twenty-one for boys and eighteen for girls, the government returned the young people to their communities and, in theory, sent civilization with them. This practice continued throughout the nineteenth century with up to 2,500 indigenous children placed in settler homes at any given time. Ward programs proved a mixed success yet constituted one of the few ways an indigenous person could achieve citizenship in Liberia until the second half of the twentieth century.[23]

Positive aspects of the apprentice and ward systems coexisted alongside abuses, yet the recaptured slaves had few options, since many lost their families and it was impractical to send them home. It was different for the indigenous children who were separated from their families and villages and given up as wards to settler families. In some cases the settlers treated them well, but many Americo-Liberians viewed the indigenous children as a source of cheap labor to be mistreated at will. Almost all suffered the indignity of having their names changed to better suit their new Americo-Liberian social status. However, almost all wards received an opportunity for education they would not have had otherwise. Perhaps most important, it gave the children access to eventual citizenship, something not available to other indigenous people.[24]

By the first decade of the nineteenth century, Monrovia was forced to take measures to restrain the indigenous groups, control its borders, and establish a measure of domination over the interior. To this purpose, the Liberian legislature passed a resolution and allocated funds for the creation of a Liberian Frontier Force (LFF) in February 1908. The force was to be "employed in garrisoning the posts on the frontier and maintaining public order," even though the Constitution of the Republic of Liberia prohibited standing armies in peacetime as a danger to liberty. Previously, Monrovia had depended on a ragtag militia force drawn from the Americo-Liberian citizenry in emergencies.[25]

The British loan agreement of 1906 and the Binger-Johnson Treaty signed in Paris in 1907 compelled Monrovia to create a Frontier Force to occupy posts along the border with garrisons. In ratifying the Binger-Johnson Treaty, Monrovia signed away more than two thousand square miles of territory to the French colonies of Ivory Coast and Guinea, so it could ill afford to ignore this demand to control its boundaries and risk losing more. The treaty warned that if the Liberians did not have the faculty to occupy the border garrisons, the French would assume the obligation. London applied equal pressure on Liberia's western border with Sierra Leone.[26]

The British government demanded that competent European officers lead this new Liberian Frontier Force. Since it had no experienced military personnel, the government of Liberia accepted the recommendation of the British consul general in Monrovia, Braithwaite Wallis, to appoint as commander a white English militia officer named Robert Mackay Cadell, who had served in the Boer War in South Africa. The British gave the president of Liberia little choice in the matter, and Cadell arrived unannounced in January 1908 to assume command of the Frontier Force with two other white British officers. Cadell claimed to be under the authority of the British receiver general in Liberia, who administered the loan agreement, and not answerable to Monrovia, a troubling arrangement for the Liberian government.[27]

The British also demanded that Liberia control its coastal commerce, and to that end sold Monrovia a ship to replace the two cutters sunk in 1900. The yacht *Eros*, built in 1895 for Baron A. de Rothschild and sunk in an accident under a different owner in 1907, was refitted by London in 1908 as a gunboat and sold to Monrovia under the new name RLS *Lark*. The Southampton shipyards fitted *Lark* with an armament of two six-pounders, two three-pounders, and several machine guns to be employed against smugglers and to transport troops. It arrived in Liberia on October 24, 1908, fully manned with a British crew under Lt. J. M. Bugge.[28]

Major Cadell betrayed the Liberian government's trust within a year of assuming command of the Liberian Frontier Force. He modeled the new force after the colonial British West African Frontier Force created in Nigeria in 1898, comprising black soldiers recruited from local ethnic groups led by white officers. Cadell enlisted ten sergeants and about one hundred veteran Mende soldiers from the neighboring British colony of Sierra Leone, dressed them in British colonial uniforms, equipped them with British weapons, and openly wielded too much authority.[29]

Cadell's overreach became too much to ignore. On his own authority and with the support of the British consul general, Cadell assumed the duties of chief of the city police, street commissioner, tax collector, and treasurer. After replacing the loyal Kru police force with his own Mendi soldiers and compelling the citizens of Monrovia to use his municipal amenities, he presented a large bill to the government for his services. Finally, in February 1909 Major Cadell informed the president of Liberia that his soldiers were threatening to mutiny due to lack of pay and that he could do nothing to stop them.[30]

The British were complicit in this mutiny. The British consul general arranged for the service of Cadell and essentially controlled the Frontier Force as well as Monrovia's lone armed cutter, RLS *Lark*. As additional proof of British complicity, a British gunboat, aptly named *Mutine*, arrived off the coast of Liberia with a company of colonial troops on board at the same time as the Frontier Force's mutiny, and British colonial officials in Sierra Leone put a colonial regiment on alert to move into Liberia.[31]

Yet instead of yielding to force, the Liberian government called out four hundred members of the First Regiment of the Americo-Liberian militia, which happened to be drilling in Monrovia, forcing Cadell and the rebellious Frontier Force troops to back down. The Liberian government sacked Cadell, who departed the country, taking with him his white officers and about one hundred black soldiers who were British colonial subjects. This left Liberia with a largely leaderless and hollow Frontier Force.[32]

The British government disavowed any knowledge of the coup in Liberia and admitted that both Consul General Wallis and Major Cadell had acted beyond their authority. Cadell shipped off to Sierra Leone and a few years later returned as a businessman in southern Liberia, using the name Major R. Mackay-Mackay. British consul general Wallis transferred to Dakar, Senegal, considered the "finest consular post in all West Africa." This closed a short-lived period of British backing for Liberia.[33]

Liberia served as a refuge for American freedmen after it was established in 1822 by the American Colonial Society, supported by the United States government. The West African coastal areas picked for colonization were already home to a large population of indigenous people. The tension between the two elements of Liberia's population grew to become an underlying source of discontent and conflict and was one of the factors that led to eventual American intervention.

However, the chief threat to Liberian sovereignty that led to American action was the prospect of partition by France and Great Britain. The European scramble for colonies left no place safe on the African continent. Little more than half of Liberia's original territory remained intact by the first decade of the twentieth century, and by then even this remnant was threatened. Monrovia barely survived a furtive coup in 1909.

Monrovia learned its lesson about Great Britain and turned next to the United States for help. By the turn of the century, the United States had acquired colonies and dependencies of its own in Latin America and Asia. Liberia would shortly follow.

FIG. 1. Liberian territory taken by Great Britain and France and added to their colonies in the west, north, and south by 1909. Courtesy of the author.

FIG. 2. Liberian officials and people of Monrovia greet the American commissioners at the U.S. consulate in Monrovia in 1909. *National Geographic Magazine*, September 1910.

FIG. 3. Visit of Governor General Ponty of French West Africa in 1909 (*center*) flanked by Liberian president Arthur Barclay (*left*) and Secretary of State F. E. R. Johnson (*right*). *Back row, far left*: U.S. Consul General Ernest Lyon. *National Geographic Magazine*, September 1910.

FIG. 4. Watercolor of the RLS *Lark* by James C. Johnson. RLS *Lark* served as the only armed ship in the Liberian navy for many years. It was a pleasure yacht built for Baron A. de Rothschild in 1895 and sold to Liberia by London in 1908. Courtesy of the Moorland-Spingarn Research Center, Howard University Archives, Howard University, Washington DC.

2

American Support

Dollar Diplomacy

This policy has been characterized as substituting dollars for
bullets. The policy of dollar diplomacy is one that appeals alike to
idealistic humanitarian sentiments, to dictates of sound policy and
strategy, and to legitimate commercial aims.

—WILLIAM HOWARD TAFT, 1912

Although diplomatic support from Washington and an occa-
sional warship probably saved Liberian independence
during several crises in the nineteenth century, the policy of the United States remained one of benevolent disinterest.
A half-hearted U.S. diplomatic objection to France in a dispute
with Liberia in 1907 resulted in the loss of more than two thousand
square miles of Liberian territory. When Great Britain seemed on
the verge of virtual annexation of Liberia over a loan dispute, the
United States finally embarked on a more serious and vigorous
effort to help Monrovia in 1909.[1]

Booker T. Washington and the African American community
were aware of the threat posed to Liberia's sovereignty by France
and Great Britain and pressured the administration to act. As early
as September 1907, Booker T. Washington wrote President Theodore Roosevelt: "I have information from reliable sources that both
France and England are seeking to take large parts of the Liberian
territory. I am sure you will prevent this, if it can be done." This
letter followed the border dispute with France in 1907, when Paris

had acquired large tracts of Liberia and added them to its colonies of Guinea and Ivory Coast. Under the terms of the Berlin Conference of 1885, Liberia had lost claim to the territory because it had failed to demonstrate effective control.[2]

After the United States' Monrovia-based consul general Ernest Lyon sounded warnings that Liberia's sovereignty was threatened by European encroachment, Monrovia sent a delegation to Washington in May 1908 to request advice on Liberia's dealings with Britain and France. The task of this team, headed by Liberian vice president James J. Dossen, was to "ask for assistance in maintaining the independence of the Republic and to enable it to carry on a peaceful, orderly, and efficient government." The team arrived in Washington on May 22 and met with Secretary of State Elihu Root four days later. Afterward, Root communicated with the British government the U.S. intent to assist Liberia, guarantee its "perpetuity," and "resist all encroachment toward absorption" by European countries. The British Foreign Office responded positively to the messages and encouraged active U.S. involvement in Liberian affairs.[3]

Booker T. Washington, a close adviser to President Roosevelt on policies effecting African Americans, appealed to the president to break protocol and meet personally with the black delegation from Liberia. Washington met with Roosevelt on June 10, 1908, and convinced him to see the delegation unofficially later that evening. President Roosevelt, Secretary of State Root, and Secretary of War William Howard Taft met at the White House with the three-man Liberian delegation (Vice President Dossen, former Liberian president Garretson W. Gibson, and Liberian attorney C. B. Dunbar), accompanied by Booker T. Washington. The president gave no assurances that the country would intervene in the disputes with France and Great Britain but promised political support. After the meeting at the White House, the delegation attended a consultation with Taft at his home.[4]

Liberian vice president Dossen knew that Taft, Roosevelt's handpicked successor, held the fate of Liberia in his hands and that the best outcome would be some form of the dollar diplomacy already practiced by the U.S. in Asia and Latin America. Dossen's official statement after the two meetings was cautiously hopeful and politically astute:

> Our formal reception at the White House and Department of State was exceedingly friendly and pleasant, and although we cannot say now that success will attend our efforts, yet the well-known large-heartedness and sympathy of President Roosevelt toward weaker races and governments inspires in us the hope that he will not turn a deaf ear to the entreaties of the feeble Republic. We are glad that the prospects are that he is going to be succeeded in the Presidency by Mr. Taft, who has been the President's right arm in carrying out reforms and instituting stable government, both in the Philippines and Cuba.[5]

Booker T. Washington escorted the delegation throughout its stay and spoke in support for Liberia at all events. The Liberian delegation continued its visit to Washington DC with a public reception for African Americans there, a special meeting with the local branch of the National Negro Business League, and attendance at Howard University's commencement. Washington later hosted the delegation at the Tuskegee Institute for its commencement. W. E. B. Du Bois joined Booker T. Washington in support of American aid, giving generous coverage and "waxing lyrical" about the Liberian delegation's visit in his newspapers.[6]

Politics played a role in Theodore Roosevelt's agreeing to meet with the Liberian delegation and in his support for assistance to Monrovia. Roosevelt chose not to run for a third term in 1908 and supported Taft as his successor. Republicans needed the African American vote, as they had since the days of Abraham Lincoln. Both Roosevelt and Taft knew that Booker T. Washington and the African American community supported aid for Liberia. As a direct result of the visit of the delegation, Secretary of State Root asked Congress for appropriations to pay the expenses of a U.S. commission to visit Liberia, assess the situation, and make recommendations. Roosevelt endorsed the effort shortly before he left office, and a majority Republican Congress approved funds for the undertaking on March 4, 1909, the day Taft took office.[7]

Booker T. Washington and the African American intelligentsia at the time had mixed feelings about Liberia. Washington and much of the black elite opposed emigration as a solution to the racial problems in the United States, believing the rural South was the best place for African Americans to live and improve their lives. W. E. B. Du Bois maintained a deep affection for Liberia, though, like Washington, he disliked the idea of emigration. Even if black American leaders like Washington and Du Bois disagreed on how to improve the plight of African Americans, they agreed that an independent Liberia administered by a black democratic government symbolized hope for Africa and should be protected by the country that had encouraged the enterprise from its inception.[8]

After the change in administrations in 1909, Republican president Taft appointed a commission "to investigate the interests of the United States and its citizens in the Republic of Liberia." Dr. Roland P. Faulkner, former commissioner of education to Puerto Rico; George Sale, superintendent of education for the American Baptist Home Mission Society; and Emmett J. Scott, an African American and private secretary to Booker T. Washington, led the commission. Secretary of State Root initially selected Booker T. Washington for the commission, but President Taft decided he could not afford the absence of his chief adviser on African American affairs so soon after the election. Several others, including Maj. Percy M. Ashburn, a U.S. Army medical officer, Capt. Sydney A. Cloman, the U.S. military attaché to London, Frank A. Flower, a civilian attaché, and George A. Finch, the team's secretary, rounded out the party.[9]

Controversy about the selection of the commissioners led to a disagreement that nearly scuttled the mission before it departed. The government initially named as chairman of the commission W. Morgan Shuster, a veteran of a similar mission to the Philippine Islands. Shuster resigned on April 16, 1909, just days before the mission was scheduled to steam out of New York Harbor. The State Department offered the explanation that Shuster suffered from a fever contracted while serving in Manila as the collector of customs. The real reason, reported in the newspapers, was Shuster's aversion to serving with Emmett J. Scott, the only black member of the commission. When interviewed at his home in Atlanta, Shuster declared that his health had nothing to do with his resignation but that "he had never served on any commission or board with a negro."[10]

Shuster's resignation and replacement with Faulkner did not end the controversy. An article in the *New York Times* two days before departure suggested that the three commissioners might take passage in different vessels of the three-cruiser flotilla to avoid racial difficulties. The paper reported that Scott was initially slated to ship on board the USS *Birmingham*, whose captain and officers where southerners, but to avoid difficulties he was moved to another ship. But it appears that Faulkner was a peacemaker, and all three commissioners sailed to Liberia on board the flagship USS *Chester*. Since the official records show the three commissioners manifested on *Chester* and the balance of the team on *Birmingham*, it is unclear whether this drama truly occurred or if the newspapers created the confusion to produce a news story.[11]

The composition of the commission and background of its members bear on the eventual outcome of the mission. The chairman, Dr. Roland Faulkner, studied, taught, and wrote extensively about economics and was well suited to judge the financial predicament of Liberia. George Sale, a Canadian-born educator and former president of Atlanta Baptist College, was equally well regarded. A *New York Times* article praised him as being "most free from racial prejudice"; Booker T. Washington wrote to Sale telling him, "yours was among the names that I wanted to have the President consider." Emmett J. Scott took the place of Booker T. Washington to the disappointment of Liberians but was also well suited to the task.[12]

The mission and role of the other commission members was no less important. The army medical officer, Major Ashburn, had the task of assessing the health affairs of Liberia and dangers posed by disease. His more immediate job was safeguarding the health of the commission members. Captain Cloman, the U.S. military attaché to London, was an army intelligence officer with the mission of appraising the readiness of the Liberian Frontier Force and security situation in West Africa. The civilian attaché Frank Flower evaluated the practical economic options available to improve the lives of Liberians, and secretary George Finch took notes and collected materials for the final team report.[13]

The congressional mandate charged the commission with spending thirty days in Liberia and Sierra Leone to complete its mission. The prescribed task of the commission was to investigate the difficulties in Liberia to "determine whether the Liberians could extricate themselves from them, either by their own efforts or with a reasonable amount of friendly assistance by the United States." The implied mission was to make a recommendation on whether the U.S. should formally involve itself in Africa and effectively supplant Great Britain as the "friendly counselor and advisor to Liberia."[14]

This undertaking coincided with an era of increasingly muscular foreign policy by the United States, characterized by imperialism and expansionism. Theodore Roosevelt had just ended his presidency, a period after the Spanish-American War when the United States founded an overseas empire that included the Philippines, Puerto Rico, Guam, Hawaii, and the Panama Canal Zone. William Howard Taft succeeded Roosevelt and continued this aggressive foreign policy, expanding the use of dollar diplomacy in the Pacific and Caribbean. Taft served as the first civilian governor general of the Philippines from 1900 to 1904, where he coined the term "little brown brothers" for the Filipinos, and as secretary of war for Roosevelt from 1904 to 1908. Taft did not intend the term as an ethnic slur but as a reflection of the "paternalist racism" shared by President Roosevelt and most Americans at the time.[15]

Not everyone agreed with this policy of imperial expansion, least of all African American leaders like Booker T. Washington, who believed the United States should deal with its racial problems at home and let "our colored brothers" in the Philippines govern themselves. Yet this sentiment was not universal or consistent over time. As one author later noted, "African American leaders' attitudes toward imperialism waxed and waned according to the presence of conspicuous opportunity for themselves." And African American views about involvement in Liberia were different still because of its location in Africa, the birthplace of their ancestors. Despite his earlier anti-imperialist view, by 1901 Booker T. Washington reversed his position and advised, "I think with the experience we . . . gained in the Philippines, we could administer and self-develop Liberia."[16]

The State Department briefed the members of the Liberian commission to prepare them before their departure. Among other things, officials informed them of the "remarkably beneficial results of dollar diplomacy in the Dominican Republic." Assistant Secretary of State Alvey A. Adee informed the commission that he expected Liberia would need a receivership modeled after the one imposed on the Dominican Republic. Clearly the State Department already had a solution for the economic problems in Liberia before the commission set sail. As evidenced by the remarks of Liberian vice president Dossen after his meeting in the White House in 1908, the Liberians likewise knew what was in store for them.[17]

The commission sailed for Liberia on April 24, 1909, from the docks of Tompkinsville, New York, in New York Harbor. All three U.S. Navy vessels were scout cruisers commissioned in 1908 with crews of sixty-three officers and 332 enlisted men each, an impressive show of support for Liberia aimed squarely at London and Paris. Faulkner, Sale, Scott, and Finch shipped on board the flagship *Chester* while Cloman, Ashburn, and Flower bunked on *Birmingham*. *Salem* developed engine trouble shortly out of port and had to return home for repairs. *Birmingham* developed boiler problems during the crossing and had to put into Porto Grande in the Cape Verde Islands for repairs on May 2, where it and *Chester* resupplied with provisions and coal. The three members of the commission on board *Birmingham* transferred to *Chester*, which completed the voyage without further incident, anchoring off the roadstead of Monrovia in the early hours of May 8, 1909.[18]

The American commission arrived in Monrovia amid fanfare with the USS *Chester*'s twenty-one-gun salute answered by a thundering shore battery. American consul general Ernest Lyon and members of his staff called officially on the captain of the ship, Cdr. Henry B. Wilson, and members of the commission. The *Chester* strictly adhered to navy service etiquette, affording Consul General Lyon a thirteen-gun salute as his boat approached with its two three-pounder guns used exclusively for firing salutes. Lyon escorted the members of the commission ashore, accompanied by a thirteen-gun salute, where Monrovia mayor Thomas Faulkner met them at the city pier with much ceremony, followed by receptions, parties, and a visit to Liberian president Arthur Barclay.[19]

The commission spent three weeks in Monrovia attending meetings, interviewing foreign consular officials, and talking to trade representatives. The team spent the first few nights on board ship, but soon moved its headquarters ashore, tired of the daily round trip through the surf necessitated by Monrovia's lack of a harbor. *Birmingham*, having completed repairs, rejoined *Chester* in Monrovia on May 13. Major Ashburn set up a clinic in Monrovia to provide free medical treatment to the people of the city, and Emmett J. Scott chartered a boat and traveled up the Saint Paul River to observe the agricultural life of the Americo-Liberians and indigenous communities. On the lighter side, two sailors from *Chester* were punished at captain's mast for returning from a "baseball party ashore under the influence."[20]

The commission completed its work in Monrovia on May 29, 1909, and departed the capital to complete the mission. Chairman Faulkner, secretary Finch, and Captain Cloman sailed northwest on *Chester* to Sierra Leone to investigate the boundary dispute with Britain and meet with the lieutenant governor. The rest of the party steamed southeast on board *Birmingham* to Cape Palmas, the seat of the boundary conflict with France. On June 10 the two ships rendezvoused in Dakar, Senegal, and the commission steamed homeward. USS *Salem* rejoined *Chester* and *Birmingham* in Madeira and the squadron cruised together to the United States, arriving on July 3, 1909.[21]

Major Ashburn, the army medical officer in the delegation, filed a report with the War Department soon after his return. Ashburn's comments on the diseases and medical conditions in Liberia should have given pause to American policy planners. He wrote that the "medical conditions in Liberia are deplorable in the extreme, the amount of preventable or relievable suffering very great, and the mortality undoubtedly much higher than it should be." Ashburn noted the absence of medical care in most of the country, with only two trained doctors in Liberia, both American-educated, one in Monrovia and the other at Lower Buchanan. He claimed: "In my opinion it is safe to say that quite 90 percent, and possibly all, of the population of Monrovia have malaria." Two of the commission members contracted malaria, in spite of the care exercised to avoid it. Ashburn also mentioned that blackwater fever, a some-times fatal disease also known as malignant malaria that afflicted many new arrivals to the West African coast, occurred all along the coast of Liberia.[22]

The commission took nearly a year to complete its formal report, compiled by Secretary Finch and sent by President Taft to Congress on March 25, 1910. It recommended the U.S. government help Monrovia resolve its boundary disputes, pay off its debt by assuming as guarantee control over the collection of Liberian customs, and set up "customs receivership analogous to that now existing in Santo Domingo." It also suggested the United States organize and drill an effective constabulary force, create and maintain a research station in the country, and establish a navy coaling port on the coast. The commission noted that U.S. bankers promised to refinance the Liberian debt with a loan "if the United States will adopt measures similar to those which adjusted the Dominican [Republic] debt." The government eventually implemented many of these recommendations, though without formal approval of the Senate, which considered Liberia outside the proper sphere of influence of the United States.[23]

With the commission's recommendations in hand, the United States negotiated an international loan and set up an American-administered receivership to pay off Monrovia's foreign debts. The commission reported that the Liberian economy was enormously unstable and feared that foreign nations might use force to collect debts. Germany had a great deal of money invested in Liberia, and Monrovia owed Germany, France, and Britain accumulated debts of $1.7 million. Washington also moved to sell arms to Liberia and undertake a reorganization of the constabulary, which led it to send African American officers to Liberia to equip, organize, train, and command the Liberian Frontier Force.[24]

The Taft administration accepted the recommendations of the commission and adapted a version of the dollar diplomacy perfected previously in Central America and Asia. Washington employed a variation of a model earlier developed in the Dominican Republic, Nicaragua, and the Philippines in which U.S. bankers facilitated loans, U.S. officials administered customs receipts, and American military advisers trained and commanded the local constabulary forces. Essentially, Washington encouraged U.S. banks and businesses to invest in these risky overseas areas in exchange for military and diplomatic support to ensure stability. The only wrinkle was extending this policy of American dollar diplomacy, already employed in the Caribbean, Central America, and Asia, to the west coast of Africa.[25]

Supporting Liberia meant the United States was embarking on an extraordinary dollar diplomacy mission in West Africa, a policy that would endure for two decades. Washington agreed to help Monrovia negotiate a loan to pay off its debts, settle boundary disputes with Britain and France, and supply military officers to train an effective constabulary to protect its territory. Each one of these tasks was mutually supportive and fraught with challenges.

Had the United States not felt a strong moral responsibility for the situation in Liberia and pressure to act from African American leaders it would never have agreed to this risky and open-ended undertaking. But the United States felt an obligation to guarantee the future of Liberia based on several factors: the United States populated Liberia with freed American slaves and intervened time and time again over the years to prop up the weak government, defend it against internal threats from the indigenous groups, and protect it from the external threat posed by France and Great Britain.

This effort coincided with a period of American political and military expansion in the Pacific and Caribbean. The United States founded an overseas colonial empire after the Spanish-American War in 1898 that included the Philippines, Puerto Rico, Guam, Hawaii, and the Panama Canal Zone. Adding West Africa seemed a reasonable policy decision in 1910, especially considering Washington's historical relationship with Monrovia. The United States was unwilling or unable to cut its losses and allow Liberia to be partitioned by the European colonial powers.

FIG. 5. First Lt. Benjamin O. Davis in his office in Monrovia, 1910. He is wearing his summer white dress uniform with his pith helmet on the window sill. U.S. Army Heritage and Education Center.

FIG. 6. Group photograph on the front steps of the U.S. consulate in Monrovia in 1910. *Front row (left to right):* Nellie L. Bundy, First Secretary Richard C. Bundy, Consul General Ernest Lyon, Olive E. Davis (Davis's daughter), military attaché Lt. Benjamin O. Davis. *Back row (left to right):* Secretary of State F. E. R. Johnson, College of West Africa professor F. Parker, consulate clerk Annabel L. Walker, College of West Africa professor W. F. Walker. U.S. Army Heritage and Education Center.

AMERICAN SUPPORT

FIG. 7. Lt. Benjamin O. Davis and Consul General Ernest Lyon in Monrovia, 1910. U.S. Army Heritage and Education Center.

FIG. 8. Lt. Benjamin O. Davis (*standing, center*) with Liberian officers and officials in Monrovia in 1910. Liberian secretary of state F. E. R. Johnson is the man seated with glasses. The Liberians are likely wearing their ceremonial or militia uniforms. U.S. Army Heritage and Education Center.

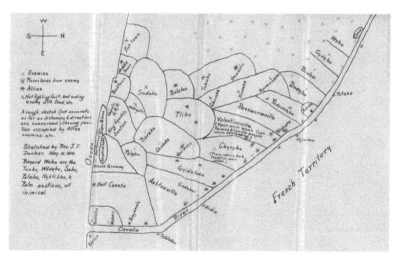

FIG. 9. Sketch map from a report by uss *Des Moines* of the area around Cape Palmas, showing the allegiance of the various ethnic groups during the Grebo revolt of 1910. National Archives and Records Administration.

3

Davis

Mission Defined

This force as it is now organized is worthless and
should be reorganized.

—BENJAMIN O. DAVIS, 1911

T he efforts of Consul General Ernest Lyon brought Benjamin
Davis to Liberia. Lyon served in Monrovia when the U.S.
commission visited Liberia in 1909, one of only two black
heads of mission then serving with the State Department. A political appointee selected for the post in 1903 by Theodore Roosevelt,
Lyon served in Monrovia until 1910. He understood the effort to
assist Liberia would fail if the country were unable to safeguard its
borders from encroachment by France and Great Britain. He also
knew the endeavor required qualified African American military
trainers and inspired leadership to guide the demoralized Frontier
Force. Therefore, Lyon wrote the U.S. War Department on November 22, 1909, even before the commission inked its final report, asking it to assign Benjamin Davis to initiate the effort.[1]

Only three African American officers served in the U.S. Regular
Army in 1909 and were candidates for the assignment: Benjamin O.
Davis, John E. Green, and Charles Young. Young, the most senior
and qualified of the three, completed his military attaché posting to
Haiti and the Dominican Republic in 1907 and rejoined the Ninth
Cavalry in the Philippines in 1908. Having been away from his reg-
iment on detached duty for nearly five years, he was ineligible for

the assignment. Green was professor of military science and tactics at Wilberforce University in Ohio, the nation's oldest private, historically black university, and was also unavailable. Davis was the only officer open for reassignment, having just completed his tour of duty at Wilberforce University.[2]

Consul General Lyon believed that Davis was up to the significant challenges of organizing the effort in Liberia but also realized he was the only man available for the job. In his message to the War Department, Lyon wrote that he considered Davis not only a "bright young lieutenant," but also "a good agent for the government to have in that Republic." The consul general sent a letter to Davis asking him to take the job, noting that his presence in Liberia would serve as an "inspiration" to the people.[3]

The choice of a black Regular Army officer was crucial for several reasons. First, only a Regular Army officer possessed the requisite leadership and professional skills for the job. Although there were black officers serving with volunteer units in the Philippines, they were not as carefully selected and highly trained as Regular Army officers. Second, Monrovia insisted the nominee be black, based on the recent experience with white officers commanding the Liberian Frontier Force that led to mutiny in 1909. Yet the most important consideration was the Liberian Constitution, which denied those "not of Negro descent" citizenship, the right to own property, or any role in government affairs. Since the military attaché had to work closely with government officials, the candidate had to be black.[4]

Benjamin Oliver Davis, born on May 28, 1880, in Washington DC, aspired to military service from an early age. After attending high school, where he excelled as a military cadet, Davis served as a first lieutenant in the Eighth U.S. Volunteer Infantry during the Spanish-American War from 1898 to 1899. He lied about his age to join without his parents' consent. After receiving an honorable discharge at the end of the war, he tried unsuccessfully to get an appointment to West Point. Despite his solid high school academic and athletic record as well as his military experience, officials told Davis it was not politically feasible for a black man to get an appointment to the U.S. Military Academy in 1899.[5]

Determined to serve as a Regular Army officer, Davis opted to enlist with the aim of taking the officer's exam once he had the requisite time in the service. He enlisted as a private in I Troop, Ninth U.S. Cavalry on June 18, 1899. Either by luck or design, he served in the same troop as First Lt. Charles Young, the only black West Point graduate then serving in the Regular Army. As Davis rose in rank from corporal to sergeant major, Young took an interest in his future, tutored him for the officer's exam, and recommended him to the board. Davis was the first of many African American officers Young would mentor. Davis passed the officer's exam, which included a written test, oral exam, and physical assessment, and won his coveted commission as a Regular Army second lieutenant of cavalry on February 2, 1901. Ironically, Davis earned his commission in eighteen months; it would have taken him four years at West Point.[6]

Davis shipped out to the Philippines and joined his new unit in the Tenth U.S. Cavalry in August 1901. The army routinely moved a newly promoted officer from the ranks to another unit to distance him from the men he had most recently served with as an enlisted soldier. He served with the Tenth Cavalry in the Philippines and later at Fort Washakie, Wyoming, before accepting an assignment as professor of military science and tactics at Wilberforce University in 1905. He had just completed his tour at Wilberforce in 1909 and returned to his regiment at Fort Ethan Allen, Vermont when the War Department enquired whether he would volunteer for the assignment as military attaché to Liberia.[7]

According to rules governing the assignment of Regular Army officers, the War Department should not have sent Davis to Liberia due to the so-called Manchu Law. Manchu Law referred to legislation passed by Congress in 1893, and strengthened in subsequent years, requiring that "no officer of the line of the army may be detached from duty with troops for more than four years out of six." It was an attempt to prevent officers from serving long stretches of their military careers away from troops in staff positions, and attaché service was considered detached duty. However, the army allowed exceptions to this rule "in case of emergency or time of war."[8]

The War Department sought to avoid situations where its three African American officers served in positions of authority over white junior officers in the black regular regiments. Only three of the roughly two hundred officers serving in the four black regular regiments were African American, while all the enlisted men were black. Some white officers objected to serving under black officers and complained to their senators and congressmen, who in turn wrote letters to the president and secretary of war. The army's promotion of Young, Green, and Davis to higher rank proved an increasing problem for Washington. The War Department solved this dilemma, in part, by rotating the three black officers between "safe" assignments to Wilberforce and Liberia, where they led only black cadets and officers. The State Department treated black Foreign Service officers similarly.[9]

The U.S. Army attaché corps, an arm of the military intelligence organization in the War Department, was small in the first decade of the century, numbering no more than twenty army officers throughout the world. In 1909 eighteen army officers served as military attachés in the capitals of six European countries, nine Latin American countries, two Asian countries, and one African country. Those officers posted to Europe reported chiefly on developments and technology with a goal of improving the U.S. military. The U.S. military attachés in Latin America, Africa, and Asia gathered intelligence mainly on the geography, resources, and military affairs of nations with whom the U.S. might form alliances, come into conflict, or impose dollar diplomacy dependencies.[10]

The military attaché system at the time of Davis's appointment was in the early stages of development. The War Department had established a formal system of military attachés in 1889 with five army officers posted to European capitals, and the organization saw limited growth after the Spanish-American War in 1898. The U.S. Navy and State Department created similar intelligence activities about the same time. However, the value of the information provided by the military attachés depended on the quality of instructions given and questions posed by the War Department, as well as the initiative of the individual officer assigned. The military officers accredited as attachés received no specialized training or education and were often sent overseas without special instructions or briefings in Washington.[11]

Fortunately for Davis, the army provided him with briefings before his departure. It notified Davis in late November that he had been designated an attaché "to obtain military information from abroad" and instructed him to report to the War Department to prepare for the mission in Liberia. After he reported to Washington on January 4, 1910, Capt. Matthew E. Hanna and Maj. Henry D. Todd Jr. presented Davis with a series of background briefings on the organization of the War Department, the situation in Liberia, and his duties at a military attaché. Hanna and Todd belonged to the Military Information Division (MID) of the War Department General Staff, the group that administered military attachés abroad. Davis's assigned duties included an investigation of the Liberian military establishment's organization, strength, training, morale, staff, mobilization system, and transportation network.[12]

The military attaché mission in Liberia proved similar to those in Latin America, where attachés gathered information on the country's geography, resources, and military affairs. Davis was lucky to have Capt. Matthew Hanna serving in the MID and preparing him for his mission in Liberia. Hanna served as the military attaché to Cuba from 1902 to 1904, where he established an outstanding reputation for his fluency in Spanish and rapport with the people. While serving in Havana, Hanna provided accurate reporting on the political affairs in Cuba and worked diligently to reorganize the Rural Guard of Cuba, a mission comparable to retraining the Frontier Force in Liberia.[13]

The War Department wanted Davis to test the waters and assess the new expansion of dollar diplomacy policy to Liberia. The department needed to know specifics of the challenges ahead in Liberia before settling on a detailed plan to support the military mission for the State Department. This was a new operation for a U.S. military that had little experience training and equipping foreign military forces. The U.S. Army had equipped and trained constabulary forces in Cuba after the Spanish-American War and the Philippines after the Philippine War but only after invading and occupying these countries with large military forces. The expansion of U.S. policy to include the military mission in Liberia would be quite different and far more challenging. The fact that it involved only African American officers as military attachés and trainers made it doubly difficult, as this limited and complicated the selection process.[14]

Davis traded ideas on the current situation in Liberia with Consul General Lyon, who was in the United States lobbying for support to Monrovia. They exchanged letters during the first two months of 1910 to review the problems in Liberia and debate the best approaches to accomplish the mission. Lyon cut short his stateside visit because of new trouble in Liberia. Because Davis had not completed his briefings or his preparations to move his family, he did not accompany Lyon to Liberia as previously planned.[15]

Lyon departed the United States early because a serious tribal revolt by the Greboes erupted in the southeast of Liberia. The threat to the regime was so great that Booker T. Washington persuaded the State Department and U.S. secretary of the navy to dispatch the scout cruiser USS *Birmingham* to assist Monrovia in suppressing the revolt. The captain of *Birmingham*, Cdr. William B. Fletcher, reported to Washington for consultations at the State Department before he sailed. Consul General Lyon boarded the cruiser before it departed on March 20, 1910. *Birmingham* sailed from Hampton Roads, Virginia, and arrived in Monrovia on April 4, 1910. This meant that Lyon and *Birmingham* arrived two weeks ahead of Davis.[16]

Lyon and Fletcher went ashore to meet with American and Liberian officials on the situation before embarking on the mission. While in Monrovia, the crew of *Birmingham* drilled landing force operations to prepare for contingencies. *Birmingham* and other visiting U.S. Navy ships always hired crews of Kru oarsmen to man boats in the unpredictable surf in Monrovia and elsewhere on the Liberian coast. After Fletcher sent a preliminary report of his findings to the Navy Department, *Birmingham* weighed anchor and steamed south on April 12 with Consul General Lyon and Liberian special commissioners Vice President James J. Dossen and Attorney General C. D. B. King on board. The cruiser anchored off Cape Palmas and the city of Harper the following day.[17]

Vice President Dossen and Attorney General King immediately went ashore to attend to their peace commission duties while *Birmingham* prepared for military operations. Dossen was from Harper and established the commission headquarters at his home there. *Birmingham* encountered the Liberian gunboat RLS *Lark* soon after arrival and anticipated working with the small armed schooner in action along the coast. *Lark,* with a German captain and Kru crew, was smaller and more suited for the shallow waters near the coast and the rivers penetrating the interior. The schooner was used mainly to ferry troops along the coast, resupply isolated garrisons, carry dispatches back and forth to Monrovia, and cut communication lines along the coast long used by the seafaring Greboes.[18]

The Americo-Liberians, claiming insufficient troops and ammunition, pressured the Americans to intervene, but Fletcher refused to be drawn into active participation until he fully understood the facts on the ground. To this end, Fletcher held meetings with the Grebo king of Rocktown as well as Vice President Dossen and Liberian secretary of war G. Stanley Padmore. There was sporadic fighting ashore, and *Birmingham* reported on April 14 that "several shots were fired ashore at irregular intervals." Commander Fletcher took a boat on a scouting mission up the Hoffman River, which emptied into the ocean at Harper, the main Americo-Liberian city in the south. While he was away, a boat conducting practice landings on the beach swamped, and two American sailors drowned, a reminder of the danger of the surf. After a memorial service on board ship, the crew buried both sailors ashore at the Americo-Liberian cemetery in Harper.[19]

At about the time Fletcher buried his dead in Harper, Lieutenant Davis arrived in Monrovia. Not knowing the extent of the primitive conditions awaiting him in Liberia, Davis decided to bring his wife, Elnora, and five-year-old daughter, Olive. He and his family had steamed out of New York City on April 2, 1910, for the Atlantic crossing. After three days in Liverpool, the three completed the trip to Africa on the British steamer *Landanna.* They arrived in Monrovia on April 25 to find that the city had no deep-water port facilities, so they boarded a small boat manned by Kru oarsmen, who ferried them ashore to beaches of the city.[20]

While Davis got himself and his family settled in Monrovia, trouble continued in the south. Commander Fletcher quickly assessed the muddled situation and placed most of the blame on the Americo-Liberians. He telegraphed the secretary of the navy on April 28 that the "trouble at Cape Palmas was caused by mismanagement and incompetence of the authorities here who have tried to commit me to use force and have rejected an offer suggesting a method for the peaceful settlement of the matter to which the tribe agrees." Fletcher realized that the Americo-Liberians wanted the U.S. Navy to intervene militarily to put down the revolt as it had so many times in the past.[21]

Two days later Fletcher forwarded a more ominous report of "injustice and atrocity practiced by the Liberian authorities" provided by the German captain of *Lark*, Walter Buchholz. Buchholz witnessed two Grebo workers taken by the Americo-Liberians, robbed of their possessions, and turned over to "friendly" Grebo allies to be killed. Buchholz also reported that his crew had mutinied and refused to sail to Monrovia because they were owed $2,500 in back pay. Buchholz confided to Fletcher that he wanted to resign his command, but the Liberian authorities threatened to arrest him if he did. *Birmingham* remained off Cape Palmas for another week awaiting relief.[22]

A second U.S. war vessel, USS *Des Moines*, announced its arrival off Monrovia on May 4, 1910, with a twenty-one-gun salute. *Des Moines*'s Cdr. John F. Luby immediately went ashore for briefings with American and Liberian officials and hired a crew of thirteen Kru rowers to man boats. First Lt. Benjamin Davis, who had only been in the country two weeks, boarded *Des Moines* on May 5 for passage to Cape Palmas. Davis needed firsthand knowledge of the Liberian Frontier Force and Liberian militia as well as the problems in the south. After Luby completed his diplomatic calls and paid off his Kru oarsmen, *Des Moines* steamed south and arrived at Cape Palmas on May 6, 1910, finding both *Birmingham* and *Lark* at anchor there.[23]

Commander Luby spent several days consulting with Commander Fletcher about the situation at Cape Palmas and the status of negotiations with the rebellious Greboes before *Birmingham* departed. Luby scanned reports delivered by the executive officer of *Birmingham* and made an official call ashore on Vice President Dossen. In accordance with navy etiquette, *Des Moines* fired a continuous gun salute until sunset on May 7 after receiving the news of the death of former Liberian president Garretson W. Gibson. Davis met with both American and Liberian officials to get an assessment of the situation, then reported to *Birmingham* for passage back to Monrovia along with Captain Buchholz of *Lark* and J. B. McGritty, the chief clerk of the Liberian treasury. Buchholz and McGritty traveled to Monrovia for money to pay the mutinous crew of *Lark*.[24]

Birmingham steamed from Cape Palmas on May 9 and arrived the following day for a short stop in Monrovia. Davis, Buchholz, and McGritty went ashore soon after arrival at the capital. Fletcher also went ashore to send one last telegram from Monrovia before his departure on May 11, 1910, reporting that "the Government of Liberia has received arms and ammunition from Germany" and that they were "preparing to attack" the Greboes. Monrovia had arranged the purchase of a thousand Mauser carbines and ammunition from Germany to outfit the poorly equipped Frontier Force. Lieutenant Davis dispatched a message carried by *Birmingham* to the War Department with his initial report on the Liberian armed forces recommending the United States support a campaign against the Greboes.[25]

After his return to Monrovia, Davis busied himself with completing arrangements to settle his family in quarters and get his office set up at the American consulate, a large and spacious brick building on the main street in Monrovia. Davis equipped his office with a large desk, typewriter, and other items, and tacked a large map of West Africa on the wall with a timetable of the local steamship line. Since there were no roads to speak of in Liberia, ships served as the main conveyance for trips to locations on the coast, as he had learned during his recent trip to Cape Palmas.[26]

Back at Cape Palmas on board *Des Moines*, Commander Luby soon confirmed everything Fletcher of *Birmingham* told him. The Americo-Liberian authorities had mismanaged the situation and rejected offers by the Greboes to settle the dispute without bloodshed. The commission and Grebo leaders visited the ship on May 16, and Luby and four of his officers attended a conference at Hoffman Station in Harper for the surrender of King Yado Gyude and the "Civilized Greboes of the Cape Palmas Tribe." King Gyude and the Greboes did not trust the Liberian officials and requested the presence of the U.S. officers as a third party "not concerned in the present trouble." Only four Grebo leaders showed up for the surrender, and many scattered into the jungle rather than lay down their arms. A few more showed up at a similar conference the following day, but Luby quickly tired of the palaver and wrote to the commission that he considered the business a waste of his time.[27]

Fighting erupted again, proving that the surrender of the four Grebo leaders meant little. The first indication of action was a memo in *Des Moines* log on May 19 noting that "*Lark* disembarked ashore and returned with a considerable body of men." Captain Buchholz had returned from Monrovia the previous day with German Mausers, ammunition, and about two hundred Frontier Force and militia reinforcements, whom Luby pronounced "a not very smart looking lot." On May 21 Dossen informed Luby that troops had taken and occupied Hoffman Station, Bigtown, and Puduke. Luby had already heard reports from four of his officers, who had been in Bigtown and witnessed the Grebo village pillaged, cattle shot, and goods removed by soldiers. He demanded the Americo-Liberian leaders "bring this wretched business to a close" and that they get "control the rabble brought here from Monrovia."[28]

Luby informed the secretary of the navy on May 29 that the situation in Harper was still volatile, though Liberian authorities had regained control of their troops and there were no further atrocities. Vice President Dossen rebuked General Padmore, the secretary of war who was nominally in charge of military operations, for the events in Bigtown. Dossen wrote Luby to assure him that further depredations would be avoided and the offending soldiers punished. More reinforcements arrived on board the German steamer *Walberg*, along with Liberian secretary of state F. E. R. Johnson.[29]

The Liberian Commission dispatched a force of about three hundred Frontier Force soldiers and militiamen up the Cavalla River to force more disaffected chiefs to surrender on May 31, 1910. The troops, who were owed back pay, only consented to march if they would be paid. Liberian agents borrowed the necessary funds from the German trading firm Woermann, promising to repay them through the remission of customs duties on goods imported by the company into Liberia. Commander Luby did not have much hope for the success of this expedition. The area around the Americo-Liberian settlement of Harper was surrounded by a patchwork of Grebo communes that were hostile, occupied, allied, or not involved in the fighting (see Fig. 9).[30]

In early June 1910 Luby informed the secretary of the navy that he was in Dakar, Senegal, replenishing his coal stores. He had sailed from Cape Palmas on June 5 and did not stop in Monrovia due to reports of yellow fever there. He planned to remain in Dakar ten days, grant men shore leave, and load enough provisions to last the balance of the mission. U.S. Navy ships that deployed to Liberia replenished stores periodically in Dakar, Senegal, and Las Palmas on Gran Canaria in the Spanish Canary Islands.[31]

On the return voyage to Cape Palmas, Luby stopped at the major trading posts along the Liberian coast and sent his intelligence officers, Ens. Elmo H. Williams and Paymaster Noel W. Grant, ashore to gather information so he "could report more fully on the general conditions existing in the Republic." Luby noted that the results of observations could only be "characterized as disheartening, if not disgusting. Corruption seems to run riot." Luby met only one honest Liberian merchant who admitted that nearly all Americo-Liberians were "office holders or office seekers" and that all the country's revenues went to pay their salaries, leaving nothing for public improvement. The merchant himself served as a senator from the Bassa District.[32]

Luby likewise visited with foreign merchants during his various stops along the coast to get a better assessment of the situation in Liberia. He reported that all the German merchants expressed the hope that the U.S. would take charge of Liberia. Luby calculated "the time when outside control by someone will be undertaken is rapidly approaching, if it has not already arrived." He reported that in no place did Liberian authority extend more than ten or fifteen miles from the coast. The British and French took advantage of this to tap the resources of the interior without paying duties. Luby also warned that the "slave trade is in full swing in the interior."[33]

After stopping in Monrovia on June 24 to brief Lyon and Davis and meet with President Barclay, Luby anchored again off Cape Palmas on July 2 to resume his mission. He learned that there had been two serious engagements between Liberian forces under the command of militia colonel William D. Lomax and the rebellious locals near a place called Webo, some sixty miles up the Cavalla River, in which the government troops came off the worse, suffering ten killed and fifty-six wounded. The Liberian Frontier Force and militia fell back in confusion to Cape Palmas, out of food and ammunition. A French army doctor serving with the Liberian forces treated the wounded in Harper and asked for assistance from the surgeon on board *Des Moines*.[34]

On July 18, 1910, Luby's surgeon reported that he had four cases of blackwater fever among the crew, one near death. This news induced Luby to steam north early to replenish coal for the sake of the sick sailors and the entire crew. He departed the following day, touched at Monrovia to report his situation, and arrived in Las Palmas, Canary Islands, on July 30. *Des Moines* remained in Las Palmas for two weeks to replenish and allow sick sailors to recover in a more temperate climate. One of the four crew members recovered from blackwater fever, but Commander Luby decided with the advice of his surgeon to leave three others behind in the hospital, to be collected on the return voyage after they had convalesced.[35]

Luby steamed back to Monrovia and arrived on August 23, 1910, to learn that the Grebo rebellion was over. All the Grebo kings had met with the Liberian commission on August 11, agreed to lay down their arms, renew treaty obligations, and swear allegiance to the Liberian government. Only two towns in Webo country escaped capture and remained hostile. Colonel Lomax commanded eighty-six Frontier Force soldiers left behind on the Cavalla River to watch the hostile towns.[36]

Amid the fighting against the Greboes in the southeast, the State Department appointed a new consul general to guide U.S. policy in Liberia. Dr. William D. Crum, appointed by President Taft in June, presented his credentials in Monrovia on August 25, 1910, and replaced Ernest Lyon. Booker T. Washington wrote to Lyon in June 1910 to inform him of his pending relief and to tell Lyon he had done everything to prevent his dismissal. Washington mentioned unknown charges that had been brought against Lyon as the basis for his removal. However, since Lyon was a Roosevelt appointee who served at the pleasure of the president, Taft was merely exercising his prerogative to replace him.[37]

When Commander Luby anchored off Monrovia on August 29, 1910, he went ashore to brief the new consul general on the latest developments in the Grebo affair. Luby and *Des Moines* remained at anchor off Monrovia for more than two weeks, doing very little. Commander Luby received a courtesy call from Consul General Crum on September 1, and the following day he and three officers attended a luncheon at the president's official residence, which he characterized as "distinctly creditable to the Liberians."[38]

With the Grebo rebellion over, the U.S. Navy asked for the release of *Des Moines* from her mission in Liberia. The State Department agreed but wanted the ship to remain nearby, so the navy sent Luby orders to proceed to Gibraltar to pick up stores waiting there. *Des Moines* weighed anchor on September 18, 1910, and touched at Las Palmas to retrieve its sick crewmembers from the hospital before proceeding to Gibraltar.[39]

Davis incorporated Commander Luby's reporting and his first-hand observations at Cape Palmas in his own commentary about the Grebo rebellion, the conduct of the Frontier Force, and Liberian militia. Davis drafted his initial report to the War Department in October 1910, painting a picture of a poorly disciplined, underfunded, disorganized Frontier Force with too many unqualified officers and two few trained soldiers. The Liberian militia was even worse, constituting a threat to the people it was organized to protect.[40]

Davis's comprehensive report provided an overview of the organization, equipment, pay, discipline, and administration of both the Liberian militia and Frontier Force. He noted that of one thousand Mauser carbines purchased from the Germans in May 1910 for the fighting against the Greboes, less than five hundred could be accounted for six months later. The three Krupp field guns delivered at the same time had gone missing as well, last seen on May 10 on the beach at Harper. In his messages to the War Department and conversations with Consul General Lyon, Davis made clear that both the Liberian Frontier Force and militia were useless and largely beyond the control of the equally inept central government.[41]

Lieutenant Davis and his family initially enjoyed their novel living conditions in Monrovia but soon found they had to spend a good deal of money importing canned goods from Europe and the United States since there was little they could safely eat locally. Clean potable water for drinking and cooking was also a constant problem. Boiling water or importing bottled water did not eliminate the risk, since Davis employed local Liberians in the kitchen who were not always thorough in their procedures. Davis and his wife, Elnora, also had diplomatic obligations and functions that stretched their budget further. They found the tropical climate odious, and one of them was always ill.[42]

Soon after beginning his tour in Liberia, Benjamin Davis contracted blackwater fever, a serious complication of malaria, a sometimes fatal disease that afflicted many new arrivals to the West African coast. He may have developed the disease during his trip to Cape Palmas, as did the crew members of *Des Moines*. The illness confined him to bed with fever, chills, and anemia for weeks, and he never fully recovered. Davis lost more than twenty-six pounds during his first few months in Liberia due to this illness. Blackwater fever has a high mortality rate, and symptoms include rapid pulse, high fever and chills, extreme prostration, a rapidly developing anemia, and urine that is black or dark red in color. Hence the name blackwater fever.[43]

After recovering sufficiently to continue his work, Davis witnessed a "disorderly mass" of Camp Johnson Frontier Force soldiers mutiny and picket the office of the secretary of war on October 10, 1910. The soldiers threatened violence if authorities ignored their demands for back pay. After a good deal of persuasion by the secretary of war and a senior Liberian Frontier Force officer, the mob dispersed. Davis found out later that there was no money in the treasury to pay the soldiers. This event and others reinforced his opinion that the Frontier Force was unstructured, undisciplined, and a menace to the government and people.[44]

As Davis and African American officers came to understand, there was a clear difference in the motivation and purpose that separated the officers from the enlisted men of the Liberian Frontier Force. While the Americo-Liberian officers operated under European military codes practiced by colonial forces serving elsewhere in tropical Africa, the indigenous enlisted soldiers retained their ethnic codes and practices.[45]

The difference in uniforms provided a visual clue to distinguish officers from enlisted soldiers. The Americo-Liberian officers dressed in khaki tropical uniforms, neckties, knee-high leather boots, pistol belts, and campaign hats as clear visual markers of their authority and origin. The Frontier Force enlisted soldiers, recruited from the indigenous people and referred to by locals as "red-caps," wore red conical felt hats like the Egyptian fez, khaki shirts, and knee-length shorts and went barefoot, though a few noncommissioned officers wore boots as a badge of privilege.[46]

But this duality of motivation and purpose went further. The enlisted soldiers of the Liberian Frontier Force were recruited heavily from the Kpelle, Loma, Mende, and Mano groups from the northern hinterland, who waged war based on ethnic codes and traditions of warfare. These behaviors centered on raiding enemy communities to collect booty, exact revenge, capture slaves, or liberate pawns, a West African term for someone forced into bondage. Many of the local ethnic groups remained enemies and fought allied with or against the Frontier Force to gain an advantage over their rivals or exact revenge for earlier defeats.[47]

The government in Monrovia found these indigenous practices of warfare useful and employed them because they lacked the resources to pay, train, and equip the Frontier Force in Western fashion. The Americo-Liberian governing class allowed these methods even though they contradicted the principles of "civilized" society they espoused. They deemed it more important that the Frontier Force pacify the ethnic groups in the hinterland and safeguard Liberia's borders than play by rules the Americo-Liberian officers were unable or unwilling to enforce. The American officers sent to Liberia found that the keys to transforming the Frontier Force were discipline, regular pay, and a fixed system of supply, all touchstones of a Western professional military force.[48]

Though events remained peaceful in the south, Commander Luby and *Des Moines* returned to Liberia from Gibraltar one last time to accomplish two additional missions. The first was to deliver Dr. Roland P. Faulkner, financial representative of the Republic of Liberia, who had come on board in Gibraltar on December 1910 for conveyance to Monrovia. Faulkner headed the Liberian commission of 1909 and returned to Liberia as a U.S. economic expert and adviser. *Des Moines* anchored off Monrovia on January 3, 1911, to ferry Faulkner ashore.[49]

Des Moines lingered off Monrovia only long enough for a junior officer to go ashore to make official calls, then departed the same day for Cape Palmas. Luby's second mission was to retrieve the bodies of the two sailors left behind by *Birmingham* for transport back to the United States. Luby assigned a shore party to disinter the bodies of Ira A. Benidict and William A. Jones on January 4 and departed for Boston the same day.[50]

On the return voyage to the U.S., *Des Moines* offered up one more casualty to the mission in Liberia. Commander John F. Luby died on January 8, 1911, the day before *Des Moines* arrived in Las Palmas. The ship's log listed the cause of death "inflammation of intestines," but a *New York Times* article two days later noted that while in Liberia "he was taken seriously ill with fever to which a number of the crew of his vessel fell victims." His death, in addition to that of another crewmember who had died while in Gibraltar, meant the ship conveyed four bodies when it arrived in Boston.[51]

Luby had drafted reports during his mission, and all information was forwarded to the State Department and shared with Consul General Lyon and Lieutenant Davis in Monrovia. His voluminous May 23, 1910, report was forty-five typed pages with enclosures, and he had added thirty-three more pages of detailed reporting before departing from Monrovia for Las Palmas. It was fortunate that Luby had recorded his assessments, as he did not reach the United States alive. The State Department had a rich store of frank and factual reporting on hand, to which Lieutenant Davis would soon add.[52]

Davis met with the Liberian secretary of state F. E. R. Johnson in Monrovia in February 1911 to recommend changes in the Frontier Force and was encouraged by the reception he received. He followed up the meeting with a memo to the secretary detailing his ideas for reorganizing the Liberian military. His plan began with abolishing the office of the secretary of war to encourage efficiency and cut unnecessary layers of bureaucracy. Davis outlined a military organization commanded by five Americans, comprising Davis as a lieutenant colonel and chief of staff, John Green as a quartermaster, and three African American noncommissioned officers to command the units.[53]

Though Secretary of State Johnson did not accept Davis's recommendations, the Liberian government was grateful and later asked him if he was willing to accept a commission in the Frontier Force. Johnson sent a letter to Consul General Crum, who forwarded it to the U.S. secretary of state, asking that Davis be detailed as "Senior Officer" of the Liberian Frontier Force. Cautious of endangering his status in the U.S. Army, and perhaps a little naïve, Davis informed the War Department of the offer and asked for advice. Washington responded that he could not accept pay or a commission in the Liberian service, though he could and should act as adviser.[54]

By 1911 Davis began to tire of Liberian intransigence and lack of support from the U.S. War Department. More importantly, his health continued to fail, and he wrote to Washington DC asking to be recalled. In his message to the War Department, he noted that he had been absent from his regiment for six years and that his service in Liberia was ruining his health. Despite the constant use of medication, Davis found it increasingly difficult to carry on his work. The War Department decided to withdraw Davis based on the continuing deterioration of his physical condition.[55]

The last substantive report filed by Davis with the MID reported the "opening of German Wireless Station, Monrovia." Sent on September 9, 1911, it detailed the completion of the German wireless and cable relay station put into operation that year. As mentioned in a previous chapter, Germany laid a transatlantic cable between Liberia and Brazil that connected Berlin with its colonies and other commercial interests in the southern hemisphere. The completion of this strategically important cable station would sharpen competition between the European powers in Liberia in the years to come.[56]

On October 12, 1911, just before his departure, Davis completed another report, titled "The Military Forces of Liberia." This narrative, coming at the end of his tour in Liberia, was more informed than the version written the previous year. It contained a scathing commentary detailing the many shortcomings of the Liberian militia and Frontier Force. The Frontier Force lacked administration, regular pay, training, professionalism, education, and discipline, and it habitually victimized the indigenous groups of the hinterland. But with good leadership and proper training, Davis felt with a "force of about twelve hundred men[,] Liberia would have no internal troubles." The Liberian militia was even worse, "regarded more as a menace to law and order, than as a force guaranteeing protection." Since this report is not listed on his record of dispatches to the MID, he must have carried it with him back to the United States.[57]

On October 17, 1911, Davis and his family boarded the British steamer *Cedric*, and after stops in the Canary Islands and a change of ships in London, they reached the United States on December 2. After a two-week leave, Davis reported for duty at the War Department, where he offered his recommendation that a cadre of four officers from the U.S. Regular Army train a Liberian force of 1,500 men. Davis predicted difficulties in getting the Liberian government to give the American officers sufficient authority to turn the Liberian Frontier Force into an effective organization. He opined that the key to success in this effort would be money for paying and equipping the force.[58]

Lieutenant Davis reported that Liberian officials opposed every suggestion to reform the Frontier Force. While blackwater fever was largely responsible for Davis's departure from Liberia, he had also been forced out by his difficulties with the ministries in Liberia. The roots of this resistance included anti-American feeling, resentment of foreign interference, jealousy over the loss of power and prestige, and lack of money. Most Americo-Liberians were deeply distrustful of outsiders, whether white or black. The Liberian secretary of war was incompetent and had completely lost control of the Frontier Force, having been trained as a preacher and thrust into the job with no preparation.[59]

By the end of 1911, as plans for a $1.7 million international loan to Liberia neared completion, the U.S. Department of State asked the War Department for an officer to lead the reorganization of the Liberian Frontier Force. A November 1911 letter to Booker T. Washington from Reed Paige Clark, who was appointed as the U.S. receiver of customs in Liberia, summarized the matter. Clark explained:

Yesterday Mr. [Chandler] Hale, the Third Assistant Secretary of State, Captain [Frank R.] McCoy of the War Department, and I were discussing the matter of the appointment of a military attaché to Monrovia to aid in the reorganization of the Liberian Constabulary, or Frontier Police. The military attaché would act in an advisory capacity only, but his advice, if the services of the right man can be secured, would have great weight and would be invaluable.[60]

After explaining the problem, Clark identified the "right man" for the job and his qualifications. Clark continued:

There seems to be one colored officer on the active list of the Army who is especially well fitted for the work and that is Captain Charles Young, Ninth Cavalry, U.S.A., who was recently attached to our legation at Port au Prince, Haiti. He has made an admirable record and is apparently just the man for a position where considerable tact and great executive ability are required. Captain Young is a graduate of West Point. He was highly recommended by Mr. Justice Stewart, of the Liberian Supreme Court, who was in Washington last week.[61]

Of the three African American Regular Army officers serving in 1911, Charles Young was by far the most senior and qualified. Young, as a senior captain with twenty-two years of commissioned service, had commanded units ranging in size from platoon to battalion, experienced intense combat as a troop commander in the Philippine War, and served ably as the military attaché to Haiti and the Dominican Republic. Perhaps as important, Young spoke French, Spanish, and German fluently and had earned a first-class education from West Point. Davis and Green, by contrast, each had barely ten years of commissioned service, no unit leadership experience above platoon level, and little education beyond a year or two of college. Clearly Young was competent in ways that Green and Davis were not, and Clark knew this.

With these qualifications in mind, Clark asked Booker T. Washington to contact Young and persuade him to undertake the mission. Booker T. Washington wrote to Young, and he replied from Fort D. A. Russell, Wyoming, on November 24, 1911. Young wrote: "I wish to state that I am always willing to aid in any work for the good of the country in general and of our race in particular, whether that race be found in Africa or in the United States." Young was clearly attracted to the idea of serving in Africa. He concluded: "Now if you and the War Department think I can be of more good to the country and our people on the African detail with Mr. Paige [Clark], I am perfectly willing to go, and shall render him faithful and loyal service."[62]

The wording of Young's response to Booker T. Washington revealed that he was loyal to the country he served as well as an activist supporter of African Americans. The term Young used in his response to Washington was telling: he wondered where he could "be of more good to the country and our people." By this Young meant people of color on both sides of the Atlantic, a clear indication of his advocacy of Pan-Africanism, a concept then being hotly debated in the African American community. Young had to decide if the best use of his next three years would be serving in the United States or Liberia. He chose Liberia.

The War Department complied with the State Department's request, naming Captain Charles Young to the post and issuing orders on December 14, 1911, to assign him to temporary duty with the army chief of staff in Washington DC to prepare for the mission in Liberia. There he met with Lieutenant Davis and got a first-hand account of his experiences in Liberia. In January, Young took his examination for promotion to major, appeared before a board of officers, and was found eligible for promotion. He had to wait until the following year in Monrovia to pin on his gold major's leaves and celebrate the milestone of achieving field grade rank in the Regular Army.[63]

The new U.S. policy involving dollar diplomacy in Liberia stood little hope of success without an effective military leader like Young and a competent military training team to stabilize the security situation in Liberia. The newly appointed U.S. receiver of customs, Reed Paige Clark, realized this better than anyone. It was his mission to oversee the customs receipts and supervise the administration of the international loan agreement being negotiated with American, British, French, and German banks. Clark needed Young to serve in Liberia to enable the success of this fresh diplomatic effort on the African west coast.

Benjamin O. Davis proved a good choice to investigate the military assistance mission in Liberia and lay the groundwork for the reorganization of the Liberian Frontier Force. One of only three black Regular Army officers serving at the time, he was well suited to the task of setting up the military attaché office in Monrovia, establishing working relationships with American and Liberian officials in the capital, and assessing the difficulties the U.S. government would experience in training, maintaining, and leading the Frontier Force. Blackwater fever and intransigence on the part of the Liberian government prevented him from making more progress.

The commanding officers of both USS *Birmingham* and USS *Des Moines* provided the navy and State Department with detailed reporting on the situation in Liberia and the maladroitness with which the Americo-Liberian regime dealt with the Grebo rebellion. Luby wrote that a "very unsatisfactory state of affairs exists in the territory of Liberia, and it is just a question of time when some exterior action will be taken." Both commanders shared their reporting and observations with newly arrived Consul General Crum and Lieutenant Davis, so both were cognizant of the challenges ahead.

Lieutenant Davis traveled extensively throughout Liberia and reported many of the shortcomings and problems that would plague African American officers in the years to come. He also devised a detailed and comprehensive plan to reorganize, equip, and lead the Frontier Force, and most of his recommendations were eventually followed. His warnings about the obstinacy and inflexibility of the Americo-Liberian establishment in Monrovia proved prescient; however, it would be left to others like Charles Young to carry the mission to the next phase.

FIG. 10. Liberian Frontier Force officer (*left*) and enlisted soldier (*right*) with a German Mauser carbine, 1912. Courtesy of the National Afro-American Museum and Cultural Center, NAM_MSS22_B12F34.

FIG. 11. Capt. Charles Young was featured on the February 1912 cover of *The Crisis*, announcing his assignment to Liberia as military attaché. *The Crisis*, February 1912.

FIG. 12. Capt. Richard H. Newton Jr. before his departure for Liberia, 1912. *The Crisis*, May 1912.

FIG. 13. Maj. Wilson Ballard (*left*), Capt. Arthur Browne (*center*), and an unidentified man in Monrovia, 1914. Courtesy of the National Afro-American Museum and Cultural Center, NAM_P3_B02F05.

FIG. 14. *Floor:* Nellie L. Bundy, Maj. Charles Young. *Seated, in chairs:* Richard C. Bundy, Pearle Ballard. *Standing:* Maj. Wilson Ballard, Ada Young. On the second-floor balcony of Young's home in Monrovia, 1914. Courtesy of the National Afro-American Museum and Cultural Center, NAM_MSS22-P3_B02F03Pg05.

FIG. 15. Maj. Wilson Ballard, Nellie L. Bundy, "Hurt," Maj. Charles Young, Pearle Ballard, and Capt. Samuel B. Pearson in front of the Young home, 1913. Courtesy of the National Afro-American Museum and Cultural Center, NAM_MSS22-P3_B02F03Pg05.

FIG. 16. Maj. Wilson Ballard meeting with British officers on the Anglo-Liberian Boundary Commission, 1912. Courtesy of the National Afro-American Museum and Cultural Center, NAM_MSS22-P3_B01F03.

4

Young

Rescuing Liberia

No man can lift himself by his own boot-straps, neither
can a nation or people. Liberia must be essentially and
materially aided, and that right early, or we shall all be made
ashamed, while the English, French, and Germans rejoice
at our weakness and discomfiture.

—CHARLES YOUNG, 1912

When Capt. Charles Young reached the U.S. consulate in Monrovia, Liberia, in 1912, the country was torn by internal strife and threatened by external incursion. Having served as the military attaché to the island of Hispaniola (Haiti and the Dominican Republic) under similar difficult circumstances, Captain Young was up to the challenge of this assignment. As always, Young approached his new duty as a practical man and consummate, professional military officer. Nevertheless, he must have been deeply moved by the opportunity to overhaul Liberia's military and help the small African republic survive.

The War Department assigned Young and his officers to Liberia based on significant geopolitical and military considerations, as well as the policy decision to extend dollar diplomacy to Monrovia. The United States had a special relationship with this troubled country that had been colonized by freed American slaves, Africa's first republic. However, sending African American officers to train the Liberian Frontier Force opened a new and complicated chapter in the relationship between Washington and Monrovia.

Charles Young's early life was remarkable. He was born into enslavement in Mays Lick, Kentucky, on March 12, 1864, near the end of the Civil War. His parents escaped enslavement when he was six months old, and Charles grew up and attended school in Ripley, Ohio. After graduating from an integrated high school and teaching in a black school in Ripley for a few years, Young won a nomination in 1884 to the U.S. Military Academy at West Point, New York. Enormous hardships, academic challenges, and social ostracism dogged him at West Point, but he succeeded through a combination of focused intellect, hard work, and a sense of humor. Upon graduation in 1889, the army assigned Second Lt. Charles Young to the Ninth U.S. Cavalry, one of the well-known Buffalo Soldier regiments.[1]

Young enjoyed an extraordinary military career in the twenty-three years between commissioning and assignment to Liberia. He served on various western frontier posts, at Wilberforce University in Ohio as professor of military science, as commander of a black Ohio National Guard battalion during the Spanish-American War, in combat against guerrillas in the Philippine War, as acting superintendent of Sequoia National Park, and as military attaché to Hispaniola. Young was a captain and senior troop commander stationed at Fort D. A. Russell, Wyoming, when he was called to serve as the military attaché to Liberia in 1912.[2]

Captain Young was uniquely qualified to undertake the difficult mission of launching the military assistance enterprise in Liberia. He was the most senior and competent of the three African American Regular Army officers on active duty at the time and the only one of the trio with the prestige of being a West Point graduate. He boasted more than two decades of active duty training and leading troops in war and peace. Finally, his previous military attaché tour in Haiti and the Dominican Republic prepared him for the diplomatic and political challenges he faced in Liberia.[3]

Young was well educated, spoke several foreign languages, and mastered the knack of picking up new vernaculars and dialects. He possessed an intellectual curiosity and was deeply interested in the history and culture of Africa. In 1912, the year he arrived in Liberia, Young published a book titled *Military Morale of Nations and Races* which he called a "psycho-military study of the morale of nations and races," intended to systemize the qualities of people, measure their effect in battle, and argue that military virtues could be cultivated. Most of his thinking as revealed in this book was mainstream, though he argued that a soldier's effectiveness had nothing to do with race and everything to do with preparation and training. He tried unsuccessfully to get the U.S. Infantry and Cavalry School to adopt it as a text.[4]

What Young said about Liberia in his book reflects the mindset with which he arrived for service in Monrovia. He said "The civilized people, the Liberians, are mostly descendants of the freedmen from the United States and Christian natives; these do not differ in their aspirations and mental and moral makeup from the same class in the United States." The indigenous population he lumped together with the rest of African people and classified as "tribal," with some being "barbarous and very little lifted above the animal in the scale of humanity, and others progressive, displaying an aptitude for agriculture, commerce, even government." His ideas of the relative strengths and weaknesses of the two classes of society in Liberia would be challenged soon after his arrival.[5]

Young carried with him to Monrovia a unique prestige among the African American intelligentsia at the time, and the black press reported on his achievements wherever the army sent him. He was acquainted with Booker T. Washington, having hosted him on at least two occasions, and was a close friend of W. E. B. Du Bois, having taught together with him at Wilberforce University. A bachelor, Du Bois often found refuge from the parochial and sometimes hysterically religious atmosphere at the university in Young's home in Wilberforce. Biographer David Levering Lewis noted, "Young's was the first genuine male friendship in Du Bois' life, one of a handful in which there was genuine affinity." Young and Du Bois carried on this friendship and corresponded throughout their lifetimes.[6]

Captain Young reported for duty at the U.S. consulate in Monrovia on May 1, 1912, and immediately set about getting organized for the mission. He rented a two-story brick house, known as the

General Sherman house, that overlooked the ocean on Ashmun Street and moved in with his wife Ada and two small children, Charles Noel and Marie Aurelia. Young spent much of his initial time setting up his quarters, office, and liaison with both the U.S. consulate and the Liberian government. Because of the sensitivity of his mission with the Liberian Frontier Force, Captain Young took care to establish good relations with Liberian government officials. In time, he developed access and a close personal relationship with the president of Liberia, Daniel E. Howard, which facilitated his difficult task.[7]

Three men whose cooperation would prove critical to Young's mission waited for him at the American consulate in Monrovia. The first, William D. Crum, had served as the consul general to Liberia since presenting his credentials in August 1910. Crum was an African American from Charleston, South Carolina, who had studied at the University of South Carolina and earned a Doctor of Medicine degree from Howard University. A staunch Republican, he practiced medicine in Charleston until President Roosevelt appointed him collector of the port there from 1904 to 1910. Selected as consul general by President William Taft, Crum followed a long line of African Americans who had served as ministers to Liberia after Republican president Ulysses S. Grant appointed the first in the Reconstruction era.[8]

The deputy to Minister Crum at the U.S. consulate was First Secretary Richard C. Bundy, who was also black. Young referred to Bundy as "the brains of our ministership here." He ran the legation for two long periods in the absence of a resident consul general as the chargé d'affaires, from September 1912 to December 1913 and from April to December 1915 (the term *chargé* was only used when the consul general was absent and the deputy took charge of the consulate). Born on January 31, 1879, in Wilmington, Ohio, Bundy grew up in Cincinnati. He received an appointment from an Ohio congressman to the U.S. Naval Academy in 1897 but failed the entrance examination. Bundy graduated from Wilberforce University, where he and Young later taught at the same time, and both were active with the Beta Kappa Sigma fraternity, also called the Black Cats. They worked hand in glove together the next four years in Liberia.[9]

The third man at the consulate who was critical to Young's mission was the American in charge of the receivership in Liberia, Reed Paige Clark. The United States facilitated the international loan to Monrovia on the condition that it accept a U.S.-led receivership. Clark filled that role, assisted by deputies from Great Britain, France, and Germany, and these men took in all Liberian income from the collection of customs and distributed the money. Essentially, a first lien on all export and import duties secured the loan agreement of 1912 and was the key component of the new dollar diplomacy policy in Liberia, just as in Nicaragua and the Dominican Republic. Letters from Booker T. Washington to American consul general Crum and Liberian president Howard spoke highly of Clark's earnestness and qualifications and found him "without race prejudice." Clark was the only member of the consulate leadership who was white.[10]

Young counted on Clark's receivership to pay his American contract officers and to finance and equip the Frontier Force. When Young and his American officers assumed control of the force in 1912, some of its soldiers had not been paid in three years, and there were endemic shortages of food, uniforms, kerosene, medicine, and other essential materials. Regular pay and a steady flow of supplies were important to restoring the morale and effectiveness of the Frontier Force and restraining it from preying on the indigenous populations in the interior. It was essential for Young to stay on good terms with the receiver, and this was an easy task because Clark had been an early advocate of Young's selection. Moreover, Clark depended on the security provided by the American-led Frontier Force to ensure stability and allow the economy to thrive.[11]

Young quickly struck up a friendship with two other men in Monrovia: fellow American Frederick Starr and Liberian Supreme Court associate justice Thomas McCants-Stewart. Both as highly intelligent and naturally inquisitive as he, they carried on a connection and correspondence for the rest of their lives. Young probed Starr, who was white, regarding his knowledge of Liberia and the Congo, where Starr had traveled extensively as a University of Chicago anthropologist. McCants-Stewart, a former African American who became a citizen of Liberia, was one of the few Liberians in a position of influence who acknowledged the potential value of the indigenous population and rejected the government's short-sighted maltreatment of them . Judge McCants-Stewart and Young worked together, often covertly, to improve Monrovia's treatment of the indigenous people.[12]

Within four months of his arrival, the army promoted Young to major in the Ninth Cavalry on August 28, 1912. This promotion made Young the first African American to achieve field grade rank as a line officer in the Regular Army. Field grade rank, from major through colonel, represented a watershed for officers in the old army, especially those who were West Point graduates. The army promoted officers to major, lieutenant colonel, and colonel if they performed their duties well and stayed healthy long enough, and to general if they were lucky and served in coveted staff or detached duty positions.[13]

Young did not take on the mission to reorganize and rehabilitate the Liberian Frontier Force by himself. Rather, he personally picked three black former officers and noncommissioned officers to train and command the Liberian Frontier Force. After Young selected the three, the U.S. War Department forwarded the names of the men, the State Department approved the choice, and the president of the United States nominated them. The three served under contract with the Liberian government, who paid them from the funds collected by the U.S.-led receivership. While Young advised on training and organizing, these Americans officers commanded the force. The difference was important, as Young was a military attaché and member of the Regular Army and therefore forbidden to command the Frontier Force, while the contracted officers were civilians and under no such restriction.[14]

Young selected three African Americans with whom he had very close personal connections. The War Department allowed him to choose from a diverse pool from his service with the Ninth Cavalry, former cadets at Wilberforce, and subordinates from his command of the Ninth Ohio Battalion during the Spanish-American War. Young knew the importance of picking experienced officers who were willing and able to undertake challenging missions thousands of miles away in Africa with little guidance or support. Young's mission would succeed or fail based on his choice of personnel.[15]

The War Department sent Young a letter in mid-January 1912 instructing him to select three officers and set sail as soon as practical. Washington began receiving letters from volunteers soon after an article appeared in the *Army and Navy Journal* in November 1911 on the U.S. commission's recommendation. Young had full discretion to select one major and two captains to lead his effort. His freedom to pick is notable; in fact, it may be that that the War Department did not care about the mission that had been forced on them by the State Department and were happy to have Young deal with details.[16]

Major Young selected his old friend and longtime colleague Wilson Ballard to lead the effort and command the Liberian Frontier Force. Ballard was a Louisianan who had served as Young's cadet adjutant at Wilberforce, as a volunteer officer under Young's command in the Ninth Ohio Battalion during the Spanish-American War, and as a first lieutenant in the Forty-Eighth Volunteer Infantry Regiment during the Philippine War. Born in 1877, Ballard earned his bachelor's degree at Wilberforce in 1899, and after his Philippine service, attended Ohio State University to earn a degree in dentistry. Ballard left his dental practice in Louisville, Kentucky, in 1912 to serve in Liberia. Young chose him to command the Frontier Force because he had confidence in his abilities and because Ballard had served long and competently as a field officer during the Spanish-American and Philippine wars. Ballard brought his wife with him to Monrovia.[17]

The second officer Young selected, Arthur A. Browne, had somewhat less military experience than Ballard. Browne was born in Nebraska on January 7, 1880, and served under Young as a cadet first sergeant at Wilberforce and as a corporal in the Ninth Ohio Battalion during the Spanish-American War. Browne returned to Wilberforce after the war to finish his bachelor's degree and military cadet training in 1902, followed by graduate work at Howard and Kansas State University. He taught mathematics and natural science at several schools before opening a private practice in podiatry in Chicago in 1911. Unlike Ballard, Browne had not served as an officer in the field or in combat. Not everyone applauded Young's choice of Browne. Booker T. Washington, who made it his business to know all African American professionals, noted privately that Browne was "a bumptious, troublesome, sensitive foolish fellow," and predicted "he would not be in Liberia ten days before he would give you and everyone else concerned all kinds of trouble."[18]

The third of Young's officers was Richard H. Newton, who hailed from Baltimore, Maryland, where he was born in 1878. Newton, though less educated than the others, boasted more active duty military experience, having served two three-year tours in the Ninth Cavalry beginning in 1900, and in the Philippine War, where he fought under Captain Young. He also spent three years as lieutenant in the Philippine Scouts training Filipino soldiers. Toward the end of his enlisted service, Newton worked at the Army War College Detachment in Fort Myer, Virginia, as a noncommissioned officer. The army discharged him in 1911 so he could take a job as a printing clerk with the U.S. civil service in Washington DC. Both Newton and Browne sailed to Liberia without their wives.[19]

All three of these officers and subsequent candidates accepted their positions with the Liberian Frontier Force for similar reasons. First and perhaps most importantly, they were asked to do so by Young, a man they all knew, respected, and had served with. As with Young, the powerful draw of service to black Africa influenced them. The salary and status that came with the commissions were also a strong incentive for the three. The commander of the Frontier Force received a major's pay of $2,000 and the others a captain's wage of $1,600 annually, the same rate as in the U.S. Army and more money and prestige than they could hope to earn at civilian jobs in the United States. And certainly the draw of adventure was a strong factor for young men who had worked previously as dentists, podiatrists, and printing clerks in a racially segregated society.[20]

There is record of at least one other qualified U.S. officer who volunteered for service in Liberia but was not selected. Captain Samuel "Jackie" B. Pearson, a white officer from the Ninth Cavalry and close friend of Young, wanted badly to join him in Africa. As a young lieutenant, Pearson had volunteered to serve under Captain Young because of the black officer's reputation as an effective leader, unlike other white officers who shunned the black officer.

Pearson, a troop commander with the Ninth at Fort D. A. Russell, wrote at least twice begging Young to consider him for a position and visited Young in Liberia. Yet Young knew that Regular Army officers were not eligible for the detail, and a white officer was not suitable for the complicated situation in the Frontier Force in 1912. The Liberian Constitution denied those "not of Negro descent" any role in government affairs, and since the contract officers serving with the Frontier Force had to work closely with government officials and carry out the directives of the Liberian War Department, they had to be black.[21]

Major Young and his American officers faced unexpected delays in getting to work after their arrival in Liberia on May 1, 1912. Though they met with the Liberian president and minister of war within a week of reaching Monrovia and expressed their willingness to go to work immediately, the war ministry told Young's three colleagues they would have to wait until their Liberian Frontier Force officer commissions were issued. Young complained, "The Liberians, following the custom of all tropical peoples, are given to tedious delays." They waited a month to get the commissions and another month before they were given anything meaningful to do. Young had foreseen this possibility and "laid out a course of study for them, which they took up and this broke the tedium of waiting." With his officers thus occupied, Young was free to devote his energies to assessing the mission.[22]

One of Young's first challenges was to evaluate the state of the Frontier Force and the obstacles to his task, and he wrote a detailed assessment for Chargé d'Affaires Richard C. Bundy on October 9, 1912. Bundy had been the temporary head of the consulate since Consul General Crum departed sick with blackwater fever on September 17; Crum died in Charleston three months later. Chief among the challenges listed by Young was a lack of money to fund the project, as the promised U.S. loan had been delayed. Some of the Frontier Force soldiers had not been paid for years, with the money for their pay diverted by their officers. Young prioritized setting up a training academy for the development of a generation of honest and competent young officers because he found that the "Liberian officers of the old force cannot be trusted." There were also problems with bureaucratic foot-dragging on the part of the Liberian government, continuing interference by the British, French, and Germans, and a lack of serviceable equipment to supply the force.[23]

Amid these problems, Young and his African American officers kept busy training the Frontier Force and responding to crises. By October 1912 Young, Ballard, Browne, and Newton had increased the effective strength of the force from 354 men and 4 officers to 540 men and 17 commissioned Liberian officers, though they had only 400 Mauser carbines with which to arm them and very little ammunition. While recruiting and training, Young and his officers had to keep on their guard for trouble in the hinterland. It would not take long for Young and all three of his officers to see significant action.[24]

The first serious crisis occurred along the western Anglo-Liberian border with the British colony of Sierra Leone. The Anglo-Liberian boundary situation was one of the key issues that prompted the United States to negotiate the loan agreement for fear that Great Britain would seize more territory adjacent to Sierra Leone and eventually annex part of Liberia. For some time, the British and Liberians had endeavored to agree on the border between Liberia and Sierra Leone, define it with surveyed markers or stone cairns, and provide effective control on their respective sides of the frontier.[25]

The requirement to settle the boundary dispute between the British and Liberians fell to an Anglo-Liberian Boundary Commission, comprising American, British, and Liberian members. The delay in finalizing the loan agreement and receivership held up money that had been allocated to pay for an American civil engineer for the commission. Though the American consulate wanted to send Young to serve on the boundary commission, the State and War departments refused to let him represent Liberia based on his active duty status. Therefore, Ballard filled in temporarily as the American representative on the commission, taking him away from his primary job commanding the Frontier Force.[26]

Before the arrival of the American officers, there was a great deal of fighting along the Anglo-Liberian boundary. A contingent of Frontier Force soldiers attacked the town of Behlu in the border area and were repulsed by British colonial troops with four Liberians killed in action on January 1, 1912. The general state of unrest continued for several months, and two of the chief mischief-makers were Col. William D. Lomax, the Liberian militia officer in command of local Frontier Force troops, and J. W. Cooper, the Liberian frontier commissioner. They did everything in their power to obstruct the marking of the boundary and participated in the execution of eight Kissi chiefs at Kolahun in January 1912. Witnesses swore that Lomax shot some of the chiefs himself. The Liberian government finally dispatched the Liberian secretary of state to the border to arrest Lomax and Cooper, though they defiantly refused to come to Monrovia as ordered.[27]

These events led Monrovia to dispatch American Captain Browne with British and Liberian officials on a fourteen-day march into Loma and Belle country to arrest the renegade Liberian officials in May 1912. They caught up with Lomax and Cooper in the border area and escorted them back to Monrovia a month later. On August 1 the government jailed Lomax and Cooper to await the September term of the circuit court. The court tried the men, who admitted to killing the local chiefs, and a jury of their peers acquitted them based on a plea of justification due to a military emergency. This was an example of the Americo-Liberians' idea of "justice" and disregard of the rights of the indigenous people, as well as an early indication of the challenges the American officers would face in the years to come.[28]

With Captain Browne dispatched to the interior and Captain Newton sent to Cape Palmas to replace mutinous troops, Major Ballard was the only officer available to tackle new troubles on the central coast after his return from duty with the Anglo-Liberian Boundary Commission. Fresh unrest began at the end of September 1912 when Liberians, worried about the situation in the country and impatient with the delays in the loan agreement, began attacking westerners and their property in Monrovia. There were four nighttime stone-throwing incidents aimed at English, German, and Dutch nationals in September, and in early October the malefactors targeted the U.S. consulate. In November the unrest moved to Brewerville, fifteen miles north of Monrovia, where locals looted a German store. Concurrently, Kru people rebelled at River Cess, seventy-five miles southeast of Monrovia, when the government refused to permit foreign merchants, mainly Germans, to sell gunpowder to them. There was a similar uprising at Grand Bassa, just south of Monrovia.[29]

The unstable conditions, disorder, and loss of goods caused the German merchants to complain to the German consulate in Monrovia and directly appeal to Germany for a war vessel. The merchants exaggerated their reports, leading the German government to query the German consul general about the real situation in Liberia. The situation was aggravated by the fact that two German newspaper correspondents were in Monrovia and took embellished reports of the disturbances back to Hamburg. Even though the German merchants were partly responsible for the uprising and sympathetic to the local Krus, they worried at the prospect of a general uprising, fearing for their lives and property.[30]

Major Ballard set out from Monrovia to River Cess on October 25, 1912, with seventy-five of his best-trained Frontier Force soldiers and quickly suppressed the unrest with steady leadership and good tactics. Ballard then moved on to Grand Bassa with fifty handpicked men to restore order there. The Krus and other communities learned to respect the leadership and fighting ability of the American officers. Conversely, the indigenous people had nothing but contempt for Americo-Liberian officers. This set up a situation in which the American officers were kept busy putting down insurgencies in hot spots, yet as soon as they moved on to other regions, the locals took advantage of their absence to incite turmoil again.[31]

Although Ballard succeeded in putting down the revolt among the Krus, the discontent among the local Germans nationals spiraled out of control. The appeal by the German merchants and an overreaction by Berlin led to the dispatch of the German gunboat SMS *Panther*, which glided ominously into the open roadstead of Monrovia late in the evening of November 11, 1912. White missionary Emory Ross recalled seeing the *Panther* "put a formal visiting party ashore and that night play its searchlights over the palms and houses and promontory of that city." Ross sat on the second story balcony of the home of his friend Maj. Charles Young and "watched the unwonted pencil of light write upon the face of Monrovia, and talked of what this portended for Africa and the world."[32]

The captain of *Panther* demanded that the Liberian government take energetic and decisive measures to guarantee the safety of Germans on the Bassa coast. He warned that if satisfactory assurances were not given within twenty-four hours, he would make an "armed intervention." Liberian president Howard responded that the situation was under control and respectfully declined German assistance, and the *Panther* departed for the Bassa coast the same night. By the end of December 1912 two other German ships, SMS *Bremen* and SMS *Eber*, joined *Panther* in Liberian waters. Berlin never took half measures when German honor and money were at stake in Liberia.[33]

On December 26, 1912, Chargé Bundy cabled the State Department with news that the Germans were demanding punishment after an alleged assault by an Americo-Liberian officer and his soldiers on a German officer at River Cess. Captain Ballard was not present at the time of the incident, but the Liberian government quickly dispatched him to the scene to investigate. The Germans delivered an ultimatum that they would be satisfied with nothing short of dismissal of the officer in question, despite Ballard's findings, which exonerated the officer. After weeks of exasperating negotiations between the U.S. State Department and the German foreign office, Berlin finally agreed to dismissal, an apology, and a promise not to employ the officer again in the Frontier Force.[34]

The German ships remained on the Liberian coast to pressure the Liberian authorities to make good on the German merchants' claims of property losses during the rebellion. The Germans, not surprisingly, objected to having the claims decided by the Liberian courts and insisted on forming an international commission. Haggling dragged on for months, so the commission did not convene until March 1913. The commission finally delivered its findings after a month of deliberation and awarded $5,601.77 to the German merchants, hardly a sum that justified the deployment of three warships. With German face saved, the troubles on the Bassa coast ended for a time.[35]

With the crisis on the Bassa coast still festering, Young had to overstep his advisory bounds and command the Frontier Force in the field. With Major Ballard engaged with the Krus and Germans at River Cess, and Captain Newton holding down Cape Palmas, Young felt he had little choice but to march to the rescue of Captain Browne and his Frontier Force troops, surrounded in a place called Tappi (Tapete), deep in the interior, by a group of rebellious Gio and Mano fighters. Liberian president Howard asked Young to lead a relief party, telling him the only available troops were one hundred men garrisoning the town of Zorzor, near the boundary with French Guinea. This meant Young would have to pick up the reinforcements en route on a circuitous path that took him many miles out of his way.[36]

Young pleaded with President Howard to send reinforcements and ammunition from nearby Frontier Force garrisons in Grand Bassa to assist Browne until his relief column arrived. Young argued that those bases were in no danger and that quick support might tip the balance and help Browne hold out until he arrived. He worried that Captain Browne might "surely try to cut his way out toward Grand Bassa" and had no confidence in the "untrained men" in Zorzor. Young warned "that it will court but disaster if I cut my way through to Tappi and instead of finding Browne, have but a desolate country devastated where I cannot feed my men while getting out."[37]

Major Young accepted the mission, yet took only six dependable Frontier Force soldiers and two carriers when he departed on November 25, counting on speed and picking up reinforcements on the way. The small party stumbled onto numerous villages along the route, some friendly but many hostile. The report of his encounters reads like something out of Conrad's *Heart of Darkness*, complete with man-eating indigenous groups and skulls displayed on the entrance of a stockade. Still, Young hired six hammock-bearers in one town, bought rice and supplies in another, and picked up reinforcements in several others. Some of these reinforcements were government troops, others were local chiefs and their men, and still others were prisoners pressed into service.[38]

The farther Young and his company moved inland to pick up reinforcements, the fewer signs they saw of the Liberian government. When Young reached the walled town of Zorzor, comprising about four hundred homes and a garrison of Frontier Force troops under Americo-Liberian lieutenant J. B. R. McGill, he encountered Muslim Mandingo merchants. The Mandingoes monopolized trade to the detriment of the Liberian government and established a high degree of political and religious control over the people of the northern hinterland. Nonetheless, the relief party departed on December 9, strengthened with a contingent of eighty-six uniformed Frontier Force troops plus ten carriers and a band of ten chiefs and their warriors, boosting strength to about 120.[39]

With his intelligence mission in mind, Young took the opportunity to make observations on the situation in neighboring French Guinea. On December 11 Young and his party moved down the Saint Paul River to the French border post of Tinsou. There he found French colonial troops constructing an earthwork, so he chatted in French with the lieutenant in charge of the post, the only white man present. Young later observed that the French exploited their side of the border more effectively than Liberia did. Liberia lost a great deal of trade to the French due to Guinea's better roads and management.[40]

Back to the task at hand, Young moved south to Dingama (Dingamo) and Sanquilly (Sanniquellie), where he encountered the Mano people. Young recorded that he was the second American the Manos had ever encountered. Young reported: "They are man-eating folk. But few graves are to be seen and those are the graves of the heads of chiefs, their bodies of even these having been eaten. This practice can be educated out of them, they being tractable and industrious people." The Manos feared the French and welcomed Young in their towns, seeking his aid and protection. Young took the time to mediate a conflict between the elder chief and some exiled chiefs before he moved on.[41]

When Young reached the village of Taymou on January 21, a welcoming line of Mandingoes dressed in their finest clothes greeted him. Though they pledged their loyalty to the Liberian government, a French flag flew over the entrance of the town. When Young asked why, the Mandingo merchants told him "that they had put up the French flag to show that they were French citizens." Since they claimed to be French, Young asked for a trading permit, which they could not produce. He then counted the people, inventoried and secured their goods, and "sent the women north over the French lines under the escort of one Mandingo man of their choosing." Young then pressed forty Mandingo prisoners into service as carriers for himself, the sick, and the rice. Young, like white Europeans and Americo-Liberians in this part of Africa, frequently had himself carried in a hammock through the bush.[42]

Young's troops numbered about 150 by December 23, 1912, when they arrived at Maingosha's Town. Young and his relief party had been trekking the hinterland of Liberia for nearly a month by this time. They had taken many false trails and did not know the exact location of Tappi, where Captain Browne and his men lay besieged by Gio and Mano fighters. Young was running out of time and worried that he would arrive too late, so he pushed on.[43]

On Christmas Eve an old woman they had captured led them into an ambush, and they had to fight their way out. Young wrote in his diary:

> We fought from town to town all that day. Had three men shot and wounded. While leading the advance guard into the town, I myself was shot in the right arm. At about three o'clock in the afternoon we stopped in a town (name unknown) about fifteen miles from the place where we had started from in the morning. I was now convinced that I was going in the wrong direction. I made up my mind to rest and capture some prisoners.

The slug Young took in his arm, fired by an old musket, was the two-inch rusty leg from a cooking pot that entered his arm below the elbow and lodged in his shoulder. It remained there for three weeks until he reached Monrovia, where a doctor removed it.[44]

Young turned south with his party and, after encountering a few small villages, reached Tappi on December 29, 1912. There he found Captain Browne and his seventy-eight men alive and delighted to see them. A contingent of forty-nine reinforcements had arrived the previous day from Grand Bassa with additional weapons and ammunition; President Howard had heeded Young's warnings. Young let Browne employ the now-reinforced body of about two hundred men to sortie out and drive away the hostile Gio and

Mano surrounding the town for the next three days. The crisis in this section of the hinterland was over for the moment.[45]

Young commended Browne's ability to hold together his command under such a difficult siege and applauded the grit of his Liberian Frontier Force soldiers. He specifically mentioned in his diary two Frontier Force noncommissioned officers as standouts: Sgt. Ganteh Vamon and Sgt. George Boyde, who "both should be given a medal and sent back to Mano country with troops." Young spent about a week in Tappi before leaving Browne in command of the now-pacified garrison. He departed on January 5 with 125 men, indigenous allies, and prisoners and arrived in Monrovia ten days later. The return trip to Monrovia was quicker because Young took a direct route via Grand Bassa to the coast.[46]

Young received good news about the American effort in Liberia when he reached Monrovia. On November 26, 1912, the day after Young had departed on the relief expedition, the 1912 loan agreement and the receivership under Clark finally took full effect. Young had supported his three American officers with money out of his own pocket for food and billeting until loan money began to arrive. Young and his officers had been in Liberia seven months by this time, but could not be fully operational without money. With cash on hand, Young and his officers could pay their soldiers and buy necessary equipment and supplies.[47]

Approval of the loan agreement also led to hiring an American engineer to work on the Anglo-Liberian Boundary Commission. This resulted in the dispatch of African American engineer James G. B. Lee from Brooklyn, New York, to work on the commission with his British counterparts. Lee, who arrived in January 1913, was a trained civil engineer who had studied at the Polytechnic Institute of Brooklyn. With Lee in Liberia, the border problems between Liberia and Sierra Leone would be addressed without the diversion of American officers, leaving them free to focus on the Frontier Force.[48]

President Taft, in his fourth and final annual message to Congress on December 3, 1912, mentioned the progress in Liberia. He cited the completion of negotiations for the $1.7 million loan and activation of the new receivership under U.S. control. Taft also noted that "three competent ex-army officers are now effectively employed by the Liberian government in reorganizing the police force of the Republic, not only to keep in order the native tribes in the hinterland but to serve as a necessary police force along the frontier." He concluded:

> It was the duty of the United States to assist the Republic in accordance with our historical interest and moral guardianship of a community founded by American citizens, as it was also the duty of the American Government to attempt to assure permanence to a country of much sentimental and perhaps future real interest to a large body of our citizens.

Taft's mention of Liberia in his State of the Union address was noteworthy. However, it was more significant that he had only three months left to serve in office.[49]

Amid these positive political developments in the United States, Young dictated a report of the expedition and submitted recommendations to the Liberian government on how relations with the indigenous groups might be improved to avoid future conflict. After his hinterland trek, Young was convinced the brutal, corrupt Liberian government and Frontier Force were squandering the country's agricultural potential as well as the goodwill of the local ethnic groups. Monrovia was also losing revenue and trade to the French.[50]

Young also submitted a preliminary message to the U.S. War Department on January 19, 1913. He wrote: "Full report of this relief expedition will be made as soon as my right arm, which contains a ball received in a four (4) days' fight with the tribesmen, sufficiently recovers to permit me to write." He had to dictate all correspondence to his friend, white missionary Emory Ross, because of the bullet in his writing arm.[51]

Young composed a letter to Booker T. Washington on January 25, 1913, just two weeks after his return from the Browne expedition. The letter was a recommendation that Richard Bundy replace Crum as the new consul general in Monrovia. Young conveyed to Washington that the president of Liberia and leading citizens wanted Bundy to stay on as consul general and praised his knowledge of Liberian affairs, "singular tact, good sense, and patience." Young asked Washington to use whatever influence he might have with the new Wilson administration to make Bundy the consul general, believing that "all United States politics should be taken away from this post until Liberia is thoroughly straightened out."[52]

Liberian president Howard was so impressed with the performance and professionalism of Major Young during his first nine months in the country that he appointed him as "Military Advisor to the War Department of Liberia," with broad powers and free access to formulate plans, write regulations, and administer the payrolls. One of the first things Young established was a "very rigid system of money accountability" in the department, with the acquiescence of receiver Reed Clark, to offset the "gross irregularities, lax methods, and inefficiency" in handling funds. Howard gave Young the power to act in the secretary's name in his absence, clearly beyond the scope of his duties as a military attaché. Later, Liberian secretary of war Wilmot Dennis complained to President Howard that Young was exercising excessive authority in his department, and when Howard refused to act on these complaints, the secretary submitted his resignation on March 29, 1913.[53]

Young needed more American officers, so he recruited a volunteer from the small African American staff of the consulate in Monrovia. Eldridge T. Hawkins resigned from his job as a clerk at the consulate on March 15, 1913, and accepted a commission as a captain to help buttress the hard-pressed American leadership. Hawkins was born in 1888 and grew up in Washington DC, graduating with military cadet training from M Street High School in 1907 and working as a public stenographer and clerk in a legal office until 1911. After he was appointed clerk at the consulate, he arrived in Liberia in March 1911. Young informed Bundy that Hawkins had sufficient military training and knowledge of Liberia to command troops immediately.[54]

Hawkins replaced Capt. Arthur Browne, who had become an increasing liability to the American mission in Liberia by early 1913. The Liberian government was not satisfied with Browne's performance and notified Bundy that at the end of his initial contract in March 1913, his services would no longer be required. Monrovia judged his "temperament unsuited to the work assigned" and cited his "failure to get along acceptably with Liberian officials." This was precisely the outcome Booker T. Washington had predicted in his letter a year earlier. Browne proved himself a good fighter at Tappi, yet made many enemies among the Americo-Liberian elite.[55]

Young put Hawkins right to work commanding a Frontier Force detachment sent north to suppress a renewed uprising by the Gbandis in the triborder area, where the territories of Liberia, British Sierra Leone, and French Guinea intersected. The Gbandis and the Kissis had been in sporadic rebellion against the government of Liberia since 1911. A bigger skirmish broke out after the March 1913 murder of an unpopular paramount chief who had been imposed on the Gbandis by Monrovia. In answer Major Young dispatched the newly commissioned Captain Hawkins with a force in April. Hawkins successfully suppressed the uprising but failed to catch the popular Gbandi chief Bombokoli, who fled across the border to Sierra Leone with many of the other rebels.[56]

Shortly after he sent Hawkins north, blackwater fever afflicted Young in April 1913. This was the same disease that forced the recall of Davis in 1911 and killed Consul General Crum in 1912. Young likely contracted blackwater fever while on his expedition to rescue Captain Browne. Young was also recovering from the bullet wound and subsequent infection and had his arm in a sling. Young requested sick leave in the United States, but his health deteriorated so precipitously that Bundy sent him home sooner than planned, on June 1, 1913. Accompanied by Emory Ross, Young spent much of the voyage lying delirious in his cabin.[57]

Bundy wrote a private letter to Ada Young confiding that her husband was a "very sick man." Bundy said that Young's "kidneys were very much involved and his slow recovery has been due, so the doctors say, to 'uremic poisoning' which set in after the fever was broken." He told her she should heed the doctor's warnings and make sure Young rested and did no work. He also warned her, "I honestly believe that he should not return to Liberia, unless you come with him. He is too disregardful of his personal welfare and needs some one ever-present to make him more careful. Successful living in Liberia is as much a matter of temperament as anything else."[58]

In June 1913, after the departure of Young, Major Ballard sent Hawkins with one hundred Frontier Force troops to put down a rebellion by the Kissi. The fighting was interfering with the work of the Anglo-Liberian Boundary Commission of black American engineer James G. B. Lee and British major E. L. Cowie. This was an echo of the trouble caused by Colonel Lomax and Commissioner Cooper and their execution of eight Kissi chiefs in 1912. Liberian special commissioner Massaquoi accompanied Hawkins to help arrest the new commissioner Dihdwo Twe, who replaced Cooper and instigated the new trouble with the Kissis.[59]

Hawkins skirmished with the Kissi and re-established order in the region. Kissi rebels later murdered the Liberian collector of customs, A. D. Thomas, at Laingedue (Linkadu) on the Sierra Leone border and looted the customs house at Foya. Captain Hawkins finally captured Commissioner Twe and sent him back to Monrovia for trial. Hawkins remained in Kissi country to keep the rebellious locals in line, which allowed Lee and the British members of the commission to complete their work delimiting the frontier.[60]

With American officers occupied elsewhere, the Kru insurgents attacked River Cess on the Grand Bassa coast on June 30, 1913. Garrisoned at the time with about eighty Frontier Force soldiers commanded by an Americo-Liberian officer, the force might have been overwhelmed by the attacking body of fighters, estimated at three to four hundred. By chance, Captain Newton was in River Cess at the time, paying troops at the post and intending to proceed on to Cape Palmas the following day by ship. The Krus did not know of his presence, so Newton was able to surprise and defeat them.[61]

After settling affairs in River Cess, Captain Newton returned to Cape Palmas to resume his mission of expanding government control. One method he used to improve control over the Grebo communities near the southern border with the Ivory Coast was roadbuilding. Liberian newspapers praised Newton in September 1913 for building a road 150 miles-long from the coast into the interior, using Grebo laborers. Though this was hardly a road by western standards, just six yards wide and suitable for pedestrians, roads would come to symbolize Monrovia's attempt to extend its reach into the hinterland and control the local ethnic groups. Newton could move troops along that road quickly when the Grebo settlements inland rebelled.[62]

While his American officers put down indigenous revolts in Liberia, Young convalesced in Ohio. After reaching his home in Wilberforce, Young requested a two-month extension in August 1913. During this time, War Department records show that Major Young submitted bills for medical care for a "gunshot wound" and "for illness from black water fever." While recovering, Young screened available applicants for two new officer positions he had asked President Howard to approve before he left Monrovia on sick leave. It appears that Ada was unable to keep Young under a strict regime of rest and recovery for long, and he was back in Liberia by September 1913. Fortunately for Young, Ada heeded Bundy's warnings and accompanied her husband to Monrovia to make sure he looked after his health.[63]

Young's home leave in 1913 coincided with a foreign policy shift in the U.S. government regarding dollar diplomacy in Liberia. Woodrow Wilson, the first southern-born and Democratic candidate elected president since the Civil War, took office on March 4, 1913. Wilson, a leader of the Progressive movement, was critical of American imperialism and campaigned against Roosevelt's "big stick" policies and Taft's dollar diplomacy. Wilson espoused a foreign policy, later called "missionary diplomacy," based on morality and pushed currency and banking reforms. Wilson opposed the kind of under-the-table deals that were common at the time and advocated that U.S. business be conducted fairly on a level field. Though his administration supported sound private investments in places like Latin America and Liberia, it gave higher priority to promoting democracy.[64]

It did not take long for Booker T. Washington to catch wind of possible policy changes regarding Liberia. In a May 1913 letter to Reed Clark, Washington welcomed the news that progress was being made since approval of the loan agreement, and assured him that "Liberia's salvation lies with the bond of friendship with the United States." Washington continued: "I confess that I have become a little troubled about the future of Liberia since the change of policy on the part of Mr. Wilson which gets rid of what is termed 'Dollar Diplomacy.' I presume, however, that the loan is too far on the way to be affected now by this change of policy." Indeed, officials worked through the initial problems and delays in implementing the loan agreement, and money began to flow in 1913. Dollar diplomacy continued in Liberia for the time being, and the American program stayed on track.[65]

Washington wrote in the same letter about a pending change in U.S. leadership at the consulate in Monrovia. On March 1, 1913, Taft had appointed Fred R. Moore, who had served on the board of directors of the National Negro Business League, organized by Booker T. Washington. However, with the inauguration of Wilson three days later, Moore never had a chance to take his post and present his credentials.[66]

President Wilson finally appointed a new consul general for Liberia on September 10, 1913, naming George Washington Buckner to the post. Buckner was born in into enslavement in Kentucky, like Charles Young, in 1852. After the Civil War, he attended a freedman's school in Greensburg, Kentucky, and later taught school nearby. He moved to Indiana to attend Indiana Normal School (now Indiana State University), earned a medical degree from Indiana Eclectic Medical College, and practiced medicine in Indiana. Buckner, a staunch member of the Democratic Party, arrived in Monrovia and presented his credentials on December 8, 1913. He was the first African American Democrat to be appointed consul general to Liberia in the post–Civil War era.[67]

Major Young and nearly everybody at the American consulate in Monrovia began to have problems with Buckner soon after he arrived. The first indication of trouble came in a progress report filed by Young with the War Department on April 20, 1914. In this comprehensive forty-page report, the military attaché detailed the progress made by the American officers with the Liberian Frontier Force over the past year and provided a full account of political opposition within the Liberian government to U.S. efforts to restructure and rationalize spending on the Frontier Force. However, a full third of the report blasted the leadership of Buckner and questioned his ability to carry out American policy in Liberia.[68]

The portion of the report on the progress of the American officers was straightforward and positive. Young reported that he had completed a manual of regulations for the force, deployed contingents to strategic points throughout the country, employed soldiers to do meaningful work, and purchased five hundred new carbines with bayonets. The Frontier Force strength stood at one thousand men who were "fed and paid regularly, clothed, moderately well-drilled, under good discipline," and led by five American officers assisted by six Liberian officers. There were also "ten young college men in training for six months as cadets for the making of intelligent and honest officers for the force." Young made a special effort to mentor bright young Americo-Liberian officers, who he employed as his orderlies. These young men, who later attended the officer academy, included Isaac Whisnant, Moses N. Grant, and Thomas Webster.[69]

Young then devoted a portion of the report to describing the opposition of the Liberian government to American efforts to strictly account for American loan money spent on maintaining the Frontier Force. Young took vigorous steps beginning in 1913 to reform accounting practices after Liberian president Howard appointed him as military adviser to the War Department of Liberia with broad powers. Young provided proof of graft in the report, showing that loan money had been skimmed and bills inflated to line the pockets of dishonest Liberian officials. Young and Reed Clark instituted a system through which they controlled the money spent on the Frontier Force, rather than passing the money to the Liberian treasury and War Department for dispersal.[70]

Young reported that Liberian officials forced President Howard to change the scheme of American control over loan money in March 1914. With Clark on home leave and Young unwilling to bend to pressure, the Americo-Liberians turned to the new consul general for support. Young and Clark warned Buckner in advance of the attempt by Liberian officials to change the rules of the game, but he disregarded their advice. Buckner supported the Liberian officials against all advice from Clark, Young, and Bundy.[71]

This power struggle over money between Liberian and U.S. officials and Washington caused a temporary stop in the flow of funds to the Frontier Force. Young cabled the U.S. War Department in mid-April: "Troops Liberian Frontier Force unpaid for last month, unfed for last 15 days." Young appealed to Buckner "in vain for aid in settlement. I fear rioting as consequence of suffering of troops—half civilized natives."[72]

This was essentially where the situation stood when Young wrote his April 20, 1914 report questioning Buckner's ability to lead. He then presented his evidence of the ineffectiveness and ineptitude of Buckner in detail. Young confessed:

> I feel confident that something is radically wrong with the Minister [Buckner] and in this opinion, I am borne out by both the French Consul and the British Consul General. I have as a consequence of my fears in this regard had a reliable foreign physician to kindly look in upon him occasionally. I apprehend that over-medication, he being a medical doctor himself, and the trying climate have done this destructive work, as it did in the case of the late Dr. Crum.[73]

Young detailed several events as proof of Consul General Buckner's lack of fitness. In December 1913 Buckner gave an inappropriate and incoherent speech at a diplomatic function followed by a toast to which the guests refused to drink. Thus, wrote Young, "Foreign representatives reported this speech to their Governments, commenting upon the misfortune in having such a man as their dean; and they have not hesitated to say, on any occasion where it comes up, that the interests of the U.S. are not being subserved nor can ever be by this gentleman." Young reported that Buckner's British and French counterparts refused to have anything to do with him and declined to go to the American consulate for any reason.[74]

Buckner was not popular at the U.S. consulate, flying into rages so often that his entire personal staff and all his servants quit. He even attempted to "pick a quarrel and oust" his deputy, Richard Bundy, who had served at the consulate loyally the past four years. Young judged Bundy "a man bearing the good will and esteem of the Liberians, foreign representatives and merchants as well as the Americans." Young went so far as to suggest that it might be necessary "to send the Consular Inspector, Mr. Gottschalk, here to look over matters and verify the facts stated."[75]

For his part, Consul General Buckner was critical of Young and his management of the Frontier Force in official dispatches. A week after Young sent his forty-page report to the War Department, Buckner filed a two-page diplomatic note with the secretary of state giving his impressions of the Liberian government and the American officers serving there. He opined, "There seems to be a very general feeling among Liberian officials that the Liberian Government has been over advised and overly helped by our American military officers, because the Americans 'have an ax to grind' as the Liberians think." Buckner continued, "I have seized upon the opportunity more than once to assure Liberians that our Government and people have only a moral and religious interest in Liberia." Buckner felt that Young and Clark had assumed too much authority in Liberian affairs, though he admitted the country had improved under American influence. He hinted at the end of his note that Young had threatened to quit, so they must have had a difference of opinion.[76]

Buckner wrote a second diplomatic note to the secretary of state in mid-June 1914 reporting a British inquiry into the official status of Major Young with the Liberian government and Frontier Force. This and a similar complaint by the German government voiced concern about the extraordinary authority given to Young and Clark to administer funds and the March 1914 reversal of this authority by President Howard. Buckner noted Howard was forced to make the change under pressure from members of the ruling True Whig Party to prepare "the way for his re-election and to save himself from impeachment by the Legislature." Buckner thought the British, French, and German authorities were jealous of American influence in Liberia, an opinion not shared by Young. Young wrote that "England, Germany, and France have made up their minds to allow a fair show here as long as the U.S. remains as chief sponsor."[77]

The verbal sparring between Major Young and Consul General Buckner continued throughout the year. In October Young responded to a letter from Buckner, who had forwarded a complaint from Mayor McGritty of Monrovia accusing Young of using his residence as "a harbor for criminals." Young sarcastically thanked

Buckner for "the oil you threw upon seemingly troubled waters" and went on to explain that his servant Frank, who had been accused of criminal behavior, had only been carrying out his wife's instructions "to protect our property from the petty thefts of our neighbors' children." Young also noted that Mayor McGritty's children attended a school run by Major Ballard's wife, Pearl, on the premises of the home and "harbor for criminals." Young rankled at being referred to as an "employee" of Buckner, correcting that he was only "attached to the Legation." It was not an exchange of letters between two colleagues on friendly terms.[78]

Whether this damaging infighting at the American consulate in Monrovia and lack of clear leadership resulted from Buckner's shortcomings, medical condition, policy instructions from the Wilson administration, or some combination of the three, it muddled U.S. efforts in Liberia. The Americo-Liberian regime clearly used Buckner's limitations and the consulate discord to change the rules Young and Clark so carefully crafted to eliminate graft in the Liberian War Department and the Frontier Force. The timing could not have been worse since the outbreak of war in Europe was just months away, and what little policy focus Washington had on Liberia would soon shift entirely to Europe.

In late 1913 at about the time Consul General Buckner arrived, two new American officers disembarked in Monrovia to assist in reorganizing the Frontier Force. Young felt that his contingent of three American officers—Ballard, Hawkins, and Newton—was stretched far too thin. He complained in a letter to Bundy that the Liberian lieutenants were of "doubtful efficiency." Chargé Bundy convinced the State Department and the government of Liberia to approve contracts to hire two American first lieutenants with a pay of $1,400 annually, the same rate as in the U.S. Army. Young initially proposed Harry P. Woodson of Wilberforce, Ohio, and Joseph H. Martin of Washington DC as his selections. Martin accepted, though Woodson turned down the appointment because his wife was ill. So Young selected William H. York of Chicago, Illinois, as an alternate, and he accepted.[79]

Joseph Martin, the first of the two officers, had less military experience than his predecessors. Born in 1885, he was a native of

Washington DC, where he attended military training at M Street High School. He served with the District of Columbia National Guard and earned promotion to first lieutenant. Unlike the previous African American officers in the Frontier Force selected by Young, Martin had not served with black regular or volunteer regiments during the Spanish-American or Philippines wars, a sign that the available pool of recruits was limited. Martin traveled by ship with the new consul general Buckner and arrived in Liberia in December 1913.[80]

The second new officer was better suited for the job based on his military training and experience. William York was born in Springfield, Illinois, in 1884. Young noted in a letter recommending York that he was "a man of good education, good character and who has seen service in the Spanish American War, in the National Guard, and in the Military Department at Wilberforce University under lieutenants Davis and Green." York graduated from Wilberforce University in 1912, where for two years he served as the cadet commander of the student battalion. Unlike Martin, he had a college education and schooling that prepared him as an officer, and he quickly earned promotion and increasing responsibilities in Liberia. York arrived in Liberia in early January 1914.[81]

Major Young's officer shortage did not end with the arrival of Martin and York. Capt. Richard Newton, at the point of resigning after growing increasingly frustrated with his Liberian masters, grew ill in April 1914 and moved from his command in the southeast to Monrovia for medical treatment. Newton died at Young's home of pulmonary tuberculosis in July 1914, depriving the American team of one of its most effective leaders. Young buried Newton with full military honors in Monrovia and promoted the newly arrived York to captain, filling Newton's vacancy.[82]

Newton achieved a great deal in the south against the Greboes before his death. He had subdued the Cape Palmas Greboes to the extent that they gave up their rebellion, petitioned the Liberian legislature for restoration, and pledged to "henceforth conform more fully to the laws and polity of the Government of Liberia." In October 1914 the Liberian legislature authorized President Howard to restore and reinstate the Cape Palmas Greboes and return the property and towns that had been taken from them. The Cape Palmas Greboes also promised not to retaliate against the Grebo communities that had aligned themselves with Monrovia in the revolt. As a final affront, Monrovia forced the Cape Palmas Greboes to pay for the flagpole that flew the Liberian flag at the signing ceremony on January 29, 1915.[83]

Young's officer situation deteriorated further when Maj. Wilson Ballard, commander of the Frontier Force and Major Young's right-hand man, resigned in 1915. Ballard was anxious to get back to the United States to resume his dentistry practice, worn out after three years campaigning in the bush and disillusioned with the way the ruling Americo-Liberians treated the ethnic groups of the hinterland. Bundy reported that Ballard voiced disappointment with the Liberian government's refusal to undertake serious reforms in the Frontier Force and felt it was "useless for him to expend any further energy in attempts to correct abuses that are both flagrant and vicious." Monrovia valued Ballard's service, and President Howard offered to make him secretary of war if he would take the oath of allegiance and stay in Liberia. Nonetheless, Ballard resigned and departed in June 1915.[84]

Captain Hawkins and Lieutenant Martin also left the force in 1915. Chargé Bundy explained in a note to the State Department that Hawkins felt, as the senior remaining American captain after the resignation of Ballard, that he should have been considered to command the Frontier Force. When he found out that the Liberian government favored York as the new commander despite Hawkins's seniority and proven record, he quit in August 1915. Lieutenant Martin had issues managing his Liberian lieutenants, carried more men on his books than could be paid, and had trouble balancing his pay accounts. Clearly overmatched by his duties, Martin resigned in November 1915.[85]

After the Liberian War Department promoted William York to major and appointed him commander of the Frontier Force in July 1915, he faced several immediate challenges. York took command just as a new Kru revolt broke out on the southeastern coast in September 1915. The departure of Ballard, Hawkins, and Martin in 1915 left York the only American officer in the Frontier Force for a period of several months. Chargé Bundy notified the State Department of the pending loses in June 1915 and requested three replacements, but the selection process took time. The changes in American leadership caused command and continuity problems in the force, whose strength was reduced in 1915 from one thousand to six hundred because of shortages due to the war in Europe.[86]

The American team in Monrovia suffered a significant loss in 1915 with the death of James G. B. Lee. The American civil engineer and his British colleagues completed their work on the Anglo-Liberian Boundary Commission to delineate the frontier between Sierra Leone and Liberia, and he signed the agreement for the Liberian government on August 5, 1915. Lee completed the work with the British so well that the French requested his help on the Franco-Liberian Boundary Commission. Regrettably, after he arrived in Monrovia on August 20 to arrange for a trip back to the United States, he fell ill and despite all medical efforts died on September 2 at the age of thirty-one. The cause of death was "Hemglobinuric fever," probably blackwater fever. Young buried Lee next to Newton in a small cemetery near the consulate and mourned the loss of another American in Liberia.[87]

The outbreak of World War I in Europe in August 1914 had a profound and detrimental effect on Liberia in the years following. The war severed trade with Germany, which had accounted for three-fourths of Liberia's prewar foreign commerce. In a few years, overall trade revenues plummeted to less than half their prewar level. Liberia remained neutral during most of the war, while British and French forces fought against German colonial troops in the nearby German colonies of Togoland and Cameroon. Young sent messages to Washington DC explaining the adverse effects of the war on Liberia and suggesting ways the United States could mitigate these in the form of support, loans, and increased trade. He even went so far as to write a personal letter in December 1914 to Maj. Charles Crawford, secretary of the war college division and former West Point classmate of Young, asking for assistance. These appeals by Young and the U.S. consulate in Monrovia fell on deaf ears in Washington.[88]

The U.S. consulate lost the problematic leadership of Consul General Buckner in 1915 due to sickness, adding credibility to

Young's earlier suggestion that illness contributed to Buckner's difficulties in Monrovia. Buckner, who arrived in Monrovia in December 1913 and caused so much turmoil in 1914, resigned and departed Liberia in April 1915. Like Young and many other westerners who served on the west coast of Africa, Buckner frequently fell ill and suffered bouts of fever. After Buckner's departure Richard Bundy once again took charge of the consulate as the chargé and acting consul general until the end of the year when a new consul general arrived.[89]

Chargé Bundy, Major Young, and General Receiver Clark held a meeting in September 1915 to discuss needed reforms to deal with the shortage of money and continuing abuses in the interior by Americo-Liberian officials. They drafted a memorandum to send to Washington DC and read the draft to President Howard and his cabinet. Along with cutting costs, the memorandum addressed the need to reform the administration of the interior ethnic communities. The report recommended that most of the Liberian commissioners be fired "to get rid of a horde of inefficient, dishonest trouble-makers at one stroke." They recommended that the "unscrupulous parasites" be dismissed, and this report led to the assignment of American commissioners of the interior in Liberia a few years later.[90]

In September 1915 Young wrote a detailed message to Chargé Bundy summarizing the grave state of Liberian affairs. Certain Kru settlements in the south had been in revolt for a week and had cut off communication between the capital and the "civilized people" living in southeastern Liberia. Other Kru groups from the regions around Picaninny Cess and Grand Cess were also hostile. The Liberian militia, over which Young and the Frontier Force had no control, ran amok in Sinoe, killing innocent members of the Kru community of Rock Cess, who were well armed by the Germans and likely to rise in response. There was no way to rush reinforcements to these areas from the woefully inadequate six hundred members of the scattered Frontier Force, who had not been paid in six months. There was also a shortage of Mauser carbine ammunition, which was manufactured in Germany and embargoed due to the war. Young ended his report with: "Can't we have the moral support of an American warship at this the most serious juncture in the affairs of the Republic since I have been here?"[91]

Young took some initial steps to deal with the Kru revolt he mentioned in his September letter to Bundy. Angered by years of mistreatment by Monrovia and taking advantage of Liberia's weakness as the result of World War I, the Krus rebelled in 1915. After a meeting with Liberian president Howard, Young recommended that Major York shift two hundred of his men and all available ammunition south to counter the Krus. He informed York that an American warship would cover his movements south and that two additional American officers had been dispatched to assist in the emergency. He told York to abandon outposts if necessary, leave a small force at Tappi in the interior under the command of a reliable Liberian lieutenant, and make all haste south.[92]

Just before his departure, Young described his mission in Liberia in letters to two West Point classmates. In a July 1915 letter to Col. Alexander Piper, Young described the soldiers of the Frontier Forces as "not one unit inferior to the soldier spirit to our best black troops." While this is a bit hard to believe at face value, perhaps Young was exaggerating to make a point. In a letter the same month to Col. Delamere Skerrett, he devoted two paragraphs to his accomplishments in Liberia, stating that he was in the process of completing a road from Monrovia through to the interior, had reorganized the Frontier Force, and had concluded work on a map of the country. Once finished with the road, he told Skerrett, he was ready to yield himself to the Manchu Law the following year.[93]

On October 19, 1915, the War Department relieved Major Young of his attaché duties in Monrovia. The Liberian government and the U.S. State Department requested an extension to Young's mission in West Africa to no avail, and he departed Monrovia on November 25, 1915, for the United States. Just before his departure, he witnessed the arrival of the cruiser USS *Chester* on November 8, sent to help put down the Kru rebellion. The president of Liberia mentioned the loss of Young in his message to the annual session of the legislature on December 5, 1915. Liberian president Howard regretted the departure of Young, who had "rendered such unselfish and constructive service" and who had "worked with such unflagging zeal to assist in the bringing of the Frontier Force up to a remarkable state of efficiency and system." He predicted that Young's counsel, cooperation, and optimistic energy would be sorely missed.[94]

In final recognition of Young's exemplary work in Liberia, W. E. B. Du Bois informed Young in mid-January 1916 of his selection to receive the Spingarn Medal, given by the National Association for the Advancement of Colored People (NAACP). The gold medal was "awarded annually to the man or woman of African descent and of American citizenship who has made the highest achievement during the year in any field of elevated or honorable human endeavor." The award committee included ex-president William H. Taft, Dr. James H. Dillard, Oswald G. Villard, John Hope, and Bishop John Hurst. This was only the second award of the Spingarn Medal and clearly reflected approval by the African American community for Young's achievements in Liberia. The Spingarn Medal was not bestowed on a military man again until presented to Gen. Colin Powell in 1991.[95]

Maj. Charles Young's military assistance mission to reorganize the Liberian Frontier Force was a limited success. Despite all the obstacles thrown in his path along the way, he and his American officers turned the force into a viable constabulary with indigenous soldiers and noncommissioned officers who fought effectively when well led. He received high praise for his outstanding work from the president of Liberia, and the American minister to Liberia wrote to him: "The actual result of work so well performed through your boundless energy and personal application leaves behind you a testimonial of your true work."[96]

Charles Young was fortunate to have the services of a dedicated and talented staff of African American officers in Liberia. Young handpicked these men, so he knew what he was getting for the bargain. He referred to his American team as "The Bunch" and later dedicated a draft volume of impressions on Liberia to Newton, Ballard, Hawkins, York, Lee, Martin, and Browne. These officers and men served Young to the best of their abilities, risked their lives in battle, suffered the ravages of disease, and two of them, Richard Newton and James Lee, died and were buried in Liberia.[97]

There is no record from his time in Liberia that Young had any misgivings about supporting a government in Liberia that was corrupt and mistreating its indigenous population. It could be argued that he was serving as an agent of Americo-Liberian elites to suppress the ethnic groups, but Young worked tirelessly with the Liberian government and urged them repeatedly to improve the treatment of the indigenous people of the interior. He realized that whatever the problems and abuses, a black ruling regime in Liberia was preferable to colonial control by France or Britain. This was certainly a position shared by Booker T. Washington, W. E. B. Du Bois, and other African Americans who viewed the black republic in Africa as a beacon of hope.

The African American community, press, and intelligentsia followed Young's achievements in Liberia with a great interest. Booker T. Washington asked Young to undertake the mission and supported the U.S. efforts to safeguard the independence of Liberia, provide loans to pay off Monrovia's debts, and extend dollar diplomacy to the west coast of Africa. Booker T. Washington died and was buried just a week before Young departed Liberia, and leadership shifted firmly to more activist leaders like Young's friend W. E. B. Du Bois. This new generation of African American leaders respected and venerated Young's accomplishments in Liberia, as evidenced by the Spingarn Medal awarded to him in 1916.

FIG. 17. Capt. Eldridge T. Hawkins standing in front of Charles Young's home in Monrovia, 1913. Courtesy of the National Afro-American Museum and Cultural Center, NAM_MSS22-P3_B02F03Pg03.

FIG. 18. Capt. Eldridge T. Hawkins in his Liberian Frontier Force uniform, 1914. Courtesy of the National Afro-American Museum and Cultural Center, NAM_MSS22-P3_B02F03Pg03.

FIG. 19. Indigenous recruits for the Liberian Frontier Force at Camp Johnson, 1914. Courtesy of the National Afro-American Museum and Cultural Center, NAM_MSS22_B09F31-05.

FIG. 20. A formation of Liberian Frontier Force soldiers equipped with German Mauser carbines, Camp Johnson, 1914. Courtesy of the National Afro-American Museum and Cultural Center, NAM_MSS22-P3_B02F03Pg10.

FIG. 21. Maj. Charles Young, shown here in 1916, served as military attaché
to Monrovia from 1913 to 1915. Library of Congress, Library of Congress
Prints and Photographs Division, George Grantham Bain Collection,
LC-DIG-ggbain-21286.

5

York, Green, Anderson

War and Peace

The situation is critical. To attempt to keep the Force up to the
current strength without paying them is to invite trouble.

—JOHN GREEN, 1917

After the departure of Maj. Charles Young in late 1915, the
American commander of the Frontier Force, Maj. William
York, continued U.S. efforts to advise and lead in Liberia. He did so as the sole American officer serving in the country
for a time. To make matters worse, the U.S. War and State departments allowed a gap of six months after Young departed before
they replaced him with First Lt. John Green. The absence of the
consulate's Regular Army attaché adviser came at a critical interval in the political and economic affairs of Liberia. The combination of the ruinous impact of the war and the events of this period
had a negative ripple effect on later years.

After the Kru revolt broke out in the fall of 1915, the U.S. consulate in Monrovia determined that immediate assistance was essential to save the situation in Liberia. The country had a full-blown
revolt on its hands with a shortage of American leadership, troops,
and ammunition. Monrovia also contended with a British government looking for an excuse to undermine Liberian authority. The
Kru rebels openly flew the Union Jack in Sinoe and petitioned the
British for support. London responded by sending HMS *Highflyer*
into Liberian waters, causing U.S. Secretary of State Robert Lan-

sing to issue a warning to the British concerning its neutrality. The British ship subsequently departed.[1]

As the situation on the Kru coast worsened, Liberian president Daniel Howard declared martial law in Sinoe, Grand Bassa, and Rock Cess counties. He also placed the region under the authority of Major York, who had commanded the Frontier Force since the departure of Major Ballard earlier in 1915. York did his best to stabilize the situation in the south by shuttling reinforcements and supplies to threatened garrisons on board the Liberian two-masted schooner RLS *President Howard*.[2]

President Howard sent a delegation south comprising three Liberian officials and Reed Clark, the American receiver of customs, on October 28, 1915. They sailed on board RLS *President Howard* with a contingent of Frontier Force troops under Major York, the president instructing York to "accompany the Commission with an armed force sufficient to enable them to carry out" the mission. The objective of the delegation was to restore order peacefully. Nonetheless, Howard authorized York to put down any opposition with the Liberian Frontier Force, supported by the Sinoe County militia of the Third Regiment. The delegation had only limited success, and sporadic fighting continued.[3]

In answer to the U.S. consulate's call for support in the Kru revolt, Washington DC dispatched the American light cruiser USS *Chester*, which arrived in Monrovia late on November 8, 1915. The captain of the ship, Cdr. Frank H. Schofield, put ashore the following day to confer with the Liberian president and the senior representatives of France, Germany, and Great Britain. U.S Chargé Bundy, running the consulate since the departure of Buckner the previous year, paid an official call on the ship to brief Schofield. The Liberian secretary of state also visited the ship to discuss the Kru matter with the captain.[4]

On November 9, at the request of President Howard, a peace commission boarded *Chester* for transit to the Kru coast. The commission comprised Reed Clark, the American receiver of customs, minister of the interior Dr. B. W. Payne, the Liberian commission chairman, and several others. Major York was already in the south, struggling to deal with the Kru revolt. The ship departed late and anchored off the mouth of the Cestos River the following day. Commander Schofield paused long enough to send ashore his intelligence officer, Ensign Mason, to gather information in city of River Cess.[5]

Chester steamed south the following day and anchored off the mouth of the Sinoe River in Sinoe Bay on November 11 to begin the peace negotiations. Their destination was Greenville, a major America-Liberian town and capital of Sinoe County, situated on the north bank of the mouth of the Sinoe River. First, a representative of the Krus named Tom Peter came on board to confer with Schofield. Later, the commission members went ashore to assess the situation and find a way to end the fighting.[6]

The next day, negotiations and efforts to restore the peace continued. A chief of the local Krus named Jargbah came on board the ship with interpreter Tom Peter to confer with Commander Schofield. Additionally, the schooner RLS *President Howard* arrived, and *Chester* sent an officer to pay a boarding call on the Liberian ship. RLS *President Howard* anchored for the night and departed the following day, carrying messages and personnel back to Monrovia.[7]

The situation around Greenville remained calm, so *Chester* sent ashore liberty parties of sailors to enjoy the local sights. On five days between November 13 and 21, Kru oarsmen ferried sailors ashore for liberty, though not all obeyed the navy regulation covering deportment. On one occasion, the ship's log recorded, "Crew member returned from Liberty intoxicated and 2 bottles found in 2nd cutter." Commander Schofield held "captain's mast" several times a week to hand out punishment for such offenses.[8]

However, in other areas away from Greenville, fighting continued, and *Chester* kept busy. On November 18 the ship's surgeon treated a Liberian Frontier Force private for a gunshot wound, but the private later died "from shock of the operation." On November 22 RLS *President Howard* returned from Monrovia with reinforcements and ammunition. The commission returned to *Chester* from Greenville and both vessels weighed anchor and steamed south to Neatano Point (King Williams Point). There, *Chester* picked up eighteen Frontier Force soldiers for passage. After a short stop at Cape Palmas, *Chester* returned to Sasstown on November 24 to pick up Major York, then sailed back to Monrovia.[9]

The presence of *Chester* and its ability to assist in transporting soldiers to troubled areas on the Kru coast kept the peace for a period; however, fighting broke out again in late November while *Chester* was away resupplying its coal stores. Chargé Bundy reported on November 28 that the port at the mouth of the Sinoe River at Greenville was open again after a battle resulting in the deaths of twenty Kru fighters and two Frontier Force soldiers. However, York reported the Frontier Force was running critically low on ammunition for its Mauser carbines and unable to undertake further offensive operations. Bundy, supported by the captain of *Chester*, asked the United States to lend the Frontier Force five hundred American Krag-Jørgensen carbines and 250,000 rounds of ammunition to remedy the situation.[10]

Just a day after it returned to Monrovia on December 15, 1915, USS *Chester* sailed south to the Sinoe River with two officers and fifty-five Frontier Force soldiers commanded by Americo-Liberian lieutenant Robert L. Kennedy to reinforce the port city of Greenville. Major York, who was in Greenville, had moved 160 soldiers out of the city a week earlier to other areas. On December 17 the Krus took advantage of this vulnerability and attacked. *Chester* ferried ashore thirty soldiers just in time to reinforce the weakened garrison and defeat the assault. The ship surgeon treated a gunshot wound for one Frontier Force soldier, who later died. The tide turned on the fighting ability of the Frontier Force, naval transport, and support by the U.S. warship.[11]

On December 18 *Chester* reboarded one sergeant and thirty Frontier Force soldiers for transport to another trouble spot on the Kru coast. *Chester* weighed anchor and steamed south to Nannakru (Nana Kru) and ferried the soldiers ashore for another engagement. The ship surgeon treated one Frontier Force soldier for a gunshot wound and he survived. After spending the day at Nannakru, *Chester* moved north to Baffu (Bafu Bay). This part of the coast was peaceful, and *Chester* spent the day there, sending a liberty party ashore.[12]

On December 23 *Chester* anchored again in Sinoe Bay to retrieve the peace commission from Greenville and return its members to Monrovia. With the fighting in Sinoe County around Greenville in a lull, the commission returned to the ship. *Chester* then transported the commission, led by Dr. Payne and accompanied by Major York, back to the capital. *Chester* anchored off Monrovia on Christmas Eve and ferried all passengers ashore.[13]

With the U.S. Navy pressuring the State Department to release the uss *Chester* for use in Haiti, the newly arrived U.S. consul general to Liberia, James L. Curtis, convinced officials to postpone the ship's departure until March 1916. He also arranged for the Liberian government to purchase five hundred used but renovated Krag-Jørgensen carbines and 250,000 rounds of ammunition in answer to Major York's appeal. The arms and munitions shipped on board the U.S. collier *Sterling*, along with coal and supplies for the *Chester*, which departed the eastern seaboard in mid-February 1916.[14]

Consul General Curtis, who landed in Liberia at a perilous time, was a highly respected attorney. President Wilson appointed Curtis, a black Democrat, on October 25 and he presented his credentials on December 27, 1915. He was one of a dwindling number of African Americans appointed to positions in the Wilson administration, which was actively segregating federal departments. Curtis, born in Raleigh, North Carolina, on July 8, 1870, graduated from Lincoln University in 1889 and earned a law degree from Northwestern in 1894. He later practiced law in Columbus, Minneapolis, and New York City.[15]

Curtis arrived in the same ship from Liverpool as two new American officers who had been sent to bolster the effort in Liberia. Both men had a great deal of military experience with the black regular regiments. James R. Gillespie, who enlisted in the army in 1881, boasted twenty-six years of service as a noncommissioned officer and a short stint as a first lieutenant with the Eighth Volunteer Infantry in Cuba. William Rountree was younger, a former noncommissioned officer who had served under Charles Young in the Ninth Cavalry. Both officers had combat experience in the Spanish-American War, Philippine War, or Indian Wars.[16]

Major York was initially delighted to see the new officers, though he soon learned that they possessed dissimilar qualities. Shortly after Gillespie and Rountree arrived, York took them to meet President Daniel E. Howard and Secretary of War Henry L. Morris.

Gillespie, having only just arrived in Monrovia, spoke out of turn and had a "hundred recommendations" about how to improve the Frontier Force. Rountree, on the other hand, had two practical suggestions and promised he would do his best. This was a foretaste of events to come.[17]

Rountree, who was young and eager for combat, showed his spirit early, while Gillespie quickly showed himself an old fuss-bucket. York took Rountree down the coast on January 18, barely two weeks after his arrival; there, the newcomer saw action four days later against the Krus. York left Gillespie in charge in Monrovia, where he soon got into trouble picking a fight with Americo-Liberian captain William Boyle. Boyle fled to the home of Liberian secretary of state Charles D. B. King, his patron. When Gillespie sent soldiers into the house to arrest Boyle, King judiciously defused the situation.[18]

Meanwhile, USS *Chester*, having been resupplied by the collier *Sterling*, arrived in Monrovia on March 17, 1916, loaded with American arms and ammunition for the Frontier Force. The following day *Chester* steamed south to the mouth of the River Cestos with Liberian president Howard, American consul general Curtis, Major York, and Liberian Frontier Force reinforcements on board. Howard, Curtis, and York went ashore briefly at River Cess, then reboarded. *Chester* then steamed south to Rock Cess and Sinoe Bay the following day. At Sinoe Bay Major York and the detachment of Frontier Force soldiers disembarked.[19]

With the reinforcements and supplies of arms and ammunition delivered, *Chester* made several other brief stops on the Kru coast before its mission ended. The ship departed Sinoe on March 19 and touched briefly at Nannakru on March 20, Sasstown on March 21, Cape Palmas on March 22, and Grand Bassa on March 23. At each stop, President Howard and American consul general Curtis went ashore to confer with officials. These stops were aimed at rallying Americo-Liberians forces, consolidating support among friendly Kru communities, and demonstrating American support.[20]

Finally, *Chester* returned to Monrovia on March 24, 1916, where Howard and Curtis left the ship and Schofield went ashore briefly. *Chester* departed Liberia the same day for the return voyage to the

YORK, GREEN, ANDERSON

United States, with Vice Consul General Bundy and his wife on board. Bundy had served without a break in Monrovia since 1912 and was due home leave. This ended *Chester*'s mission in Liberia.[21]

The decisive battles of the Kru revolt began shortly after *Chester* delivered critical arms, ammunition, and reinforcements and departed. York directed the operation but let his two new American officers lead the actual fighting. The first attempt in early April misfired when Captain Gillespie attacked Rock Cess, took the Kru positions, then abandoned them a few days later in confusion. Two months later in early June, Lieutenant Rountree led a detachment of troops from Sinoe Bay and sent another from River Cess against Kru strongholds in Sangwin and Rock Cess. After three days of hard fighting, the Kru rebels fled, and the Frontier Force troops occupied the enemy's former redoubts.[22]

This victory was significant and displayed the fighting ability and determination of the Liberian Frontier Force; much of the tough fighting at Rock Cess and Sangwin led by young Americo-Liberian officers. The Frontier Force beat the Krus in a "sanguinary battle lasting three days, in which the troops, flushed with victory, pursued them and practically massacred them," per consulate reporting. Consul General Curtis cabled the State Department after the event, noting that the southeastern coast was under the control of the Liberian government for the first time since the republic's founding.[23]

Monrovia regarded Major York's victory on the Kru coast as a coup de maître, even more extraordinary because nobody in the capital gave the order to go on the offensive. The attack took the Krus completely by surprise, as it came during the rainy season when offensive operations in Liberia were not customarily undertaken. Dispatches from the U.S. consulate gave Lieutenant Rountree much of the credit for the leadership and initiative he showed in the decisive attack.[24]

The butcher's bill was unusually high in the Kru revolt. The fighting killed hundreds, and the government tried, convicted, and sentenced to death sixty-two Kru rebel leaders. Although President Howard commuted the death sentences of forty-seven to life imprisonment, word did not reach Greenville in time, and executioners hanged all but twenty. The Liberian Frontier Force crushed the insurgency in the south but at an exceedingly high price not foreseen by the government in Monrovia or the Kru leaders on the coast.[25]

At about the time the Kru rebellion ended, First Lt. John E. Green landed in Monrovia. The War Department had few choices other than John Green for assignment to Liberia because there were only three serving African American Regular Army officers. Charles Young had shipped stateside to rejoin his regiment after four years in Liberia, and Benjamin Davis had replaced Green as an instructor at Wilberforce University after three years with his regiment. Service in Liberia and blackwater fever nearly killed both Davis and Young; it was Green's turn in this pestiferous rotation.

John Green, like Benjamin Davis, began his service as an enlisted soldier in 1899 and earned his officer's commission in 1901. Born in Murfreesboro, Tennessee, on April 27, 1878, Green joined the Twenty-Fourth Infantry Regiment on his twenty-first birthday. Black chaplain Allen Allensworth recruited Green, who was then attending college at Walden University in Tennessee, hoping that Green would compete for an officer's commission as soon as he was eligible. Pvt. John Green joined the Twenty-Fourth Infantry at Alcatraz Island, California, before it shipped out to the Pacific to fight in the Philippine War in 1899.[26]

Two years later, Cpl. John Green was called back to Manila to take his officer's exam and was accompanied there by an armed escort in case of a Filipino ambush. He passed the written and oral examinations in April and May 1901, and after joining his new unit in the Philippines, accepted a commission as second lieutenant in the Twenty-Fifth Infantry on July 8, 1901. As with Davis, the U.S. Army moved the newly commissioned Green to another regiment so he would not command men with whom he had formed bonds as an enlisted soldier.[27]

The newly commissioned Green served for another year in the Philippines, assigned to Company H, Twenty-Fifth Infantry before rotating back to the United States with his regiment. Subsequently, Green served with the Twenty-Fifth in Oklahoma, Texas, and Hawaii and on detached duty at Wilberforce University before his posting to Liberia. He was formally notified of his military attaché detail to Monrovia on February 10, 1916, and traveled to Washington D C for consultations at the War Department before shipping out to Liberia in April.[28]

The composition of the officer corps of the Regular Army in 1916 had not changed fundamentally since the late nineteenth century. Though the Regular Army expanded from approximately 2,200 officers before the Spanish-American War to about 3,600 in 1902, West Point graduates still predominated. As an officer commissioned from the enlisted ranks, known as a "ranker," Green operated at a disadvantage when it came to peer connections and career enhancing assignments. That he was one of only three black Regular Army officers in the service at the time made this doubly disadvantageous. Even when the army began to expand in 1916 in preparation for the war in Europe, officers commissioned from the ranks found opportunities only after their West Point brethren had taken their pick. Black officers found them last of all.[29]

Lieutenant Green confronted a host of intractable problems when he arrived in Monrovia on May 16, 1916, not least of which was the economic trouble caused by the war in Europe. There was no money to pay the Frontier Force, causing morale problems after its recent successes against the Krus. Green did not have personal connections with the three American officers serving in Liberia who were embroiled in a leadership struggle. Lately arrived and struggling to master his new responsibilities and understand the Byzantine politics of Monrovia, Green was in no position to immediately resolve these calamities.

Green's most immediate challenge was advising the consulate and Liberian government on the leadership crisis among the American officers. Captain Gillespie continued to cause trouble after the Kru revolt, thinking he was more qualified to lead the force than York. Unhappy with his service in Liberia, Gillespie sent a letter of resignation to President Howard in September 1916 giving his notice and accusing York of cowardice in the Kru rebellion, mishandling the Frontier Force during the revolt, and misconduct administering operational funds. Howard held Gillespie's resignation, pending a formal investigation. Green watched much of this from the sidelines, as the American officers worked under contract for the Liberian government.[30]

York responded to the charges in a rebuttal to President Howard later in September. He admitted that Gillespie had a great deal of military experience, but reminded the president that Gillespie had caused considerable mischief since his arrival. Among other things, Gillespie had insulted the Liberian secretary of state, challenged the Liberian associate chief justice to a fistfight, struck one of his Americo-Liberian officers with the butt of a carbine, and proved unable to face the hardships of field duty because of his age. York considered Gillespie a failure in action on the Kru coast, a "self-conceited coward," and "the greatest hindrance to our success."[31]

Second Lt. Isaac Whisnant, an Americo-Liberian protégé of Charles Young and graduate of the officer training academy, provided the most balanced account of the conduct of the American officers during the investigation. In a sworn statement, he gave Rountree credit for conceiving the plan for the two-pronged attack on Rock Cess and Sangwin in June and rousing the dispirited Americo-Liberian officers and soldiers to fight. But Whisnant made it clear that junior officers provided most of the actual leadership in the fighting. Rountree led the attack against Sangwin while Whisnant and Americo-Liberian officers assaulted Rock Cess without American leadership.[32]

Whisnant's statement was a scathing condemnation of Gillespie's conduct. He described Gillespie's role in the April attack on Rock Cess as an unmitigated disaster. Major York conceived the April scheme but let Gillespie talk him into commanding the force to burnish his reputation. Gillespie then showed himself a coward incapable of following a plan or leading men, running from the first hail of bullets, cowering in the baggage train during the fight, and fainting near the end of the battle, only to be carried to safety by his men.[33]

Curtis reported in February 1917 that Gillespie had finally resigned from the force, his letter accepted effective March 31, 1917. The Liberian government demanded his resignation after Gillespie challenged the integrity of the secretary of war in front of members of the cabinet. He charged the secretary with graft via a deal with a

YORK, GREEN, ANDERSON

merchant for the purchase of cloth for uniforms but was unable to substantiate the charges. This ended Gillespie's hugger-muggery in Liberia, and he departed in late March 1917.[34]

However, Gillespie's accusations resulted in the Liberian government's proffering court-martial charges against Major York for embezzlement of Frontier Force funds. The best attorney in the country, former Liberian president Arthur Barclay, represented York in the court-martial that followed. Pending resolution of his case, York resigned his commission on January 10, 1917, but the case dragged on for months. York eventually settled out of court and agreed to pay $1,000 restitution in March 1917.[35]

Oddly, York stayed on in Monrovia with his wife and engaged as a businessman afterwards. He later petitioned President Howard for reinstatement in his old position as major in the Frontier Force, but Howard politely declined. York departed Liberia in June 1917. Years later, York operated an enterprise out of New York City that aimed to bring black American tourists and settlers to Liberia.[36]

The year 1917 proved a difficult and demoralizing one for the Frontier Force. Captain Green reported that about 120 Frontier Force soldiers mutinied in March 1917, taking control of the arsenal and streets in Monrovia for two days. The soldiers had been paid three months' back pay but demanded five. The Liberian government feared violence and met the soldiers' demands, so no blood was spilled. Captain Rountree was the only American officer serving in the force after the departure of York and Gillespie, and he could not be everywhere. The loss of American leadership and lack of money to pay the soldiers did a great deal of damage to the morale and discipline of the Frontier Force during the war years.[37]

To remedy the situation, U.S. Secretary of State Robert Lansing demanded in April 1917 that Liberia institute reforms. The United States made it clear that further "fraternal assistance by the United States" depended on Liberian compliance. Among other things, he demanded an expansion of the power of the U.S. receiver of customs, reform of the Liberian militia, revocation of the authority of the Liberian secretary of war to spend money on the Frontier Force, restoration of the officer academy, and reorganization of the Frontier Force, albeit at a much-reduced strength.[38]

Under American president Woodrow Wilson and prompted by the demands of World War I, the State Department transformed the dollar diplomacy of Taft into "strong quasi-colonial financial and military control of Haiti, the Dominican Republic, Nicaragua, and Liberia." The United States sent dozens of economic and military advisers to each of these countries. They controlled every aspect of the host country's revenue collection, budgetary expenditures, accounting, and tax systems. The United States also sent a group of white interior commissioners to Liberia to report on excesses by Liberian officials and improve the treatment of the indigenous groups in the hinterland.[39]

The economic troubles caused by World War I forced Green to advise the Liberian government to trim the Frontier Force to half the size originally recommended by Benjamin Davis in 1911 to police the hinterland and control the borders. By 1917 American officers and about a dozen Liberian lieutenants commanded a force of about six hundred that was dangerously scattered, inadequately paid, and badly supplied with ammunition. The Frontier Force posted roughly two hundred soldiers each to the troubled western and eastern border areas of Liberia and dispersed the balance throughout the hinterland, with a small recruiting and training base near the capital of Monrovia at Camp Johnson.[40]

With the force so thinly spread, the indigenous groups of the interior soon took advantage of the situation to settle old scores. The first challenge came in May 1917, when Monrovia sent Frontier Force troops into Nimba County to put down a rebellion by the Gios and Manos. This was the same area where Major Young had marched to rescue Captain Browne in 1913. In this northeastern wedge of Liberia between French Guinea and the Ivory Coast, the Manos and Gios had been in sporadic revolt against Monrovia since 1916. Directed by the American commissioner of the interior, Thomas C. Mitchell, the initial campaign failed, though the Frontier Force put several towns to the torch.[41]

The second attempt to subdue the rebellious groups in Nimba succeeded. In August 1917 troops under Americo-Liberian lieutenant Alexander Harper returned and defeated the Gios and established a fortified camp. By November 1917 Mitchell declared that all of Mano country and thirty-seven Gio settlements had surrendered. Mitchell forced the Manos and Gios to give up their muskets, which were melted down and fashioned into tools with which to build roads and work government farms.[42]

Another reform demanded by Washington D C in 1917 was that the "cadet school organized by Major Young should be continued by the Military Attaché." The academy had foundered due to economic shortages and lack of an American officer's steady hand to maintain standards. However, by October 1917 Consul General Curtis reported that "Captain Green has taken charge of the school for cadets, who are officers of the Frontier Force in embryo, and is making commendable progress in his efforts to have the military arm of the Government service approximate American standards."[43]

The U.S. State Department similarly forced Monrovia to restructure the Liberian militia, an organization considered worthless by both Davis and Young. The militia comprised most able-bodied male citizens of Liberia between the ages of sixteen and fifty and was organized regionally into brigades, regiments, battalions, and companies. An August 1917 progress report by Curtis noted that the militia had been placed under the supervision of the War Department and was now subject to the orders of the new commander of the Frontier Force, Maj. John Anderson, "in consequence of which a wonderful transformation in its bearing and esprit de corps is apparent to the most casual observer."[44]

This was the first mention in consular dispatches of the new commander of the Frontier Force, John H. Anderson, who had arrived in Monrovia on May 20, 1917. Anderson, born on September 12, 1871, was educated in the public schools in Alexandria, Virginia, and taught in black schools in Fairfax County, Virginia, in 1887. He enlisted in the Twenty-Fifth U.S. Infantry in 1890 and served his first enlistment in Montana at the end of the Indian Wars. He served on and off with the Ninth Cavalry and later the Twenty-Fifth Infantry for more than twenty years as an enlisted soldier, post teacher, saddler sergeant, and, finally, sergeant major, when his unit deployed to Cuba during the Spanish-American War.[45]

Anderson, retired from the army when he arrived in Liberia, also boasted experience as a volunteer officer. The army rewarded his service in Cuba with a commission as a first lieutenant in the Tenth U.S. Volunteer Infantry from 1898 to 1899. The army commissioned him again in 1899 as a first lieutenant in the Forty-Eighth U.S. Volunteer Infantry, in which he served for two years during the Philippine War.[46]

Anderson retired from the army in April 1915 and accepted the position in Liberia two years later. After landing in Monrovia in May 1917, he led the Frontier Force with Capt. William Rountree for the next eight months. He later served as the solitary black American officer with the Liberian Frontier Force for more than two years after the departure of Captain Rountree.[47]

William Rountree, who had been promoted from lieutenant to captain, was the only officer to escape the campaign against the Krus with his reputation intact. Rountree had submitted his resignation in December 1917 at the expiration of his two-year contract but was asked by Monrovia to extend his contract to command an expedition against rebellious Greboes near Cape Palmas in the southeast. He reluctantly agreed to stay on.[48]

Rountree's expedition achieved only partial success due to a shortage of ammunition and disagreements with local Liberian officials. Thus, in March 1918 President Howard relieved Captain Rountree of his command and turned it over to an Americo-Liberian officer. Rountree returned to Monrovia, resigned his commission, and caught the first steamer home. Bundy noted in a letter that Captain Rountree left voluntarily and had accomplished "some exceedingly effective work" with the Frontier Force.[49]

American officers like Anderson and Rountree who served with the Frontier Force from 1916 to 1918 experienced a more difficult command climate than those who had served previously. The six-month gap between the departure of Young and the arrival of Green was partly to blame. During this time officers began to report directly to the American receiver of customs, whose decision-making power increased in 1917 under the new Wilson administration policies.

The lack of personal connections between Captain Green and the American officers serving with the Frontier Force also contributed to the challenges. Unlike Young, who recruited officers with whom he had personal relationships and trained as a team, Green arrived alone and had no say in the choice of his officers. This certainly had a great deal to do with the leadership turmoil among the African American officers in Liberia during this period.

External events added to the difficulties faced by the American officers in Liberia. Monrovia declared war on Germany on August 14, 1917, but the pronouncement brought no relief to the Liberian economy—quite the contrary. The U.S. consulate reported in November 1917 that "two vessels which should have brought some forty thousand dollars' revenue to the Republic have been recently sunk by German submarines." Commercial shipping virtually ceased between Europe and Liberia. Even after the Liberians deported all German residents, there was no respite, and the country continued to suffer economically with no trade or aid coming from the Allies. The resulting shortages rippled down to the Frontier Force.[50]

As a further blow to the effort in Liberia, the American consulate suffered a terrible loss of leadership in 1917 with the death of Consul General Curtis. He fell ill in mid-October and officials evacuated him for medical treatment to Sierra Leone by ship. He died en route on October 24, 1917, a reminder of how vulnerable westerners were to disease.[51]

Consul General Curtis's widow, Helen, was determined to return his body to the United States despite the shortage of coffins and dangers to shipping during the war. After receiving permission from British authorities in Freetown, she acquired a metal rum barrel to serve as a temporary coffin and set sail on a tramp steamer for the United States, an unfortunate and undignified final journey for the career of a U.S. diplomat. After six weeks, she reached home to bury her husband in his native land.[52]

Chargé Richard Bundy again assumed leadership of the American consulate from October 1917 until the arrival of a replacement for Curtis in October 1919. Bundy and his wife, Nellie, had returned to the United States on board USS *Chester* the previous year for a long period of home leave, their first after four years in Liberia. In Washington he spent time at the State Department, where he was debriefed and "made some very frank statements about the situation in Liberia." Bundy sailed back to Liberia supplied with the latest guidance from the State Department on policy aims in Liberia, braving the submarine-infested waters of the Atlantic.[53]

After declaring war, Monrovia feared an attack, especially after Germany designated the Liberian coast as part of the submarine interdiction zone in January 1918. A British admiral commanding the West African Squadron visited Monrovia in January to confer with Liberian, American, British, and French representatives about the defense of the Liberian coastline. Neither the French nor British had the resources to station ships, aircraft, or gun batteries along the three-hundred-mile coast of Liberia. Admiral Thomas D. L. Sheppard advised that he thought an attack on Liberia unlikely anyway.[54]

He was wrong. Without warning, the German submarine U-154 surfaced off the roadstead of Monrovia on April 10, 1918, and attacked the capital. First, it seized and scuttled the Liberian schooner RLS *President Howard*, then sent the Liberian crew ashore with a demand to haul down the French flag and destroy the French cable station. When President Howard refused his demands, German Korvettenkapitän Herman Gerche opened fire with his 150-mm deck gun, destroying the French wireless station and damaging the cable station. The hour-long shelling caused extensive damage to buildings and killed four people, three of them children.[55]

The British ss *Burutu*, an armed steamship of the Elder Dempster Lines, ended the shelling when it brazenly responded to a Liberian sos and steamed toward the German submarine. U-154 dived to pursue *Burutu*, missed with a torpedo, and expended sixty rounds of 150-mm cannon fire trying to sink the ship before darkness ended the engagement. The encounter resulted in extensive damage to the British ship and two crewmembers killed, one a Kru boy who jumped overboard and drowned. London awarded British captain H. A. Yardley the Distinguished Service Cross for his bold engagement with U-154.[56]

In response to the German attack, the American cruiser USS *Raleigh* steamed into the estuary off Monrovia on May 7, 1918. The captain of USS *Raleigh*, Cdr. Frank E. Ridgely, came ashore for a conference with the Liberian president, his cabinet, Bundy, and Green. The Liberian president refused Ridgely's offer of a five-inch gun for the defense of the city, on grounds that it would be

YORK, GREEN, ANDERSON

ineffective against the greater firepower of a German submarine. President Howard did accept his offer of 15,600 rounds of badly needed Krag-Jørgensen ammunition, 15,600 rounds of 1901 Springfield rifle ammunition, and one Colt automatic machine gun.[57]

The one person in Liberia who benefited from the war was John Green, since it led to his rapid promotion. As the American officer corps expanded to meet the requirements of a wartime army, the promotion of Regular Army officers accelerated. Green had waited six long years for promotion to first lieutenant and another nine to captain, the rank he assumed two months after his arrival in Monrovia. The War Department notified Green of his temporary appointment as major on August 5, 1917, and as lieutenant colonel on July 30, 1918: two ranks in two years. Green retained these temporary promotions and the welcome increase in pay until the wartime commissions ended on February 9, 1920, shortly before he departed Liberia.[58]

John Green had one other reason to celebrate. On February 22, 1917, he married Julia Ernestine Whitman in a ceremony at the American consulate in Monrovia officiated by Liberian bishop A. P. Camphor. Green had met his future wife while serving as professor at Wilberforce University in Ohio, where they later became engaged. Ernestine joined John Green in Monrovia on the very day they were married. It was no small feat to cross the Atlantic in 1917 with German submarines prowling the waters in search of Allied shipping. She braved the Atlantic once again when she returned to Ohio at four months pregnant to have her baby in a healthier setting.[59]

By 1918 the efforts of Major Green and Major Anderson to improve the organization, discipline, and training of the Frontier Force began to pay off. Anderson, forced to reduce his roster for lack of money, rid himself of many mutinous and substandard soldiers. Green also purged the force of many unacceptable and corrupt officers in training by raising the standards of the officer academy. Yet there was still work to do, and Anderson noted, "I do not know one officer among the Liberians who could take the Frontier Force now and run it without a breakdown."[60]

The government in Monrovia acknowledged the improvements

in the Frontier Force during the difficult war years. At the end of 1918, the president of Liberia proclaimed in his annual message:

> The Frontier Force has rendered very excellent service during the year; and when it is remembered that here-to-fore numerous complaints were made against officers and men of the Force by both Americo-Liberians and Natives, and that now but very few complaints are received by the Department, I must commend the Major of the Force for its present standard of discipline which he has spared to little pains to realize.[61]

Monrovia celebrated the end of World War I on November 11, 1918, though the war's end did little to improve the economic situation in Liberia. The European economies took years to recover and the trade with Africa suffered consequently. Also, the focus of the United States shifted to rebuilding Europe through loans and reshaping the political landscape through deliberations over the Treaty of Versailles and the League of Nations. Liberia suffered as a result.[62]

By the end of the war, Liberia was more firmly under American economic control than ever before. In 1919 the United States had two colonies (the Philippines and Puerto Rico) and two protectorates (Cuba and Panama) and held complete fiscal oversight in four countries (Dominican Republic, Haiti, Liberia, and Nicaragua). Of these eight, the position of Liberia was perhaps the weakest and American economic control the most complete. Washington used the damage done to Liberian trade during the war to tighten the mechanisms of control. The only area where the United States seemed to lose ground during World War I was in control of the Liberian Frontier Force.[63]

However, even with the war over, the Frontier Force had internal difficulties to deal with. In late 1918, the Grebo communities around Cape Palmas challenged the authority of the central government in Monrovia again. American chargé Bundy reported that "for more than two years past the native tribes in the region of Cape Palmas, Liberia, have been in more or less open rebellion against the Government." The shortage of money, personnel, and ammunition in the Frontier Force compelled Monrovia to delay action to restore control and good order. Beginning in January 1919 matters took a turn for the worse, and the "civilized population of Cape Palmas could not go one-half mile beyond the town limits without being fired on from ambush by the natives who had closed all the roads."[64]

Bundy sent a request to the State Department for the purchase of arms and ammunition, always in short supply, to aid the effort to counter the Greboes. The United States agreed to sell the Liberian government one hundred Krag-Jørgensen rifles and 250,000 rounds of ammunition, but the British refused permission to ship them to Monrovia on one of their West African steamers. So the U.S. Navy shipped the cargo to Liberia on board the cruiser USS *Chattanooga*, which anchored off Monrovia on April 19, 1919. Lieutenant Colonel Green paid a courtesy call on the ship to brief the captain shortly after its arrival. The cargo was unloaded the following day, and the warship departed shortly thereafter.[65]

It did not take long for the infusion of arms and ammunition to tell on the effort against the Greboes. Monrovia shipped the munitions that had been delivered by *Chattanooga* south. Major Anderson was already in the south at Cape Palmas with 126 men and limited supplies dealing with the rebellion. Through good strategy and a wise disposition of the Frontier Force at his command, Anderson completely overwhelmed the Grebo opposition.[66]

Bundy reported two notable results of the expedition in a June 1919 cable. First, Anderson captured a large quantity of arms and ammunition in the process of defeating the rebellious communities around Cape Palmas. The list included nearly 4,000 small arms, 42 cannons, 1,200 rounds of ammunition, and 78 revolvers; one-third of these were "improved" or modern weapons. The surprising quantity and quality of weaponry in the hands of the indigenous groups revealed a serious illegal arms trade across a porous border. Bundy considered this achievement by Anderson impressive, as the government in Monrovia had been trying to subdue and disarm these groups in the southeast since 1910.[67]

The second achievement Bundy reported was more constructive and long lasting, though not necessarily legal under the laws of war. Major Anderson set the prisoners to work and completed construction of twelve miles of road from Cape Palmas into the hinterland by June 1919. Twelve additional miles of road were later hacked out of the jungle by this Grebo press-gang. Bundy noted "by means of this road it is expected that troops may be moved with such facility that in future it will be difficult for a native uprising to gain any headway in the immediate vicinity of Cape Palmas." Anderson's road north from Cape Palmas along the Cavalla River, which ran parallel to the border with the Ivory Coast, also enhanced control over that frontier.[68]

The Gola and Gbandi uprising of 1918 to 1919 in northern Liberia erupted at about the same time as the Grebo rebellion in the south. This unrest was a continuation of the Kpelle, Gbandi, and Gola troubles between 1911 and 1914 near the Anglo-Liberian boundary. Because Major Anderson was busy in the south pacifying the Greboes, he ordered his America-Liberian officers in the north to negotiate and remain on the defensive. He hoped to finish with the Grebo troubles in the south before shifting his scarce resources north to deal with problems there.[69] From July to August 1918, Frontier Force troops under America-Liberian captain Samuel L. Smith, Capt. Moses N. Grant, and Lt. John G. Watson set up camps in troubled areas in the north. They remained strictly on the defensive as directed by Anderson. The Frontier Force expected the Golas and Gbandis in these areas to supply them with rice and carriers, but they often refused, leading to conflict between the soldiers and local inhabitants.[70]

The local Frontier Force contingents in the north were too small, so the America-Liberian officers put local auxiliaries to good use. Major Anderson authorized Capt. Samuel Smith to "employ one or two thousand Buzi [Loma] warriors to assist you should you deem or consider the same necessary. The only compensation to these auxiliary troops being that they can hold whatever they catch." Major Anderson had little recourse since he had no other American officers and insufficient funds with which to lead and pay a larger force. He resorted to fighting with supplementary troops under the indigenous rules of warfare using raid and plunder tactics.[71]

By March 1919 the Liberian Frontier Force and its auxiliaries had crushed the Gola and Gbandi resistance. These forces burned rebel towns, disarmed rebel warriors, expropriated rice to feed soldiers and allied troops, and took war booty and captives as plunder. President Howard justified the drastic military measures in his December 1919 message to the Liberian legislature as stern but necessary measures to maintain the republic. He warned that half measures only confirmed to the indigenous groups that the government was weak and incapable of keeping them under authority. At a peace conference in December 1919, Howard forced the defeated rebel chiefs to submit publicly to authority and pledge to pay all hut taxes in arrears for 1916 to 1919.[72]

With these two rebellions ended, Chargé Bundy cabled the State Department in June 1919 with an urgent request for American officers to leverage Anderson's gains and supply much-needed leadership for Frontier Force detachments in other parts of the country. Bundy called Major Anderson "a much-overworked man" and claimed the Liberian government was anxious to fill the vacancies that had existed for more than two years. He noted that the Frontier Force had put down several rebellions in the north and southeast and captured more than fifteen thousand weapons over the course of four years. He closed his dispatch with the news that Anderson had renewed his contract for another year and had been commended by the president of Liberia for his service to the republic.[73]

World War I created a temporary shortage of black American officers willing to sign up for the hardships of service in Liberia. The U.S. War Department established a training camp for black officers at Fort Des Moines, Iowa, in 1917, which attracted the best and brightest the African American community had to offer in the way of potential officers. Even Regular Army officers like John Green and Charles Young volunteered to serve with the black National Guard regiments raised for European service. The close of war in November 1918 ended this dearth of officers willing to sign up for the dangerous duty in Liberia.[74]

Near the end of Green's tour in Monrovia, the U.S. State Department asked Col. Charles Young in March 1919 to comment on a proposed list of new U.S. officers for the Frontier Force. Young responded with a letter setting out his advice on the type of officer to send to Liberia. Colonel Young rejected outright the list of twelve men proposed by the State Department on grounds that they were inadequately educated, unfit by temperament, too old, or physically not up to the rigors of life in the bush. Young warned: "I have the case of Gillespie in mind, which would prove a typical one as to the outcome of your applicants, I fear."[75]

Young made clear in his letter the criterion for a successful candidate and provided his own list of possible selectees. Young's touchstones of success are noteworthy because they directly influenced the success or failure of the enterprise in Liberia. Young noted, "Youth, activity, resourcefulness, initiative, education, and a love and sympathy for the work must characterize every man sent there, because of the trying climate and the difficulty of getting on with the people both Liberians and Natives." He stressed, "This work requires continuous training, hiking through the jungle, and almost incessant fighting; and without the man who is the leader [and] possesses pep and push and can convince the native soldier of his bravery in the field and his love of his men, he will be a failure." Lastly, Young warned against aspirants who were "desk-men" who sat in Monrovia while things around them went to pieces. Young's list of "proper fellows" included Emanuel Romero, Ennis Warrick, Henry O. Atwood, Oscar J. Price, Wilson P. Carry, Miles Green, and Julius B. Matthews.[76]

With these officer selections in the air, Lt. Col. John Green's time in Liberia ended. Before his departure, President Howard appointed Green a Knight Official of the Liberian Humane Order of African Redemption on July 25, 1919. The War Department notified Green of his pending relief by Col. Charles Young on November 12, 1919, almost one year to the day after the armistice that ended World War I. Green had spent nearly four years in Liberia and was due for reassignment to his regiment. He applied for an emergency passport for himself, his wife Ernestine, and infant son in February 1920. Bundy approved the application, and Green departed Liberia after filing his final reports to Washington on February 23, 1920.[77]

Major York and the black American officers under contract with the government of Liberia continued to lead the Frontier Force during the six-month interval between the departure of Young and the arrival of Green. However, they sorely missed the steady hand of an attaché during a challenging period, one that led to the early departure of several American officers.

Even after his arrival, Major Green could not sustain the ambitious work begun in 1912 by Charles Young to train and maintain the Liberian Frontier Force. He lost ground due to U.S. policy shifts in Liberia, a war raging in Europe, the collapse of the Liberian economy, indigenous revolts, and leadership challenges among the American officers of the Frontier Force.

Near the end of Green's four-year tour in Liberia, he and Major Anderson had little choice but to reduce the Frontier Force to half the size necessary to carry out its missions. Nevertheless, the Frontier Force fought and defeated two serious challenges to the sovereignty of the Liberian government in the south and north. Anderson achieved these successes with the help of an increasingly capable group of Americo-Liberian officers.

When Green departed in early 1920, he did so with the knowledge that Charles Young would replace him in Monrovia with a new team of officers. This must have given him confidence that the hard work accomplished during the war years would not go to waste. Davis outlined the plan for rebuilding and leading the Liberian Frontier Forces but Young was the architect who drafted the detailed strategy. Now Young would get a second try at leading the enterprise to completion.

FIG. 22. Maj. William H. York, who commanded the Liberian Frontier Force from 1915 to 1917, shown here in 1917. Courtesy of the National Afro-American Museum and Cultural Center, NAM_MSS22_WilliamHYorkLFF1914-17.

YORK, GREEN, ANDERSON

FIG. 23. William Rountree, who served as a lieutenant and captain in the Liberian Frontier Force from 1915 to 1918, shown here in 1917. Courtesy of Keith Rountree.

FIG. 24. First Lt. John E. Green (*with saber*), marching in front of his platoon of the Twenty-Fifth Infantry Regiment in Hawaii circa 1913–16. Courtesy of the U.S. Army Tropic Lightning Museum.

FIG. 25. Lt. John E. Green, who served in Monrovia as military attaché from 1916 to 1919, and his wife, Ernestine, in a passport photo from 1919. National Archives and Records Administration.

YORK, GREEN, ANDERSON

FIG. 26. French wireless towers near the beach in Monrovia, shown here in 1914, were shelled by the German submarine U-154 in 1918. Courtesy of the National Afro-American Museum and Cultural Center, NAM_MSS22_B09F71-04.

FIG. 27. Passport photo of Maj. John H. Anderson, 1920. National Archives and Records Administration.

6

Young

Final Post

If the Black World is not to be made ashamed, then Liberia
(for whom some good can be said), can do better, should
do better, and must do better. I submit that the Negro
people of the United States cannot afford to back with
their influence the present corrupt system.

—CHARLES YOUNG, 1921

I n 1920 Charles Young got a chance to finish the job set in motion a decade earlier. He had served capably as a soldier-diplomat in Liberia during his first assignment, providing the enterprise with a promising start. The war in Europe, near economic collapse of Liberia, policy changes in Washington, and political resistance in Monrovia set back the program of transforming the Liberian Frontier Force in the intervening years. John Green had certainly done his best during his four years in Liberia, helping defeat several indigenous revolts, mitigating the effects of no money, and working through a grave leadership crisis in the Frontier Force. Yet there was much hard work left to be done.

Before Young's second assignment to Liberia, the U.S. War Department asked the State Department if it could discontinue the military attaché position in Monrovia in 1919. The military faced deep cuts in post–World War I budgets, and the army leadership wanted to use the scarce position in other more important capitals of the world. Congress controlled the number of officers serving abroad as military attachés by establishing strict upper limits and funding controls. Despite this, the State Department refused and requested that Young return to Monrovia, based on the continued need for U.S. military help in Liberia. The military attaché position in Liberia would not escape the next round of congressional budget cuts.[1]

The MID sent a telegram to Young in Wilberforce, Ohio, on October 29, 1919, informing him of its wish that he return to Monrovia. Young wasted little time in deciding, accepting the detail as military attaché on November 3 and receiving orders the following day. It is unclear what the War Department would have done if Young had refused to serve again, with Green departing Monrovia and Benjamin Davis serving with his regiment in the Philippines and likely unwilling to return to Liberia to risk his health and career.[2]

Young's quick assent should not have surprised anyone because his military career options in 1919 were few. The army forced him to retire after a promotion physical in 1917 found that he had chronic nephritis (Bright's disease), high blood pressure, sclerotic arteries, and hypertrophy of the left ventricle. In Young's mind his medical condition indicated the possibilities and not the probabilities; he believed his iron constitution would see him through another tour in Liberia. A man of action, he could not bring himself to sit in his comfortable home in Wilberforce and enjoy his retirement, even with the war over. He should have looked forward to a well-earned rest, but could not bring himself to give up service to his country and to his people on both sides of the Atlantic.[3]

The War Department maintained throughout the period after his promotion board in June 1917 that Young was physically unfit for the rigors of active duty in World War I. Yet in 1919 it deemed him fit for duty amid the primitive living conditions and tropical diseases of West Africa. These two irreconcilable decisions indicate the army was disingenuous about its decision to keep Young out of active service during the war. Besides, recalling Young to active duty for service in Liberia tempered the African American community's criticism of Washington DC's failure to employ him as a leader of black troops during the war.

There was no lack of meaningful civilian work for Colonel Young in the United States if he had seen fit to turn down the Liberia assignment. Arthur Spingarn told Young in a November 1917 letter that he had nominated him to join the board of directors of the NAACP . Young replied that he would join the board and "help with all of my remaining might," yet only if his new responsibilities did not conflict with his loyalties as a "Retired Officer of the Army on active duty" during wartime. Spingarn, a major on active duty himself, responded that in time of war, the "Country and Government" come first and thanked Young for his acceptance. Mary W. Ovington, acting chair of the NAACP, notified Young in a letter that he had been elected to the board for a term of three years at its annual meeting on January 7, 1918.[4]

Young's friend Du Bois worked to get Young named to the board of directors of the NAACP, hoping to involve him in the association's business. He dispatched Young across the country on fact-finding missions in 1918, hoping it would "restore perspective to his friend's options and obligations" and offset the powerful pull of Young's loyalty to the army. Young traveled "from Philadelphia to Topeka" on behalf of the NAACP and found that working-class black families "regard the NAACP as a Negro snob affair."[5]

Ultimately, Young's loyalty to service and country won the contest. Colonel Young sailed to Africa for his second tour to Liberia as a fifty-five-year old veteran of three decades of service in an army that had declared him too sick to serve on active duty. So badly did he want to serve his country, so deep was his devotion to duty, and so desperate was he to show his fitness to work, he took the assignment even though he knew it might further damage his health. When an army friend pointed out the dangers of returning to Africa, Young replied, "Chum, there is so much over there to be done."[6]

Young spent his last Christmas with his family and packed his belongings for a long stay in Liberia. He received an extra weight allowance from the War Department to take the supplies and books he would need. Young and his family made one last visit to the East Coast before departing. In Boston Young delivered the keynote address to the Grand Conclave of the Omega Psi Phi fraternity, of which he was an honorary member. After the conclave, he accepted an invitation to dinner at a local chapter house where he had a "heart to heart" discussion with the young brothers for what he feared would be his "last opportunity" to talk to them. He also traveled to Harlem to address a meeting of the National Urban League.[7]

Colonel Young and his family boarded the Cunard Line ship *Orduna* bound for Liverpool on January 3, 1920, for the first leg of their journey. On board were three of Young's new African American officers, who would help train and command the Liberian Frontier Force: Henry O. Atwood, Allen C. Bean, and William D. Nabors. After the ten-day crossing, Young bid farewell in Liverpool to his family, who were bound for France, where they would live while the children attended school. Unlike his first tour in Liberia, Ada Young did not accompany her husband to Liberia. Young and his officers caught the Elder Dempster steamer *Onitsha* to Monrovia four days later.[8]

Young arrived at the U.S. consulate in Monrovia in February 1920 and spent his first months setting up his office and quarters. Green's last dispatches had concerned a requisition of quinine, and one of Young's first was a bill for the purchase of distilled water and ice. Both men knew the dangers of disease and sickness that threatened visitors to the West African coast. Young was especially vulnerable due to his previous bout with blackwater fever and because he suffered from the effects of Bright's disease and high blood pressure. Young had never doubted the doctors' diagnosis that he suffered from these diseases, so he knew the risk.[9]

Just three months before his arrival, President Daniel E. Howard appointed Charles Young a Knight Commander of the Liberian Humane Order of African Redemption on November 15, 1919. Young made no mention of an award ceremony after his arrival in Monrovia, but he was given the medal and certificate. Young and Howard had worked closely together during his previous tour as military attaché. Howard's term of office ended on January 5, 1920, and the new president of Liberia was Charles D. B. King.[10]

A contemporary State Department post report described Monrovia as Young saw it in 1920. The Liberian capital had a population of about five thousand and was located on a long promontory with sea on two sides, a tidal river on the third, and a mangrove swamp in the rear. The climate was tropical, with a wet season from April to November. Malaria, blackwater fever, yellow fever, and dysentery were prevalent, in part, due to the absence of public water or sewage systems. The American consul general used a portable sand toilet and bathed in a galvanized tub filled with water heated on the kitchen stove. There were no carriages and only two horses in the country; one either walked or was carried in a hammock or chair. The foreign community comprised about two hundred members who were mostly white but also included a number of African Americans. Young noted that only eight white women lived in the city.[11]

Young's first letter to his wife on March 8, 1920, gave a good summary of the situation in Monrovia and showed how quickly he returned to the routine of serious political and military affairs in the country. He wrote: "I am going in a few hours to Cape Palmas on a Commission for the President by special request and it may be about six weeks before I get back so I must write you now. I am well and so are the boys." It is an indication of Young's prestige in the eyes of the Liberian government that he was trusted to be a part of this mission in the southeast to settle the border dispute with France barely a month after his arrival in the country.[12]

The "boys," referred to the African American officers under contract with the government of Liberia to train and command the Liberian Frontier Force. The success or failure of Young's mission depended on these American officers and how they carried out their difficult duties. Colonel Young had a mostly new team of black officers. In the letter to Ada he reported:

> Nabors has gone to the Mono Country, Harry [Atwood] goes to Cape Palmas to take station, and Bean remains as Paymaster and in charge of [the] Training School at Monrovia until my return when he goes to Belli Yella [Belle Yella] in the center of the country and where the headquarters of the Force will be located. Major Anderson goes there now until he returns home in June.[13]

The commander of the Frontier Force in 1920 was still Maj. John Anderson, the lone holdover from the previous cadre of African

American officers. Anderson and Young were well acquainted from their service together in the Ninth Cavalry. Major Anderson had arrived in Monrovia in April 1917 in the wake of the leadership crisis following the Kru revolt that led to the dismissal of Maj. William York, the resignation of Capt. James Gillespie, and the eventual departure of Capt. William Rountree. It was a tribute to his health and determination that Anderson served more than two years as the solitary black American officer leading the Liberian Frontier Force under the guidance of Lieutenant Colonel Green. When Major Anderson departed Liberia in June 1920, he handed over command of the Frontier Force to Henry Atwood.[14]

Capt. Henry "Harry" O. Atwood was Young's closest confidant and the only one of the three new officers who appeared on the list of candidates Young had recommended to the State Department in March 1919. Born in Washington DC on May 8, 1881, Atwood grew up in Zanesville, Ohio, but attended high school in the District of Columbia when his father moved back to Washington to take a political job. He began college at Oberlin in Ohio but left to enlist in the Ninth Ohio Volunteer Infantry Battalion at the outbreak of the Spanish-American War, where he served as a corporal under Charles Young.[15]

After the Spanish-American War, Atwood returned to civilian life, though not for long. He completed college at Lincoln University, Pennsylvania, graduating in 1901, and later did graduate work at Howard University. His yearbook noted that he intended to study agricultural chemistry, though he really wanted to be a soldier. During World War I he attended the army officer training camp at Fort Des Moines, Iowa, and served as a captain in the 368th Infantry Regiment in France. Upon his return to the United States after the war, Young convinced him to join the effort in Liberia.[16]

Capt. William D. Nabors, the second officer to accompany Young to Liberia, also had a solid military background as an enlisted man and officer. Born on June 21, 1891, in Aliceville, Alabama, Nabors enlisted as a private in the Ninth Cavalry in December 1912 and later served under Young with the Tenth Cavalry during the Mexican Punitive Expedition in 1916 and 1917. He attended a training school for black officers established by Young at Fort Huachuca,

Arizona, and the Fort Des Moines officers' course. Nabors served in France during World War I as a second lieutenant in the 366th Infantry Regiment. After his discharge from the army he seized the opportunity to serve with Young in Liberia.[17]

Capt. Allen C. Bean, the third officer, was the youngest and least experienced. Born the son of a preacher in Davenport, Iowa, on September 5, 1896, Bean was attending school at Wilberforce University when he volunteered for service in Liberia. At Wilberforce Bean had pledged the Kappa Alpha Psi fraternity, managed the baseball and football teams, and graduated in 1918. He attended the fourth officer training school at Fort Des Moines, Iowa, which started in 1918, but the war ended before his training was complete. Bean was at Wilberforce taking postgraduate courses when he signed up to sail with Young to Liberia.[18]

It was a measure of Charles Young's status in the U.S. Army and influence in the African American community that he could select a talented team of officers to bring with him to Liberia. He had taken his own team during his first tour in 1912 with Ballard, Browne, and Newton, and did so again in 1920. On the other hand, John Green had to settle for the three officers already on the ground when he stepped ashore in 1916. All three of Green's officers were cashiered or resigned within a year of his arrival, so he was forced to operate the Frontier Force with a single American officer for two years. Young enjoyed advantages that Green never had.

Young's superior at the consulate for his entire tour of duty was Dr. Joseph L. Johnson, an African American who presented his credentials in Monrovia on October 8, 1919. Johnson, born in Washington Township, Ohio, on February 14, 1874, taught school there before getting his medical degree from Howard University in 1902. He practiced medicine in Columbus, Ohio, and served as a trustee for Wilberforce University from 1914 to 1917. Johnson and Young likely knew each other since they were both active at Wilberforce University at the same time. Johnson replaced Curtis, who had died in October 1917. Dr. Johnson was the last African American Democratic Party member appointed by Wilson during his presidency.[19]

Johnson's arrival coincided with the serious deterioration of President Woodrow Wilson's health, which ultimately affected American policy in Liberia. President Wilson suffered a debilitating stroke and collapsed on October 2, 1919, following a national tour seeking support for the Treaty of Versailles and the League of Nations. Wilson went into seclusion for the rest of his presidency, and the Senate rejected the treaty, mainly due to the Senate's opposition to the League of Nations. The resulting dearth of leadership resulted in foreign policy drift and partly led to the election of Republican Warren Harding in 1920.[20]

Richard C. Bundy remained the number-two man at the legation, as he had during Young's first tour. Aside from the home leave he took with his wife during the summer of 1916, Bundy had served continuously in Liberia since 1912. He had acted as interim consul general (chargé) for two years between the death of Curtis and arrival of Johnson. Since Bundy had grown up in Cincinnati and taught at Wilberforce at the same time as Young, the three Ohio men at the consulate had a great deal in common. Young confirmed their rapport in a March letter: "Dr. Johnson is quite a nice codger and gets along with Dick [Bundy]. . . . He boards with the Bundy's." Young was ten years older than "codger" Johnson and fifteen years senior to Bundy.[21]

Rounding out the U.S. team in Monrovia was the American general receiver of customs Harry F. Worley, who replaced Reed Clark in October 1916. Worley, who was white, had a great deal of experience as a customs official, having done similar work after the Spanish-American War in Cuba, the Philippines, and the Dominican Republic. He also enjoyed good connections with President Wilson. Worley was on home leave when World War I ended, and the United States sent him as "Minister Plenipotentiary for Liberia" to the peace negotiations in Paris in 1919, where he signed of the treaty for Monrovia. A U.S. official representing and signing for Monrovia at Versailles visibly demonstrated the role of the United States in Liberia to the world. Worley returned to Liberia in 1919.[22]

Young was well acquainted with all of the senior Liberian government officials in Monrovia. In his March letter to Ada, he noted: "Eddie [Edwin J.] Barclay as Secretary of State is the same old friend. . . . The Kings had us to dinner the other night." Charles D.

B. King was elected president of Liberia in 1920 and served as the head of state throughout Young's tour. Young and King, who had served as secretary of state during Young's previous tour, knew each other well, though they did not always see eye to eye.[23]

Under King, Liberia's seventeenth president, corruption, patronage, and mistreatment of the ethnic communities of the interior reached a highpoint. Born in Sierra Leone, King later migrated with his parents to Liberia, where he was educated. Like his father-in-law, former president Barclay, King was known for his pro-British and anti-American views. Before his election as president, he served as attorney general and secretary of state as a member of the True Whig Party. Though purportedly a moderate reformer, he continued to support a stifling political patronage that kept power tightly in the hands of a small number of prominent leaders of the ruling elite. Worse, King and the True Whig Party continued to subjugate and exploit the indigenous population and undertook few productive steps to harness tremendous potential they held.[24]

One particularly ugly example of mistreatment of the ethnic people in the hinterland occurred just before Young's arrival in Liberia for his second tour. In January 1920 Liberian district commissioner James W. Cooper complained to the interior secretary about a renegade Liberian Frontier Force officer named Lt. Alexander E. M. Rauls in Tappi. Cooper reported that Rauls had captured an indigenous prisoner, instructed the man to run for his life, and gunned him down. He killed two other men and ordered them "skinned for the drumhead." (Drums were used to communicate signals between the towns.) Rauls had other prisoners dragged out in front of his quarters in front of a crowd and with revolver drawn forced "each man to cohabit with his wife."[25]

Later, when Commissioner Cooper attempted to arrest a local man for "buying and selling slaves and not paying license to trade," Lieutenant Rauls prevented him from doing so. Cooper managed to get word back to Monrovia about Rauls's depredations and the officer was brought up on charges. However, as was the case in many other such incidents, a jury of his Americo-Liberian peers cleared him of the charges. When Young found out about the incident after his arrival in Liberia, he suspended Rawls from the force.[26]

While Young was working to improve the Frontier Force, he received some unwanted attention when the *Monrovia Weekly Review* reprinted an article from the NAACP publication *The Crisis* titled "Haiti." The author of the July 1920 article suggested that Liberia might suffer the same fate as Haiti, which had been invaded and occupied by the U.S. Navy and Marines in 1915. Young had played a key role collecting intelligence preparing for that incursion while serving in Haiti as the military attaché from 1903 to 1907.[27]

Young complained about the article in a letter to W. E. B. Du Bois, the editor of *The Crisis*. He noted that Liberians wondered whether the U.S. military attaché was in Monrovia to gather intelligence to support a future invasion of their country. This article and the controversy it created made Young's mission in Monrovia more difficult and complicated negotiations for a new loan agreement. It also fueled the ever-present xenophobia of Americo-Liberians against the United States.[28]

Du Bois, whose father was born in Haiti, criticized the Wilson administration for its invasion and occupation of Haiti. The NAACP sent an investigative team led by James Weldon Johnson to Haiti and published a scathing report in September 1920 that found little benefit to the American occupation of Haiti. Despite this criticism of the occupation of Haiti, Du Bois continued to support the United States' economic and military assistance in Liberia.[29]

Shortly before Young's arrival in early 1920, Washington sent American commissioners to Liberia to compel Monrovia to end its abuse of the indigenous people. They deployed to the interior of Liberia wherever there was friction and fighting between the Americo-Liberians and indigenous communities. Selected for their engineering backgrounds, they were recruited from the War Department's insular service; many had experience in the Philippines, Cuba, and the Dominican Republic. These white civilians faced obvious difficulties trying to enforce policies in a country where the constitution allowed only people of color to be citizens, property owners, and government officials.[30]

The leader of the American commissioners, Thomas C. Mitchell, was new to Young. Mitchell had originally sailed to Liberia in 1916 to represent the United States on the Franco-Liberian Boundary Commission. He returned to the United States in the summer of 1918 to serve in the U.S. Army during World War I, but the war ended before he could complete his engineer officer training. He sailed to Liberia again in 1919, this time as the commissioner general of the interior. In that position he worked closely with Young to settle the border disputes with France as well as mediate trouble between the indigenous communities and the government in Monrovia.[31]

Mitchell and the initial contingent of commissioners sailed on board the cruiser USS *Chattanooga* and arrived in Monrovia in April 1919. The *Chattanooga* also carried small arms and ammunition to outfit and resupply the Frontier Force. It was odd that commissioners sent to improve conditions in the interior came on the same ship with weapons to equip the Frontier Force, the very soldiers often used to exploit the indigenous inhabitants of the hinterland. The balance of the commissioners, a total of six in all, arrived in December 1919. Mitchell dispatched them to their stations in the interior while he took up his post in Monrovia.[32]

After Young and his officers arrived, the interior commissioners began to report abuses of the indigenous people by Americo-Liberian officials and the Frontier Force. Americo-Liberian officers commanded many isolated Frontier Force garrisons, far from the effective control of American officers. Horace A. Sawyer, the commissioner sent to the Liberian boundary with French Guinea, reported abuses in June 1919 by Americo-Liberian district commissioner Boimah Y. Sandimannie and Liberian Frontier Force Capt. Alexander R. Harper. The charges included theft of cattle and other property, but also trafficking in slaves, either in wars between indigenous groups or the more common practice of pawning. Other commissioners found similar abuses involving enslavement and pawning in their districts.[33]

The commissioners noted that conventions surrounding the handling of slaves and pawns were highly structured and regulated. It was customary for captives taken during fighting between indigenous communities to be ransomed for $20 to $30 each to the defeated chief; if the ransom was not paid, the captives' status as slaves became permanent. With pawning, the head of a family, village, or group would trade a marketable member of the group for cash. The victim was later exchanged for a sum ranging from $13 to $20, plus interest. If the pawn was not redeemed, he or she could be pawned to another party.[34]

In a first test of the authority of the American commissioners, Mitchell ordered Sawyer to arrest Americo-Liberian commissioner Sandimannie and send him to Monrovia for trial in May 1920. American captain Nabors arrested Sandimannie, seized his records, and transported him under guard in chains to Monrovia, where he was charged with trading in slaves, brutalizing the local inhabitants, and embezzling about $6,000. Once in Monrovia, Sandimannie, who was well connected to former president Arthur Barclay, was immediately released.[35]

The Americo-Liberian elite expressed outrage at this treatment of one of their own. They vented their fury on Mitchell, derided in the press as a white Southerner from Georgia who placed a free citizen of Liberia in chains, an echo of the treatment of black slaves in the pre–Civil War South. Not only was Sandimannie freed, Mitchell was harassed and hauled into court on a civil suit stemming from an altercation over the affair.[36]

This was the beginning of the end of the ambitious program to improve conditions in the interior using American district commissioners. Bundy, Young, and former receiver Clark were the driving forces behind this reform initiative. Most of the U.S. commissioners departed later in 1920 due to sickness, lack of pay, or the demoralized state of affairs in the interior. The reform program by the United States to improve the treatment of the interior peoples failed.[37]

One other casualty of the failure of the district commissioner program was the American receiver of customs, Harry Worley. He was described by an American colonial expert who attended the 1919 Paris Peace Conference as provincial, gullible, narrow-minded, and "entirely unsuited to take charge of Liberia." Du Bois was also critical of Worley, describing him as "a white Virginian" who as "General Receiver, is the one prominent figure and would be the real ruler of Liberia under this [Wilson] plan, together with his band of white pensioners." The "white pensioners" referred to the district commissioners, with whom Worley argued over money and record-keeping.[38]

The complaints about Worley and Mitchell led the State Department to ask the U.S. Navy to send an officer to conduct a formal investigation. The navy dispatched Capt. Victor A. Kimberly of the uss *Chattanooga* to conduct the inquiry, and he arrived in Monrovia on June 1, 1920. Col. Charles Young boarded Chattanooga to pay an official call soon after the ship's arrival, and they both returned to shore for meetings with Consul General Johnson and President King. Kimberly took a week to conduct his investigation, departing on June 8 and transmitting his official report from Freetown, Sierra Leone, on June 10, 1920. Kimberly found fault equally with Mitchell and Worley, and his report ruined the reputation of both. Mitchell stayed on until 1921, and Worley until 1922, when ill health forced him to return to the United States.[39]

Young was also active in efforts to improve the treatment of the indigenous people, and in November 1920 he wrote an impassioned letter on the issue to Bundy. Young felt duty-bound to bring the "overpowering grievances of the native population of the Liberian Interior" to the attention of American officials and provide clear proof the Americo-Liberians practiced and profited from slavery. He referred to the Sandimannie affair as a case in point and went on to quote from formal instructions issued by the Liberian president in February 1916 for dealing with prisoners of war, captives, and refugees that essentially legalized slavery and the taking of pawns. One of Young's Liberian lieutenants told him there was "not a family of any importance among the Americo-Liberians that does not hold slaves in some form or another." Young ended his note with an appeal for the United States to do everything in its power to halt the abuses, even if it meant using the $5 million loan as leverage.[40]

In January 1921, with the president of Liberia scheduled to visit the United States in connection with an agreement for a new loan of $5 million, Young sent a letter on Liberia to Dr. Robert Russa Moton, president of the Tuskegee Institute. The letter endorsed a report carried to Moton by Thomas Mitchell. The report, titled "An Exposé of the Present Liberian Situation" was a damning description of the state of affairs in Liberia. It was intended to correct "erroneous statements coming to the United States" on Liberia and encourage Dr. Moton to counter any effort to "unwittingly contribute to any fiasco in the future Government of Liberia." Young recognized that Dr. Moton had influence with the president of the United States, as had his predecessor Booker T. Washington, and hoped he would deliver the message ahead of the delegation visit.[41]

Young indicated in his letter to Dr. Moton that as a military attaché, he could not endorse the exposé publicly, yet privately stood by the facts it contained. He sent an official copy to the War Department two weeks later on February 8, 1921. Young's only interest was to find a solution to the "Liberian muddle" and maintain the honor of the United States. His goal was "the good of the Negro people on both continents to see a decent and stable Government which will protect the native population, upon which every interest of the Republic, if it survives, must depend."[42]

The sixteen-page exposé, marked "confidential" and written by Colonel Young's friend and former Liberian Supreme Court justice Thomas McCants-Stewart offered a rare window into the actual situation on the ground in Liberia in 1921. The exposé provided an accurate picture of the government in Liberia, the indigenous population, the economic realities, and the outlook for the future. Yet McCants-Stewart offered solutions, not condemnation. He felt the answer to Liberia's problems was continued U.S. support, pressure from Washington DC to reform, Americans on the ground to lead the Frontier Force, and a push to harness the potential of the indigenous people as "the greatest asset of the Republic."[43]

According to the assessment, the United States unwittingly fostered the corrupt system of government in Monrovia by intervening to help every time a foreign power tried to take advantage of Liberia, thus "strengthening the hands of the political machine in power." Every time the indigenous communities rebelled, Washington sold arms to Liberia or dispatched a cruiser to help put down the uprising. This effectively propped up the government in Monrovia, made the Americo-Liberians rich off the spoils of war, and discouraged the local inhabitants from participating in the economic and political life of the republic. The report warned that Liberia was doomed to fail and be partitioned by France and Britain if it did not work to harness the tremendous economic potential of the hinterland.[44]

The reason for Young's private endorsement of the exposé was President King's departure for the United States on January 28, 1921, to conduct the final negotiations for the new loan. The U.S. secretary of the treasury had extended the offer for this war loan in September 1918 to meet the needs of allied countries for national security and defense in World War I. The United States notified Liberia promptly, but the Americo-Liberians argued over details and did not submit the agreement to the Liberian Parliament for approval until June 1920. President King spent nearly a year in the United States waiting for the U.S. side of the negotiations to conclude, signing the agreement in October and waiting in vain for its passage in the U.S. Congress.[45]

Finally, with negotiations over the loan still in the air, President King notified the U.S. State Department that he had to return to Liberia due to the constitutional requirement for him to be present for the opening of the Liberian legislature on December 4, 1921. U.S. Secretary of State Charles E. Hughes asked the Navy Department if a ship was available to transport President King back to Monrovia, and the navy designated the USS *Denver*, then undergoing repairs in Boston, to carry the delegation back to Liberia. *Denver* departed Boston with the delegation on board on November 15 and arrived in Monrovia the morning of December 3, 1921, with just one day to spare.[46]

With his mission complete, Capt. Austin Kautz of *Denver* did not stay in Monrovia long. Once the president and his party were ashore, he paid official calls on Consul General Johnson, American receiver Worley, and Col. Charles Young. On December 5 Kautz and two of his officers attended a formal luncheon at the executive mansion hosted by the president and joined by government officials and the diplomatic corps. After the luncheon King presented Kautz with the Liberian Order of the Redemption of Africa. USS *Denver* departed the following day on December 6, 1921.[47]

Inopportunely for King and Liberia, the inauguration of Republican president Warren G. Harding on March 4, 1921, brought changes to the international financial policies of the United States. During the campaign of 1920, Harding had strongly denounced Wilson's policies in Haiti and the Dominican Republic. Harding's Republican administration followed a "cooperative approach that underlined the idea that private enterprise could carry out public purpose with some guidance from the government's hidden hand." After 1921 U.S. foreign policy encouraged private bank investment, not government loans, to stabilize the world's economies.[48]

Since the State Department could not find private banks interested in the risky situation in Liberia, it convinced President Harding to ask Congress to give the Treasury Department lending authority for Liberia. The U.S. Congress introduced a resolution supporting the agreement with Liberia on February 15, 1922. The resolution passed the House on May 11 but failed to get Senate approval and died in conference. The Senate refused to make Liberia an exception to a new American policy that barred government loans to foreign states. The United States notified the Liberian government that the loan deal was dead on December 8, 1922, and Liberia's debt crisis and security problems continued.[49]

Concurrent with the loan negotiations, some African American groups in the United States pushed for resettling U.S. blacks on the coast of West Africa. Marcus Garvey, founder of the Universal Negro Improvement Association (UNIA), led the Back-to-Africa movement in the early 1920s. Unlike Booker T. Washington and W. E. B. Du Bois, who believed blacks should find their rightful place in the United States, Garvey maintained: "If Europe is for the Europeans, then Africa shall be for the black peoples of the world." Garvey founded UNIA in Jamaica in 1914, established a UNIA division in the United States in 1917, started the Black Star Line shipping firm in 1919, and initiated his program to develop Liberia as a place to resettle black Americans in 1920. His ultimate goal was the mass emigration of black people of the world back to Africa and the continent's forced liberation from colonial rule.[50]

The Liberian administration of Charles King was ambivalent about the Garvey movement. In private meetings with UNIA officials, King encouraged the effort and promised limited support, but publicly kept a neutral face. At first, he did not want his association with Garvey to jeopardize the $5 million loan from the

United States. On April 13, 1921, while in Washington lobbying for the loan, King wrote an open letter to African Americans concerning immigration in response to Garvey's activities for printing in *The Crisis*. He cautioned that Liberia was not in an economic position to accept mass immigration but welcomed limited numbers of "strong young men trained as artisans, engineers, and merchants who can bring with them some capital for investment." He promised Liberia would never "allow her territory to be made a center of aggression or conspiracy against other sovereign states," a statement aimed to calm the worries of London and Paris.[51]

Charles Young voiced his opinion about Marcus Garvey and UNIA in a May 1920 letter to Charles S. Cuney, a lawyer in Washington DC. Cuney was a friend and former military cadet who had served under Young at Wilberforce University. Addressing him as "My dear old shipmate," Young told Cuney that Garvey had generated interest along the west coast of Africa, but hoped he would "put some business methods in it and all possible guarantees about people's capital." Young wrote, "It would be a darned shame for the project to fail now," and believed that any "all-black proposition well financed cannot fail of success in Africa."[52]

In his letter, Young displayed uncharacteristic frankness and race consciousness. He warned that any such enterprise should be "prepared to fight the machinations and commercial supremacy of the white man." He concluded, "But one thing is certain and that it will never be simple pickings for the white man alone, while the African that does the work goes half-fed and half clothed." This letter provides a rare glimpse of private views Young never conveyed in official correspondence.[53]

Colonel Young's list of reports sent to the MID the summer and fall of 1921 confirmed that he focused a great deal of attention on Marcus Garvey and the UNIA. In June he sent the MID an article titled "Universal Negro Improvement Association in the Liberian Legislature" which appeared in the *Liberian Patriot* on May 21, 1921, along with reports he wrote titled "Sociologic-Collectivism-Garveyism" and "Liberian Politics." He followed these two with a monograph in early August titled "The U.N.I.A. or Garvey Movement." None of the official copies of any of these reports survived a War Department housecleaning in the 1920s.[54]

A State Department copy of one of Young's monographs did survive; it expresses his strong concerns about UNIA and the Garvey movement in Liberia. This report, intended to update Washington on the Liberian political situation, was titled "Garveyism: The Constitution of the Universal Negro Improvement Association." He warned the State Department that UNIA representatives in Liberia and the United States were corrupt and that persuading black Americans "with delusive promises to sell their property and abandon the land where they were born, for the sickness, suffering, and loss of money and property [in Liberia] where their means of livelihood will be only too precarious."[55]

Young knew that Washington had little interest in Garvey's operations in Liberia. In the report, Young stated that the "American Minister [Dr. Joseph L. Johnson] informs me that the U.S. State Department has not asked for any report on the Garvey Movement." Still, he insisted on sending the account "in order to forestall if possible the inevitable suffering and trouble ensuing by deluding Negro American citizens in numbers to these shores where they cannot expect to find a home and happiness and ordinary conditions."[56]

In his report Young also expressed concern over the trouble France and England might cause. Both countries watched the Garvey movement with great wariness "as being wholly incompatible, and dangerous, and subversive of their policies in Africa." Young went so far as to accuse Garvey officials of lying and using false papers to pass through the passport authorities at Liverpool on their way to Liberia.[57]

By the summer of 1921, the government of President King ended any real chance that Garvey could use Liberia as a springboard for its Back-to-Africa movement. On May 24, 1921, Liberian secretary of state Edwin Barclay responded to a UNIA official that his government did not approve of the scheme of Marcus Garvey to use it as a center from which to launch a movement to drive the white people out of Africa. Later during his trip to the United States, President King urged the Garvey movement to discard its "political propaganda and the impossible talk about driving the white race out of Africa." Rather, he urged them to "enlist the aid of the American people in sending emigrants there, building up the country agriculturally, commercially, and financially."[58]

The majority of Young's reporting in 1921 was administrative reporting on accounts, codes, and supplies, but nearly a third concerned Garvey and the UNIA. Of seventeen detailed reports send to the MID in 1921 on the politics, geography, and military affairs of Liberia, five concerned Garvey's Back-to-Africa movement. He dispatched his last detailed substantive report of the year, titled "UNIA Convention Sends Message to Liberian Plenary Commission," to Washington DC on October 10, 1921. But by that time, Garvey's plans for Liberia were dead in the water.[59]

In the midst of the loan negotiations and his reporting on Marcus Garvey in 1921, Young pursued his military attaché duties. Young planned an extended intelligence trip to British, French, Spanish, and former German colonial possessions on the West African coast beginning in November 1921. He had previously visited Sierra Leone and the Ivory Coast in the course of assisting in the Anglo-Liberian and Franco-Liberian border commissions. He also wanted to visit some of the other important cultural and historic sites in Western Africa.[60]

Young's travel was primarily aimed at gathering information for monographs on the countries of West Africa. The MID compiled monographs in the areas of combat, economic, and political affairs. The MID's Monographic Section prepared a series of military handbooks and studies covering the important countries of the world. By January 1919, a year before Young's second posting to Liberia, this office had published seventeen major geographical handbooks. The chief source of information for these country studies were the overseas military attachés, who possessed first-hand information.[61]

Young completed a Liberian monograph on the "Economic, Political, and Combat Factors" and forwarded it to the MID in May 1921. The chief of the MID sent Young a letter in June 1921 commending the scope, content, and thoroughness of his work and expressed his appreciation for his "splendid, intelligent cooperation on this matter." The message ended with a reminder that Young's was "the principal outpost for collection of information on the African west coast, and that your government needs greatly pertinent first-hand information on that territory." Young required no further encouragement and began planning his trip.[62]

Young wrote his last letter to his wife on November 10, 1921, just five days before he boarded a steamer to journey south along the coast. He noted his intention to visit "Fernando Po [now Bioko, Equatorial Guinea], Cameroons, Nigeria, Gold Coast," and be gone about a month and a half. He wrote, "First-hand information is what I want. Especially do I want this kind of knowledge of the Psychology of the people."[63]

There were other reasons for the trip. The MID files on Africa include an entry dated April 12, 1921, noting a Senate Joint Resolution authorizing the president of the United States to "undertake negotiations for the purchase of territories in East, Southwest, West Africa, and Oceania, over which Germany exercised sovereignty before the war, to purchase cables etc. in payment of debt." The U.S. Navy wanted to free itself from dependence on British cables and wireless stations. It is also possible his trip to the island of Fernando Po was a fact-finding mission to investigate claims of the use of indigenous forced labor from Liberia that led to a League of Nations investigation a few years later.[64]

Young requested a four-month leave of absence beginning on April 1, 1922 to visit his wife and children after the completion of his trip. He had made an earlier request for four months of leave in June 1921, citing the need to visit Europe to take care of family affairs and to have dental work done. The State Department turned down that request in July because of the confused state of affairs in Liberia and the ongoing negotiations for the $5 million loan agreement. So instead of traveling north to Europe to see his family, Young journeyed south to meet his fate.[65]

Young departed on the Spanish steamer *Catalina* on November 15, 1921, en route to Fernando Po, Cameroon, and Nigeria. He stopped at the U.S. consulate in Monrovia on his way to the ship, showing signs of a slight cold, but was excited about the trip. Consul General Johnson later reported that Young left in spirits and boarded the steamer singing his old favorite, "The Owl and the Pussycat."

That was the last time anyone in the legation, except for Captain Atwood, saw him alive.[66]

Young kept a diary titled "African Journey" throughout his trip. The first travel notation read, "Left morning of November 15, 1921 on *Catalina* for Fernando Po. Fare 8 Pounds—6 days enroute. Cared for by Dr. Don Adolfo Amilivia, Administrator of Carreos, Joaquim Mallo Alcalde, and Consul H. H. Gibson of Liberia. Put up with Gibson, fine fellow for ten days. Left Fernando Po December 3 for Lagos via Duala." His reference to his being cared for by a doctor on the ship supports several other sources that indicate he became seriously ill during the crossing to Fernando Po. He stayed on the island for ten days to recuperate at the home of the Liberian consul to Fernando Po, H. H. Gibson.[67]

His sickness did not keep him from traveling the island and completing several pages of notes in his journal about the music, history, people, and topography. He recorded that there were about three thousand laborers from Liberia working under contract for $5 a month on the cocoa plantations. His journal is also full of details about the local people and culture. Young, an accomplished musician and composer, detailed in his diary two short tunes titled "Conko Bay Song" and "Woman Get Ashore." Maynard H. Jackson, who wrote of Young in "An African Elegy" in the *Associated Negro Press* on October 13, 1922, noted: "Every ship on which he has 'coasted it' remembers 'The Colonel's Amplified Native Songs.'"[68]

On December 3 Young boarded a ship for the short crossing to Duala, Cameroon. From that point to the end of his journal, there is no clear indication of his exact travel schedule. Immediately after his notes on Fernando Po, Young wrote five pages on the "Congo River," "Stanley Pool," and the "Katanga Plateau." He may have visited the Belgian Congo or written his notes based on others' firsthand accounts and other sources. However, the style of his comments was more clipped and choppy than the rest of his journal, as if he was recounting them secondhand. Yet there was time enough in his six-week journey to have visited the Congo.[69]

The next four pages of his diary dealt with observations of Cameroon, a former German colony. The first half concerned Cameroon's history and reads clipped and detached, like his notes on the Congo. The second two pages were clearly firsthand observations and full of Young's personal comments. He noted: "The French are extremely unpopular and the people say they prefer the Germans," and "There is a wonderfully large and well-filled market. There is a pier for landing ships right at the town [Duala]. Dredgers and dry-dock left by the German's still exist." He continued with details about railroads, crops, and exports.[70]

The last entries in the journal concern the crossing to Lagos and his visit to Nigeria. Young began, "Left Duala Tuesday and struck Victory (English) and the entrance to Buea and the Cameroon Mountain." All his comments from Duala to Lagos were exact descriptions of the geography along the route. Young arrived in the port of Calabar and made his first landfall in southern Nigeria, where he noted, "First time passport was asked for. The official kindly disposed to African people could not refrain from delivering the usual sermon on unpreparedness of the Negro for government." He also wrote: "Here as everywhere on the west coast of Africa the Negro merchant class are driving their bargains. Who said the Negro is no merchant?" In Calabar the journal portion on the "African Journey" ended.[71]

Young continued his trip north to Lagos after his stop at Calabar. Still feeling ill, he visited Dr. Macaulay's Dispensary in Lagos and paid two pounds, two shillings for unspecified "professional services" on December 15, 1921. Young wrote in his diary a last scribbled note , perhaps meant to be torn out and delivered, addressed to Mr. J. M. Stuart-Young, a British poet and friend of who had critiqued some of his verse in Monrovia. He scribbled: "Dear Friend: Can you let me have about 4 bananas and as many oranges to whet my whistle for a while until our extravaganza getup? Hope you are well today. Tomorrow I go to Kano Ward. Yours, Young."[72]

Young then began his trip to the famous walled city of Kano, a five-hundred-mile round trip by train from Lagos, though it is unclear whether he reached the city. On December 25, 1921, an American businessman named Murray G. Sawyer discovered Colonel Young sick at the train station in Zaira, Nigeria, a town on the rail line between Lagos and Kano. Young was very sick and in need of immediate medical care, so Sawyer took Young back to Lagos by train, arriving the following day.[73]

Sawyer, who later wrote to Ada Young of the incident, detailed his time with Young. He noted: "When I first met the Colonel he could speak coherently but his mind commenced to fail soon afterwards." Young told Sawyer that he had felt ill when he arrived in Lagos a week earlier and sought treatment from a doctor but didn't think the illness was serious. Young also said he stayed in what Sawyer referred to as "poor hovels" in Lagos rather than seek out the "leading black people there" for assistance. Young added that he had been robbed of $1,000 in cash in Lagos before he caught the train to Kano.[74]

Sawyer took Young from the train station directly to Grey's Hospital in Lagos, where the doctors diagnosed him as suffering from chronic nephritis. Young wrote a telegram at the hospital to be sent to the British Bank of West Africa in Monrovia that instructed, "See Doctor Johnson Capt. Atwood telegraph quickly Lagos hundred pounds. Am seriously ill hospital. Col. Chas. Young. Dec. 26. Grey's Hospital." The consulate in Monrovia received the telegram on December 27 and immediately cabled money to Young. The British gave Young the best care available: a doctor visited him daily, and nuns at the hospital cared for him constantly.[75]

When American officials heard of Young's condition, they voiced concern for the confidential notes and papers he was carrying. In a message on December 28 from the consulate in Monrovia marked "Strictly Confidential," Johnson stated that Young was "likely to have his military possessions and notes impounded" and asked the War Department for instructions. Washington responded in a cable on December 31 that if Young was unable to safeguard his confidential papers, the legation was to "take any necessary steps to prevent their falling into unauthorized hands." The legation dispatched Captain Atwood to safeguard Young's confidential papers on the first available steamer.[76]

Col. Charles Young died on January 8, 1922, at the hospital in Lagos, Nigeria. He was two months shy of fifty-eight years. Dr. William Walker signed the death certificate the following day, citing the primary cause of death as "Nephritis (chronic)" and the secondary cause as "cardiac failure." He died of the very ailments the army doctors had found during his promotion physical in 1917. The doctor attested that he attended Young and was present at his death. Young's friend Henry Atwood was also present, having arrived on board the German steamer *Jupiter*. Murray Sawyer also stood vigil and later wrote an account of the death for Ada Young.[77]

Atwood and Sawyer made funeral arrangements, and the British colonial authorities buried Young with full military honors on January 9, 1922. The British borrowed a U.S. flag from a local Dutch company to drape over Young's casket, which was also adorned with flowers and branches. Authorities provided an honor guard of that included black Nigerian soldiers, sailors, and a police band. A wonderfully carved horse-drawn hearse carried Young's body to the European section of Ikoyi Cemetery. The bishop of Nigeria presided over the ceremony and acknowledged that Young's success in the U.S. Army was "proof positive of his ability and integrity" in a country renowned for its prejudice. An aide to the Nigerian governor and several British officers attended in their dress uniforms, aiguillettes, and pith helmets.[78]

Members of the local Nigerian West African Frontier Force regiment fired a volley over the gravesite as they lowered Young's coffin into a brick and concrete vault and covered it with African soil. A Nigerian bugler sounded "Last Post," signifying that Colonel Young's duty was complete—he could rest in peace. His body remained in Nigeria until his widow petitioned the War Department for its return to the United States. When Young was reinterred with full military honors at Arlington National Cemetery on June 1, 1923, his journey finally ended.[79]

Colonel Young served skillfully as the War Department point man as well as the State Department soldier-diplomat in Liberia from 1920 to 1922. Both he and the U.S. government hoped he could finish the work he had begun with such vigor and success eight years earlier. Although he made progress, there was much more to be accomplished when his untimely death cut short his important work. It would be left to others to attempt to finish the task.

In the last year of his second tour in Liberia, Young became more and more engaged in the political struggle between Washington and Monrovia concerning the future of Liberian governance and the treatment of the indigenous people. Young supported reform efforts that led to sending white American commissioners to improve the treatment of the ethnic communities of the interior. This initiative failed in the face of Monrovian resistance and lack of support from Washington DC.

The exposé written by a former associate justice of the Liberian Supreme Court and endorsed by Charles Young raised the fundamental question about the willingness of Liberia to be rescued by the United States. The United States had unwittingly fostered the situation in Liberia by supporting Monrovia against internal revolts and external threats. Moreover, the government in Monrovia was so corrupt and set against any American effort to improve affairs in Liberia that by the 1920s, Washington wondered if the effort had any prospect of succeeding.

FIG. 28. Col. Charles Young, shown here in 1917, served a second tour as the military attaché to Liberia from 1920 to 1922. Courtesy of the National Afro-American Museum and Cultural Center, NAM_P3_B02F06.

YOUNG: FINAL POST

FIG. 29. Capt. William D. Nabors, Col. Charles Young, Capt. Allen C. Bean, and Capt. Henry O. Atwood on the Atlantic voyage to Liberia in 1920. *The Crisis*, February 1920.

FIG. 30. Maj. John H. Anderson (*seated, second from left*) and Capt. William D. Nabors (*seated, far right*) pose with Americo-Liberian and indigenous officials, 1920. Courtesy of the National Afro-American Museum and Cultural Center, NAM_MSS22-P3_B01F26.

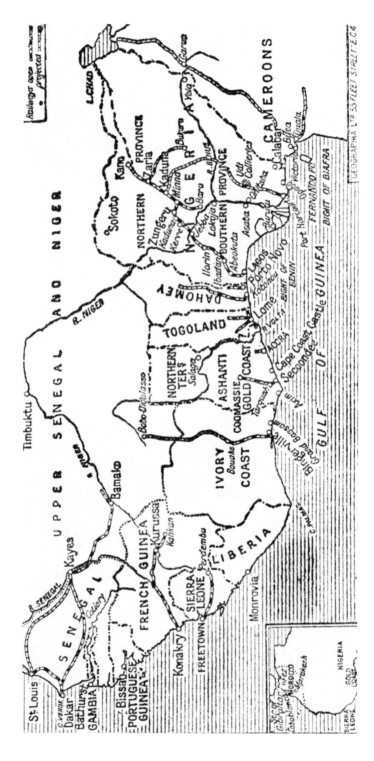

FIG. 31. Map from 1919 showing areas Colonel Young visited during his visit to Fernando Po, Cameroon, and Nigeria. Courtesy of the National Afro-American Museum and Cultural Center, NAM_MSS22_B16F05.

FIG. 32. Col. Charles Young's burial at Ikoyi Cemetery in Lagos, Nigeria, 1922. Courtesy of the National Afro-American Museum and Cultural Center, NAM_MSS22-P3_B01F05C.

7

Nabors, Staten, Outley

Mission Transition

I found the morale of the soldiers greatly shaken by treatment
of the civil officers and especially by the flogging of certain
soldiers by the District Commissioner.

—Moody Staten, 1927

The year 1922 proved a turning point for American political,
economic, and military support to Liberia. For the previous
ten years, despite changes in administration that resulted in
minor policy shifts, American support to Liberia stayed on track.
However, the mood of the country shifted in the postwar period to
isolationism and "a return to normalcy." When President Warren
G. Harding took office in March 1921, the new Republican administration espoused disarmament and rejected foreign intervention.
And finally, the Americo-Liberian regime in Monrovia had tired of
Washington's interference in its internal affairs and was anxious to
find an alternative to the $5 million American war loan.

Another reversal came after the death of Colonel Young in 1922,
when the War Department declined to replace him with a Regular Army officer. The Military Intelligence Division at the War
Department notified the State Department in April 1921, nearly a
year before Young's death, that the position in Liberia would be
excluded from its forty-three authorized military attaché officers
worldwide. The War Department reduced staff sharply beginning
in 1921 as the result of the National Defense Act of 1920, which

cut military spending. Even if Young had survived and completed his tour, he would have been the last military attaché during this period to serve in Monrovia.[1]

Most of Young's American officers departed soon after his death. Capt. Henry Atwood, frustrated and demoralized by the loss of Young and the general lack of progress, refused to renew his two-year contract and shipped out in early February 1922. Capt. Allen Bean departed soon after Atwood for similar reasons. Maj. John Anderson, commander of the Frontier Force, left in May 1922 after five years of continuous service in Liberia. Because he remained in Liberia his whole tour, he accrued more than seven months of paid home leave under his contract. Anderson's doctor in Monrovia urged him to return to the United States for at least a year to restore his damaged health.[2]

Before Anderson departed, the Liberian secretary of war, James Cooper, directed him to turn over temporary command of the Frontier Force to Capt. William Nabors. Of the officers Young brought with him in 1920, only Nabors stayed on to provide leadership to the Liberian Frontier Force. He took command of the Frontier Force on May 22, 1922, though his health, like Anderson's, suffered from years of hard service in Liberia. A doctor's certificate in May 1923 attested that Nabors suffered from "chronic malaria, leukemia, debilitas cordis nervosa" and that his "organism in general" was "run down."[3]

Despite his ill health, Nabors stayed on at the request of the U.S. consulate and Liberian government to provide continuity and leadership. He married Nakkitah E. Williams, an American citizen, in Monrovia in February 1923. When Major Anderson decided not to return after his home leave expired in May 1923, the Liberian government promoted Nabors to major and designated him commander of the Frontier Force before he shipped home on sick leave at the end of June.[4]

At the time Nabors commanded the Liberian Frontier Force, it comprised 762 enlisted men and noncommissioned officers and 37 commissioned Liberian officers. The officers included 7 captains and 30 lieutenants. Five cadets studied at the officer academy at Camp Johnson to earn their officer commissions. These 5 officer trainees remained after another 19 were dismissed or resigned during the year, a sign that the program of study was not easy, or that the candidates were not sufficiently prepared or qualified. Young and his American officer cadre had done their best to improve the training and effectiveness and overcome the detrimental effects brought on by World War I, yet the job was by no means complete.[5]

It did not take long for the loss of Young and the departure of most of the American officers to tell on the discipline and morale of the Frontier Force. For example, a troubling incident had occurred involving Liberian first lieutenant Alexander E. M. Rauls in March 1922. Two years earlier, Rauls commanded a Frontier Force detachment at Tappi and was arrested on charges that he killed several indigenous people and "made a drum-head from the skin of at least one of them." When he was tried for murder, a jury of his Americo-Liberian peers found him not guilty. Young took a deep interest in the case and made sure Rauls was suspended from the Frontier Force. A few days after the death of Young, Monrovia released Rauls from suspension and restored him to his previous rank and duty with the Frontier Force.[6]

There were also problems with the structure and conduct of the force. The American auditor in Liberia, Sydney de la Rue, noted in March 1922 that the Frontier Force comprised about 700 men, exclusive of officers. Each soldier had from 2 to 4 indigenous women living with them, totaling approximately 2,100 individuals. In addition, each soldier retained an average of 2 "soldier boys" who dressed in some sort of uniform and usually carried the soldier's weapons while in the field. This was another 1,400 boys, bringing the total of camp followers to about 3,500, attached to only 700 soldiers. Since these camp followers could not possibly live on the meager and irregular soldier rations and pay, they lived off the land and preyed on the local indigenous communities. This had the effect of depopulating areas around the military camps, as local inhabitants moved away to avoid the depredations of the Frontier Force. The American auditor recommended the elimination of these camp followers and the regular transfer of soldiers from station to station to prevent them from establishing semi-permanent camp follower communities.[7]

Without leadership and regular pay, the Frontier Force steadily regressed to the dual character it exhibited before the arrival of American officers in 1912. The soldiers lapsed into old habits and lived off the land with their Liberian officers unable or unwilling to stop them. When asked to wage war on the ethnic people by the Liberian government, they did so using indigenous rules based on collecting booty, exacting revenge, and capturing slaves. Young and his officers had attempted, with limited success, to restore regular pay and fix some of the organizational problems brought on by World War I and its aftermath. When Young died and most of his American officer cadre departed in 1922, this transformation was far from complete.

A new consul general arrived in 1922 to sort out some of the postwar challenges in Liberia. Republican president Harding appointed Solomon Hood to replace Joseph Johnson in October 1921, though Hood did not arrive in Monrovia to present his credentials until February 1922. Solomon Porter Hood was born in Lancaster, Pennsylvania on July 30, 1853. He graduated from Lincoln University in 1876, completed seminary at the same institution in 1880, and later spent four years as a missionary in Haiti. Hood served in Liberia until 1926 as the State Department's point man handling the difficult negotiations for the transition to a private loan agreement.[8]

Consul General Hood arrived a month after the death of Young in Nigeria and immediately took steps to replace American officers. With Atwood and Bean already gone, Anderson departing in May 1922, and Nabors leaving in June 1923, Hood began asking the State Department to find new candidates. He asked for at least two officers, thinking Nabors would return to Liberia after sick leave in the United States. The records show that several candidates applied for positions in the Frontier Force, but the State Department rejected most of them because they lacked the proper credentials. In June 1922 the State Department recommended one of the few who met the qualifications, Moody Staten, and offered him the position a year later.[9]

Born in Lincoln County, North Carolina, on February 18, 1891, Staten had a solid military background. He joined the U.S. Army as an enlisted soldier at the age of twenty-one and served with the

Twenty-Fifth Infantry Regiment until 1917. He then took advantage of the expansion of the army, attended the officer training camp at Fort Des Moines, Iowa, earned a commission as an infantry captain in 1917, and served with the Ninety-Second Division in Europe during World War I. After his honorable discharge in 1919, he attended Cheney State Normal School (later Eastern Washington College of Education and now Eastern Washington University) near Spokane, planning to pursue a teaching job in the South.[10]

President Harding approved the State Department's selection of Staten in June and he arrived in Monrovia in July 1923, initially with the rank and pay of captain. Hood hoped Staten could restore some of the morale and effectiveness of the much-depleted Frontier Force. The consulate anticipated that Staten could make an impact based on his enlisted service in the Regular Army and his officer experience during World War I, where he participated in the campaigns in the Vosges Mountains, the Argonne Forest, and at Metz. Staten also enjoyed the benefits of a college education, and standing six feet one, an imposing stature.[11]

Staten's transition to leadership in the Frontier Force was rocky from the beginning. It took time to familiarize himself with the situation on the ground, especially since Nabors departed before he arrived. With Nabors still filling the major's position on paper, the Liberian War Department issued Staten a commission as a captain. This put him in a position that was in theory equal to that of the seven Americo-Liberian captains then on duty with the Liberian Frontier Force. The seven Americo-Liberian captains had the added advantages of political and family connections in Liberia as well as time and experience commanding troops in the Frontier Force. The Liberian War Department aimed to wrest control of the Frontier Force from American hands, and this situation of having Staten at a relative disadvantage aided that goal.

Monrovia was not interested in creating a Frontier Force that was efficient, overly professional, or outside the firm control of the government. The Americo-Liberian minority would see such a force as a threat to the regime, based on its experience in 1909. The American receiver of customs, Sydney de la Rue, had it right when he wrote in 1924 that "the result of this situation has been that the Frontier Force is undrilled, extravagant, totally inefficient, and is frankly a disgrace. Curiously enough, the Liberians recognize this themselves."[12]

Political events in Washington aided the Liberian goal of more complete control over the Frontier Force. After the 1921 election of Harding, the Republican approach to foreign economic policy discouraged government loans and encouraged American firms and bankers to advance the national interest. The mood of the nation turned inward, evidenced by Congress's repudiation of the Treaty of Versailles and League of Nations. In 1922 the United States began the phased withdrawal from the dollar diplomacy dependencies and military occupations of Nicaragua, Haiti, and the Dominican Republic. After the failure of the government loan to Liberia, the State Department began looking for an exit strategy in that country as well.[13]

Discussions were already underway in the United States that would aid the effort to end American government economic aid to Liberia. When the British government adopted the Stevenson Plan in 1922 to regulate rubber production in its colonies, American companies voiced alarm at higher prices. This led Harvey S. Firestone of the Firestone Company of Akron, Ohio, to approach the State Department with an idea for a private loan plan for Liberia. The administration of Calvin Coolidge, who succeeded Warren Harding after he died in office in 1923, supported the deal with Firestone.[14]

Negotiations for the production of rubber in Liberia between the Firestone Company and Monrovia began in earnest in 1924. Firestone had been looking for a place to establish a large plantation to break the British monopoly on the production of rubber, which was becoming so critical for cars, trucks, and other machines. British colonial possessions produced about 70 percent of the global output during this time, while the United States consumed about 70 percent of the supply. Firestone looked at options in the Philippine Islands, Mexico, and Central America but decided that Liberia had the ideal climate and conditions for growing and producing rubber.[15]

The main attraction of the Firestone venture for the State Department, besides the prospect of breaking the British monopoly, was the hope of ending the loan agreement of 1912 and shifting responsibility for the economic well-being of Liberia. In an early example of privatization, Firestone made an offer in April 1924 to the State Department to replace the loan agreement with its own plan to pay off the debt and improve the economy of Liberia with a substantial rubber production enterprise. With the support of the State Department, Firestone submitted a draft proposal to Liberian secretary of state Edwin Barclay in June 1924.[16]

Liberian president King was anxious to find a new loan and mentioned the deal with Firestone in a letter to W. E. B Du Bois in June 1924. Du Bois had traveled to Liberia for King's second inauguration on January 1, 1924, as the official representative of President Calvin Coolidge. In an active exchange of correspondence following the visit, Du Bois warned King of the dangerous political entanglements that came with government loans and argued the advantages of private financial agreements, if carefully managed, and in July 1924 Du Bois advised King of the benefits of American capital over that of British or French. He counseled King that African Americans "have enough political power to make the government go slowly" when pressured by white American investors. This proved to be exactly the case.[17]

Years later Du Bois recalled his visit to Liberia with his usual elegance. "I remember," he wrote,

> standing once in a West African forest where thin, silver trees loomed straight and smooth in the air. There were two men with me. One was a black man, Solomon Hood, United States Minister to Liberia; a man of utter devotion, whose solicitude for the welfare of Liberia was like a sharp pain driving him on. And he thought he had found the solution. The solution was the white man beside us. He was a rubber expert sent by the Firestone Corporation of the United States to see if rubber could be grown in Liberia.

Hood's initial reports to the State Department on the suitability of Liberia for growing rubber had been shared with Firestone and led to the dispatch of Firestone representative Donald A. Ross to Liberia.[18]

Three torturous years of negotiations ensued after the initial offer, and at several points Harvey Firestone nearly gave up on the Liberians. Firestone was willing to negotiate a $5 million loan, build an artificial harbor in Monrovia, invest a great deal of capital, employ indigenous workers at rubber plantations, and improve the infrastructure of Liberia. In exchange, Firestone wanted a ninety-nine-year lease on up to 1 million acres of land for the rubber plantation, permission to build the port and transportation network necessary to run the enterprise, and some assurances that his company would be allowed to operate in Liberia profitably.[19]

Consul General Hood did not remain in Liberia long enough to see the successful end of the negotiations between Firestone and Liberia. Hood, a huge supporter of the agreement with Firestone, departed Monrovia for the United States on January 9, 1926. He wrote to Du Bois that he had been granted home leave because of ill health, noting that he had been in bed for five weeks with "African fever" before his departure. Hood, who arrived in the United States prostrate and had to be carried from the ship, convalesced through the summer but never returned to Liberia.[20]

Despite the departure of Hood, both parties finally agreed on the comprehensive agreement in September 1926, though it did not go into effect until July 1927. The agreement had four parts: the first was a ninety-nine-year lease on a former British experimental rubber plantation near Monrovia; the second a ninety-nine-year lease for up to one million acres of land devoted to rubber production; and a third covering the right to improve the harbor facilities in Monrovia. The fourth and last was a loan agreement with the City Bank of New York extending $5 million in credit to the Liberian government. This last agreement paid off the debt to the United States for the bonds issued under the loan agreement of 1912 and allowed Liberia to pay its debts to European creditors. This fourth agreement caused the most trouble for the Liberian government, as it put the country under a financial obligation to Firestone.[21]

As with the loan agreement of 1912, Firestone secured the loan by a first lien on all Liberian export and import duties and on revenues from the head tax (a poll tax levied on people rather than property). Under the agreement, the United States appointed a financial adviser to administer the Liberian income and distribute the money. Additionally, Article XII of the agreement stipulated that the Liberian government maintain the Liberian Frontier Force to provide security for the loan. As under the previous agreement, the Liberian War Department administered the Frontier Force with funds provided by the financial adviser. Finally, the president of the United States nominated "qualified and experienced" American officers to serve with the Frontier Force.[22]

Firestone and Monrovia disagreed over the number of officers necessary under the agreement. A draft produced by Firestone in 1925 initially called for the United States to appoint one colonel, two majors, and one captain, to be paid an aggregate sum of $16,000 per year. The Liberian legislature rejected this clause and altered it to read one major and one captain at a combined annual salary of $8,000. The American consulate in Monrovia cabled the State Department in 1926 during the negotiations: "It is regretted that Article XII referring to military officers will not be modified further because the Liberian Government resents the sending of U.S. non-commissioned officers, regardless of their efficiency, to reorganize the combat forces of their country."[23]

It was no coincidence that one American major and one captain were on duty with the Frontier Force at the time of the negotiation of the agreement. This was enough for Monrovia, so long as the money kept flowing. The Liberian government appeared ready to dispense with American officers altogether and take full control of the Liberian Frontier Force if allowed to do so.[24]

The Liberian War Department promoted Staten to major in January 1925, once it became clear that Nabors would not return from his extended sick leave. Major Staten commanded the Liberian Frontier Forces alone for a time, though he asked for assistance. On January 19, 1925, he wrote to Consul General Hood informing him that the Liberian government would soon ask for the services of a second American officer. Staten recommended Lewis Broadus, a colleague he had served with both as a noncommissioned officer in the Twenty-Fifth Infantry and as an officer with the Ninety-Second Division in World War I.[25]

In June 1925 Hood sent the official request for a captain to the State Department, which forwarded the request to the U.S. War

Department. The War Department responded in July with a list of eight African Americans who had prior service as both noncommissioned and commissioned officers. It also sent letters to the commanders of the Ninth and Tenth Cavalry and the Twenty-Fourth and Twenty-Fifth Infantry regiments asking for candidates. The War Department ultimately chose Hansen Outley, a noncommissioned officer recommended by the commander of the Tenth Cavalry Regiment.[26]

Born in Houston, Texas, on October 22, 1898, Hansen Outley was an experienced and decorated noncommissioned officer, though he had never served as a commissioned officer. After two years of college, Outley joined the Ninth Cavalry in 1914. He served with the Ninth for two years in the Philippines, then rotated back to the United States with his regiment and joined the cadre of the newly formed black 349th Field Artillery Regiment, organized for service in World War I. Outley distinguished himself in combat in France, earning a Purple Heart and the French Croix de Guerre. After the war, he rejoined the Ninth Cavalry and served until 1925, when he was honorably discharged to accept a commission as a captain in the Liberian Frontier Force.[27]

Upon arrival in February 1926, Outley met resistance from Liberian authorities because of his lack of commissioned service. The Liberian War Department put off issuing his commission until May 1926. During this three-month wait, there was an unfortunate incident in which guards denied Outley admittance to Camp Johnson to watch Frontier Force soldiers parade. Part of the delay had to do with the wording of his contract and questions about pay, though these were eventually resolved. Still, it was clear the government in Monrovia was piqued at Washington for sending another former African American sergeant and not a fully qualified Regular Army officer. Captain Outley faced a great deal more controversy in the years to come, though some was of his own making.[28]

Shortly after Outley's arrival, Major Staten forwarded his annual report on the Frontier Force to the president of Liberia. Staten did not paint a rosy picture. Chief among his complaints were the lack of regular pay, clothing, and subsistence. Officer and enlisted pay had been irregular since at least 1923 and was growing worse year by year. He reported that in 1925 the troops in Monrovia received pay covering nine months of the year and those in the interior eight months; in 1926 it was six months' and five months' salary respectively. Soldiers in the bush had only one set of uniforms, so threadbare that their appearance was a discredit to the force. He also noted he could adequately feed his troops in Monrovia, though most of those in the hinterland suffered shortages of such staples as rice and palm oil, not to mention soap, meat, salt, medicine, and kerosene.[29]

On the positive side, Staten reported the Frontier Force actively performed such duties as "water guards, customs patrols and guards, escorts to Civil Officials, and general police work in the Interior." Those in Monrovia were used "on patrol work in connection with the War and Interior Departments, guards at the Executive Mansion and at other important places in Monrovia." The band that Young had first organized was popular for events in Monrovia and played often at civilian functions. Unfortunately, the force was so busy and scattered that there was scarcely time to properly discipline, drill, and train the soldiers.[30]

Staten observed in his report that the only regions remaining under military control due to indigenous problems were Gbor and Geebor in Grand Bassa. Yet these two areas had been under "semi-military control" for more than eighteen months and were nearly ready for return to civil authority. Despite its shortcomings over the years, the Frontier Force had succeeded in putting down numerous uprisings and placed the Liberian government in nearly undisputed control of the hinterland and indigenous areas.[31]

This very success produced the most serious problem about which Major Staten complained: friction between the civil and military authorities in the hinterland. Staten detailed that the Frontier Force rolls carried twenty civil employees, mainly district commissioners, and these received their salaries monthly while the officers and soldiers often went unpaid. Moreover, the district commissioners were charged with providing rations and supplies to the Frontier Force in the interior, which were often withheld, diverted, or sold by the commissioners. The officers and men of the scattered detachments complained bitterly about their lack of food and about abuse by the district commissioners. The officers and men of the Frontier Force had done the hard fighting to pacify the hinterland, only to turn it over to the misrule of civilians who abused them at every opportunity.[32]

Just a month after submitting his annual report, the Liberian secretary of war sent Staten on an inspection tour of the hinterland that lasted from November 1926 to February 1927. He was expected to visit all the posts of the Liberian Frontier Force before returning to Monrovia. During his absence, Captain Outley should have commanded the Frontier Force detachment in Monrovia. Yet the Liberian War Department promoted Capt. William S. Boyle, the ranking Liberian officer in the Frontier Force, to junior major, to command in Monrovia. The consulate complained to the U.S. State Department that this was "certainly in contravention of the spirit of the existing loan agreement." The move set a bad precedent of subordinating an American officer to a Liberian officer.[33]

In fact, the extended inspection tour may have been a calculated move by the Liberian War Department to get Major Staten out of Monrovia. The Liberian government was disappointed with Staten's job performance and unhappy with what they considered inappropriate political meddling. Secretary of State Edwin Barclay later told an American official that Staten played politics and accused him of having an "ill-concealed friendship for Mr. Faulkner," who ran unsuccessfully for president in 1927 against the True Whig Party incumbent president King. Barclay considered this friendship incongruous with Staten's duties as commander of the Frontier Force and may well have been the reason the secretary of war sent him to the bush for four months.[34]

Major Staten began to have more serious difficulties with the Liberian authorities soon after his return from the trip to the interior. In April 1927, the Liberian authorities arrested Staten for protesting the detention of one of his Frontier Force sergeants. Per newspaper reports, anti-American feeling, always present in Liberia, had worsened during the negotiations with Firestone.[35]

The incident involving Staten's arrest proved serious and illustrated the complicated interplay among the American officers, Americo-Liberian elite, and ethnic Frontier Force soldiers. On April 23, 1927, an Americo-Liberian member of the United Brotherhood of Friendship Lodge dragged a Frontier Force sergeant out of his barracks, carried him to the meeting hall, accused him of possessing a copy of their rituals, and began to "brutally injure him." The sergeant sustained internal injuries, including three fractured ribs. Staten, backed by an armed contingent of his soldiers, demanded the release of his sergeant. When the lodge members refused, Staten summoned the chief of police and withdrew after assurances that his sergeant would not be further harmed. Two days later the chief of police arrested Staten and his soldiers for "infraction of peace" and released them on bond. The authorities charged Staten with assault and summoned him in a civil trespass suit as well.[36]

Staten's arrest portended the end of his tour in Liberia, and he departed three months later in July 1927. Staten, his wife, Lulu, and their eighteen-month-old son, Moody, shipped out on the next steamer to Europe on July 9, 1927. This ended Major Staten's four-year tour with the Liberian Frontier Force. As was the case with all his American predecessors, the Liberian elite resisted his attempts to improve the command and control of the Frontier Forces and carry the mission to completion.[37]

When Major Staten submitted his official letter of resignation on May 9, 1927, Liberian secretary of war James Cooper directed he turn over command of the Frontier Force to Liberian major William S. Boyle, the same Major Boyle who took command of the Frontier Force detachment in Monrovia when Staten was away on his extended inspection tour. Clearly, this was a power play by the Liberian government to seize control of the Liberian Frontier Force and put the remaining American officer, Captain Outley, in a subordinate position to a Liberian major.[38]

Shortly after Staten departed, the U.S. chargé Clarence E. Macy dispatched a "Strictly Confidential" message to the State Department titled "Demoralized Condition of the Liberian Frontier Force." Macy, who served as the acting chief of mission from May to November 1927, painted a grim picture of the Frontier Force and gave little hope for its future. He considered the force "a joke from a military standpoint" and judged that its "usefulness in suppressing a serious riot or rebellion would be less than nil." He enclosed the "Report of Inspection" Staten completed in March 1927. Staten's detailed report of his inspection trip from November 1926 to February 1927 exposed far more intractable problems with the Liberian Frontier Force and its relationship with the civil authorities than did his annual report a year earlier.[39]

According to Staten, for the first six months of 1926, the Liberian War Department paid only 25 percent of the money budgeted for the salaries of the enlisted soldiers, instead diverting that money to other purposes. For instance, Monrovia used Frontier Force funds to pay for cement used in the construction of a public square in Monrovia and for remodeling a house to be used as an administrative building by the War Department. The American consulate had little control over the disbursement of funds after they were turned over to the Liberian government. The consulate recommended that the general receiver circumvent the Liberian War Department and disburse the funds himself to make sure the money went directly to the Frontier Force. This was the same problem reported years earlier by Young.[40]

In another area of concern, Macy noted Staten's recommendation that the Frontier Force be located at strategic points for easier discipline and training. He singled out four principal camps: one in Monrovia and three advantageously placed in the interior for ease of command, control, and training. Per Staten, the system of scattered "details of from two to twelve soldiers on stations without officers" would "destroy every vestige of discipline in them." He suggested totally reorganizing the force into battalions and companies and stationing them at strategic locations. Staten complained that Monrovia granted officer commissions to political favorites with no regard for military experience or general education, resulting in the poor performance of the officer corps and the high dropout rate for cadets at the military academy.[41]

Staten emphasized that concentrating troops from the scattered hinterland outposts would minimize conflict with the civil government. When Staten visited one post in Butulu, he witnessed an Americo-Liberian station master put ten indigenous people on the ground and "give ten lashes each on their naked backs" for minor offenses. The station master explained: "The President said that you must not give them twenty-five but he did not say anything about twenty-four." At another post, Staten found the soldiers complaining that the district commissioner flogged them. A Frontier Force sergeant told Staten: "When we were fighting in the country and dying there were no civil officers to be seen, but now that the country is peaceful and quiet they have come in and assume all of the control and the soldiers are nothing."[42]

Chargé Macy forwarded another report in late July 1927 titled "Disquieting Conditions in Liberian Interior Administration," which reported many of the problems and issues noted by Staten during his inspection trip. Macy remarked that two of the five interior district commissioners were inefficient, unscrupulous, and worthless and continued to serve only because of their political connections with President King. He feared that the oppressed ethnic population would either revolt or be forced into a "concerted pilgrimage over the border into French territory." This would destroy any vestige of good will with the government in Monrovia and deprive Firestone of an adequate supply of indigenous labor. Macy noted the friction between the civil authorities and the Frontier Force and blamed both sides for the problem. He recommended the Frontier Force be allowed to feed its own men and opined that no "civil government in history enjoyed billeting soldiers, or the requisition of food, especially in time of peace."[43]

Macy's final report in August 1927 addressed the issue of "American Military Instructors for the Liberian Frontier Force." He noted that Captain Outley's agreement would expire in four months and was unlikely to be renewed. Macy had recently discussed the matter with Liberian secretary of state Edwin Barclay. Barclay confided that neither Staten nor Outley had lived up to expectations, being former noncommissioned officers and lacking the "technical training and qualities of leadership necessary to lay the broad foundations." Barclay expressed the opinion that "only a man with wide experience and the technical training of a West Point graduate, or its equivalent, would fit the bill." He cited Colonel Young as the "only American officer ever sent out here whose work, from the Liberian viewpoint, deserves commendation."[44]

This is where matters stood when the U.S. consulate in Monrovia got much-needed new leadership. President Calvin Coolidge appointed Republican lawyer and politician William Treyanne Francis as the new U.S. consul general in Liberia. Born on November 28, 1869, Francis had worked as a lawyer for the Northern Pacific Railroad and later served as a member of the Minnesota Republican Central Committee. He and his wife led the successful fight to pass antilynching laws in the Minnesota State Senate in the 1920s. Francis arrived in Monrovia in December 1927, bringing with him to Monrovia outstanding professional credentials and strong political connections.[45]

Consul General Francis sought an audience with Secretary of State Barclay soon after arrival to ascertain Liberian intentions regarding American officers. Francis knew that the Liberian government was disappointed with Outley's performance and had no plans to renew his contract when it expired in December 1927. Francis met with Barclay but received no firm answer on the matter. Francis later learned Secretary of War James W. Cooper filed a complaint about an "impertinent" letter Outley sent him complaining about the poor quality of Liberian candidates to be trained as officers.[46]

In early 1928 the plan for Outley's future employment took an unexpected twist. In January, Outley informed Consul General Francis that Monrovia had extended his contract and that a bill had passed the Liberian legislature which granted a leave of absence, with expenses allowed, to "visit France to take instructions in aviation." Both Francis and the U.S. State Department wondered what flight school in France had to do with the mission in Liberia and questioned the appropriateness of paying this out of government funds. Outley agreed to delay his departure for Europe until the matter was resolved.[47]

In June Francis met informally with President King about the Outley matter. King insisted the Liberian government had not suggested that Outley take aviation training, nor did they commission him on any mission in Europe. King told Francis he had "attempted, in a mild way, to discourage the Captain when he heard he intended to take such instruction by remarking that he, the Captain, had not yet mastered the land and perhaps he had better wait a while before he mastered the air." In the end, Hansen Outley departed Monrovia in June 1928 on "his personal leave of absence for a period of six months on no mission, aviation or otherwise, for the Liberian Government."[48]

Outley returned to Monrovia in October 1928, having visited Paris, London, Hamburg, and Berlin along the way, all at his own expense. He spent most of his time in Hamburg, where he completed a certificate in aviation instruction. In Europe Mrs. Dorothy Moll, a figure well known in Monrovia, defrauded Outley of a good deal of money, promising contacts in Germany that she never delivered. This was just as well, since Outley told her he was on assignment by the Liberian government to "purchase arms and ammunition for the Republic," a mission disavowed by Monrovia and considered by Francis as "shadowy creatures of the idle imaginings of the Captain." Moll later returned to Monrovia and reported to officials that Captain Outley had criticized the Liberian government while in Germany, further alienating him from his superiors.[49]

Francis reported in May 1928 that the Liberian government had imposed overdue reforms on the Liberian Frontier Force, including those recommended by Maj. Moody Staten in 1926 and 1927. Francis wrote that the Frontier Force completed a long-overdue reorganization on May 1, 1928. On that date the Frontier Force discharged all officers and soldiers and only permitted those considered "desirable" to re-enlist within forty-eight hours thereafter. Per Francis, no "man who had been in the service over ten years, or who was in the service during any of the mutinies or 'uprisings' within the Force in times past was permitted to re-enlist." The Firestone Agreement made these service requirements mandatory for future funding.[50]

In addition to these measures, Francis indicated the Liberian War Department had cleaned house among its officers. It mustered out all officers over the retirement age of fifty, as well as eight captains and lieutenants considered unqualified and all the third and fourth lieutenants. The department commissioned two new junior majors to command the two battalions of the Frontier Force in the interior, and retired major Boyle, the troublesome officer who challenged Staten's authority. They left vacant the position of major commanding the Frontier Force, purportedly awaiting nomination by the U.S. government, and named Captain Outley to fill the position of "American Military Instructor." The reorganization capped the total number of officers at thirty-four, including the two American officers, and the total number of enlisted men at 701.[51]

The reorganized Frontier Force concentrated in three locations: one camp in Monrovia and two camps strategically placed in the hinterland. Further, the Liberian War Department promised to provide supplies and food through the Quartermaster Department to the Frontier Force to "be prepared by the Company cook much after the system in vogue in the American Army." The War Department prohibited the earlier practice of soldiers retaining "boys" and "wives" as servants and camp followers. These changes addressed specific recommendations made by Major Staten.[52]

With Outley on leave in Europe for six months and his role minimized upon his return to Monrovia, there was no real way of verifying that these reforms were enacted. American officials ill-advisedly depended on the word of the Liberian government. By the fall of 1928, Captain Outley, consulate officials, and the handful of Americans working with the receivership learned that officials never implemented many of the reforms. On the positive side, the Frontier Force had been cleansed of many of the undesirable officers and soldiers and concentrated in three locations: one battalion in Monrovia as a general headquarters, a second in the northeast near the boundary with Sierra Leone, and a third in the south near the border with the Ivory Coast. Training was concentrated at the two battalion stations as well as in Monrovia.[53]

Francis understood the Monrovia had no intention of relinquishing control of the Frontier Force. During the six months of Outley's absence and after his return, Americo-Liberian major Lemuel L. Smith, one of the junior majors appointed under the recent reorganization, commanded the Liberian Frontier Force and the headquarters battalion stationed at Camp Johnson near Monrovia. As a further indication of the permanence of this arrangement, Major Smith received a considerably higher salary, designated on the table of appropriations for the American major ($4,369), rather than the salary of a junior major ($2,200). The other Americo-Liberian major, Alexander R. Harper, assisted Major Smith in commanding the headquarters. Under the reorganization, the two junior majors should have commanded the two battalions stationed in the hinterland.[54]

Outley identified several other problems with the Frontier Force in November 1928. The Liberian War Department never enforced the regulation prohibiting soldiers from retaining wives and boys at the stations, so the camp followers remained. The department also failed to implement the provision for more regular delivery and distribution of food. Finally, no ammunition was kept in the headquarters battalion in Monrovia due to the mutiny attempted at Camp Johnson in January 1927. The War Department stored the ammunition under its control, and the Frontier Force was never allowed to fire weapons at target practice. This was just as well because, as Outley noted, the Springfield Model 1898 rifles were too old and dilapidated to be useful.[55]

At the end of November 1928, the Liberian War Department ordered Outley on a six-month mission to train and reorganize the two battalions of the Frontier Force in the hinterland. He was first to go to the Second Battalion, headquartered in Belle Yella, about seven days' journey on foot north of Monrovia. His second stop would be with the Third Battalion in Barrabo, inland northwest of Cape Palmas, on the coast 150 miles southeast of Monrovia.[56]

Outley's orders came from the "Office of the Liberian Frontier Force" and were signed by "L.L. Smith, Major, Liberian Frontier Force, Commanding." The order instructed Outley to proceed first to Belle Yella, headquarters of the Second Battalion, commanded by Capt. Moses N. Grant. There he was to "verify the enlistment" of each soldier, identify any found below the standards of the reorganization, and replace any man so identified. He was also to pay each soldier on the rolls and spend the balance of the three months training and drilling the soldiers. He was to repeat the same process in Barrabo with the Third Battalion, commanded by Capt. Isaac Whisnant.[57]

This mission would get Outley, who was considered an incompetent troublemaker by the Liberian president and secretary of war, out of Monrovia for half a year. It put to good use the formal role and single acknowledged skill of Outley as a trainer, something U.S. Army noncommissioned officers did well. The Liberians showed the Americans that they were serious about completing the reforms instituted in May and paying the soldiers of the Frontier Force, even if for show. Lastly, the move solidified command of the Frontier Force by Liberian officers without the meddling presence of an American officer.

While Outley was away from the capital on his training mission, the American consulate in Monrovia suffered a grievous loss. Consul General Francis came down with yellow fever in mid-June, and after suffering a month of agony, died on July 15, 1929. Francis was cared for by two doctors, Rudolf Fuszek and Justice Rice, who worked for Firestone. The consul general's widow, Nellie Francis, arranged for his body to be returned to the United States for burial. His death was a stark reminder of the dangers of disease to Americans assigned to Liberia. Between 1864 and 1930, seven of twenty-one consul generals who served in Liberia died on station in West Africa, and at least one other died of disease three months after his return to the United States.[58]

Chargé Clifton R. Wharton replaced Francis in the interim to run affairs at the consulate. He was the first black Foreign Service officer after passage of the 1924 Rogers Act, which consolidated the State Department's Consular and Diplomatic Services. After passing the test in 1925, he was the only African American to enter the U.S. Foreign Service for the next twenty years. Wharton stayed only briefly in Monrovia before returning to the United States on home leave and a new assignment in the Canary Islands.[59]

As they had done for Young, Davis, and Green, the State Department shuffled Wharton and other black officials between consulates considered appropriate for African Americans. While the army moved the three black officers between assignments in the black regiments, Wilberforce, and Liberia, the State Department shuttled Wharton and his colleagues among posts such as Haiti, Liberia, the Canary Islands, Madagascar, and the Azores. This routine among African Americans in the State Department was known in the diplomatic corps as the "Negro Circuit."[60]

Around the time of Wharton's departure, the State Department finally got around to discussing the nomination of the officers required under the terms of the Firestone Agreement of 1926. The State Department decided to withdraw Outley's nomination, effective February 26, 1930, "for the convenience of the Government" to set the conditions to nominate a new officer. Outley had been nominated under the terms of the old 1912 loan agreement and never confirmed under the Firestone accord.[61]

Chargé Henry Carter, who replaced Wharton, noted in February 1930 that "Outley was at present in Cape Palmas and I do not feel that his continuation out there will serve any useful purpose." Outley had been marginalized and dispatched to a frontier outpost while Americo-Liberian officers commanded and controlled the Frontier Force from Monrovia. Captain Outley, the last officer to serve under the loan agreement of 1912, departed Liberia in October 1930.[62]

Charles Young's death in 1922 ushered in a new era in the relationship between Washington and Monrovia, causing a dramatic change in the mission of the African American officers in Liberia. No Regular Army officer replaced Young, and the remaining African American officers trained and led the Frontier Force under difficult conditions, often at odds with the Liberian government. The dwindling number of American officers serving in Liberia operated under some of the most challenging circumstances since their arrival in 1910.

The support relationship of the United States and Liberia also saw significant change in the third decade of the 1900s. The loan agreement of 1926, arranged by Firestone, replaced the inter-governmental loan agreement of 1912, which had been negotiated by the State Department and supported by the U.S. War Department. This led to a new era of private, capitalist support for the economy of Liberia with a smaller oversight role for the U.S. government. It also led to the elimination of African American officers serving with the Liberian Frontier Force under the terms of the 1912 accord.

It took nearly a decade to negotiate and implement the new private agreement with Firestone. And this meant a long and demanding period for the African American officers still serving in Liberia. A mere three officers bridged the gap between agreements for most of the 1920s, with never more than two serving together in the years after 1922. Compare this to the three Regular Army officers and ten former noncommissioned or reserve officers who served in Liberia between 1910 and 1922. Moody Staten, William Nabors, and Hansen Outley did their best in extremely difficult situations, but were clearly overmatched by the tasks at hand and outmaneuvered by their Liberian superiors.

FIG. 33. Capt. Hansen Outley, shown here in 1925, served in the Liberian Frontier Force from 1926 to 1930. U.S. Army photo.

FIG. 34. Charles D. B. King, seventeenth president of Liberia (1920–1930), with his entourage at the Peace Palace, The Hague, the Netherlands, 1927. Carnegie Foundation Photo Collection, Wikimedia Commons.

FIG. 35. Capt. William Nabors on his way to Liberia with the U.S. Army, 1943. U.S. Army photo.

8

Firestone

Privatization

At all times we should remember that Firestone went into
Liberia at its own financial risk, and it is not the business of
the State Department to pull its financial chestnuts out of
the fire as a friend of the Liberian people.

—FRANKLIN D. ROOSEVELT, 1933

A fter the departure of the last African American officer
assigned to Liberia under the 1912 agreement, the State
Department began to appoint candidates under the Firestone arrangement. The Liberian government continued to object to
the selection of black ex-noncommissioned officers and demanded
qualified Regular Army officers. Yet the pool of black officers in
the U.S. Army was limited, and with the elimination of the army
attaché position in Monrovia, Regular Army officers were not eligible for assignment in Liberia. This forced the State and War departments, as in the previous decade, to look elsewhere.

The United States began the process of appointing American
officers under the 1926 Firestone Agreement shortly before Captain Outley shipped out of Liberia in 1930. The State Department
surveyed a list of retired black officers and found them unsuitable
because of health, age, or long separation from the military. As an
alternative, the State Department proposed white officers with the
proper qualifications, but the Liberians initially refused. In Liberia only those of "Negro descent" could have any role in govern-

ment affairs. Hiring a white contractor for any leadership role in the Frontier Force would be at odds with this convention. Finally, in December 1929, Liberian secretary of state Barclay agreed to accept a white candidate. The Liberian government already enjoyed firm control of the Liberian Frontier Force, so it made this decision only to placate the U.S. government and maintain the flow of money from Firestone.[1]

Even before the Liberian government agreed to accept a white officer, Firestone identified a candidate and moved to fill the vacancy. The State Department nominated George Wilburton Lewis as a major in the Liberian Frontier Force under Article XII of the Firestone Agreement on November 20, 1929. President Herbert Hoover personally approved the selection the following day. This meant the United States selected and approved a white officer a month before Liberia formally consented to take a white applicant.[2]

Major Lewis had lately served as a colonel and as chief of the internal police of Puerto Rico when identified by Firestone as a nominee in 1928. At forty-five, he was a bit older than the ideal age of thirty-five stipulated in the agreement, but the U.S. authorities judged him healthy and well suited by temperament and training for the position. George W. Lewis, per one African American newspaper, was a "well known soldier of fortune, writer of verse, and policeman." He had served as a volunteer soldier in the Philippine War and as a paid military contractor in the Panama Canal Zone, Puerto Rico, Dominican Republic, and Haiti.[3]

Lewis proved ineffective despite his experience because Monrovia gave him no authority. Chargé Claude H. Hall, who served as head of the consulate after the death of Francis and the departure of Wharton in 1929, confirmed this shortly after Lewis arrived. He wrote that "the President of Liberia is of the opinion that Lewis is a mere adviser who is outranked by two Liberian majors and the Secretary of War here gave instructions accordingly. While the Liberian Government will be interested in the views of Lewis, it is believed that he will have little actual authority."[4]

The Liberian government showed no interest in Lewis's ideas, and his time in Monrovia was short. He served out his two-year contract, complained he was given nothing useful to do, and was never engaged by the Liberians as an adviser. Lewis sat in his office and collected his pay, and the only positive episode recorded in his personal life during that time was his marriage to his fiancé, Zoraida, the daughter of the Nicaraguan minister of war, in 1930. He resigned, effective July 1932, the end of his two-year contract, "on grounds that he was not given sufficient authority to accomplish anything." Newspaper accounts indicated that he "fell ill with a vicious fever," so sickness might have had something to do with his departure.[5]

The Liberian election of 1927 and the subsequent League of Nations investigation into allegations of slavery in Liberia contributed to the difficulties experienced by Lewis and the American consulate during this period. Trouble had been brewing on the issue of slavery for several years but came to a head after the Liberian presidential election of 1927, when Thomas J. R. Faulkner, who ran on the People's Party ticket, challenged incumbent president King of the True Whig Party. Faulkner, the former mayor of Monrovia, ran on a radical platform calling for a decrease in presidential powers, movement of the capital to the interior of the country, and improved rights for the indigenous people.[6]

The turmoil began after King won the election by a landslide, receiving twenty-four thousand votes. The problem was, suffrage in Liberia constitutionally limited voting to the roughly fifteen thousand Americo-Liberian registered voters. Thus, King earned the dubious honor of winning one of the most fraudulent election recorded in history. Angered by the results of the election, Faulkner tried to bring down the King administration by accusing it of sanctioning slavery and forcibly recruiting and selling contract laborers for employment on the colonial plantations in West Africa. He implicated both the Frontier Force and Firestone in the charges.[7]

Monrovia denied the allegations and initially refused to cooperate, though it finally acceded under pressure from U.S. and European governments. France and Britain sought to exploit the charges in the renewed hope of absorbing Liberia into their colonial holdings. The Hoover administration suspended relations with Liberia to pressure King into assisting with the investigation into human trafficking. The new League of Nations asserted itself by appointing a commission to be led by Dr. Cuthbert Christy from Great

Britain, Dr. Charles S. Johnson of the United States, and former Liberian president Arthur Barclay.[8]

Charles Johnson, a noted African American sociologist and professor at Fisk University, accepted President Hoover's invitation to serve on the tripartite commission. The commission began its work in Monrovia in April 1930. Johnson worked with ex-British explorer Christy and Barclay to investigate the allegations in the face of Liberian attempts to stall the probe. As if they did not have enough worries with yellow fever, malaria, and blackwater fever, Johnson and Christy expressed fears that the Americo-Liberians attempted to poison them during the inquiry.[9]

The commission members persisted and worked through any hurdles thrown their way. The Liberian government grudgingly gave the commission members relatively free access to the indigenous people of the hinterland, and they collected proof of widespread forced labor practices and the direct involvement of the Liberian government. Many individuals risked retribution by testifying against the regime in Monrovia. Based on the evidence collected, the Christy Commission report of September 8, 1930, revealed that Americo-Liberians had shamefully exploited the illiterate ethnic population of the hinterland for private gain.[10]

According to the findings, the exploitation of the indigenous population took many forms. The first was "pawning," a practice widely employed in Liberia and elsewhere in West Africa. A parent or guardian pawned a child or woman for an indefinite period for repayment of a debt. In some cases, the pawns were held in servitude for as long as forty years. The second and more pernicious practice was involuntary recruiting of indigenous labor to work the Spanish cocoa plantations on the nearby island of Fernando Po and elsewhere in West Africa. Monrovia employed the Liberian Frontier Force to round up ethnic people for this purpose at $45 a head. Liberian officials directly sanctioned and profited from this practice.[11]

President King at first denied the allegations and tried to fight the findings, calling the commission's accusations "malicious propaganda," used by the colonial powers to discredit Liberia. Under pressure from the United States, King finally appointed a Liberian commission to further investigate the results. The commission confirmed the conclusions and directly implicated Vice President Allen B. Yancy and other government officials with direct involvement and personally profiting in human trafficking.[12]

The League of Nations and Liberian commission findings forced Monrovia to act. Parliament began impeachment proceedings, forcing King and Yancy to resign on December 3, 1930, to avoid prosecution under the constitution. Parliament quickly swore in Secretary of State Edwin Barclay as the new head of state. Barclay accepted the findings of the League and requested help in undertaking financial and judicial reforms. Officially, forced labor was banned and the practice of pawning phased out.[13]

The investigation made clear the reason Monrovia so eagerly dispensed with American officers. After the departure of Major Staten in 1927, Liberian authorities gained full direction of the Frontier Force and put Liberian officers in command. Monrovia easily marginalized Captain Outley thereafter and maintained full control until his departure in 1930, the year the Christy Commission conducted its investigation. Major Lewis had no access to the Frontier Force during the period of his service, so the United States essentially lost any objective reporting on the Liberian military after 1927. The absence of American oversight allowed Monrovia to shield its mistreatment of the indigenous people.[14]

Liberia was able to use the Frontier Force in the manner described by the commission because of U.S. military training. By the 1920s, Liberia possessed a qualified cadre of American-coached officers with a great deal of experience leading troops and putting down indigenous rebellions. The Liberian government used these officers and the U.S.-funded Frontier Force to assemble forced labor to be shipped off to Fernando Po. Because the troops of the Frontier Force were mainly from the northern ethnic groups, Monrovia experienced little trouble using them to round up laborers from the Kru and Grebo communities in southeastern Liberia.[15]

American officers in Liberia were not entirely innocent of the practices found objectionable in the Christy report. Captain Newton, Major Young, and Major Anderson employed forced labor to build roads to the interior of Liberia. Newton and Young used laborers supplied by the government in 1913 and 1915, while Anderson resorted to employing captured rebel fighters in 1919. Moreover, during the relief expedition in 1912, Major Young pressed forty Mandingoes into service as porters during his march into the bush to rescue Captain Browne. The American officers were well versed with the laws of war and the rules governing the treatment of prisoners and civilians and their use as forced labor. However, the commission report made no mention of these cases.[16]

The Christy Commission initially accused Firestone of using of forced labor. The Liberian government supplied about 10 percent of the laborers used on the Firestone plantation, and the investigation found that Monrovia conscripted many of these workers by force. However, Firestone quickly responded that they paid their workers in cash, and all remained free to quit at any time. In the end, the commission found that "there was no evidence that the Firestone Plantations Company consciously employs any but voluntary labor on its leased rubber plantations." Firestone escaped reprimand.[17]

Washington lacked steady leadership in Monrovia during much of the forced labor scandal, so the commission findings caught the U.S. government by surprise. After Consul General Francis died in 1929, a new head of mission did not arrive for nearly two years. This dearth in leadership could not have come at a worse time in the history of the diplomatic relations between the United States and Liberia. Moreover, it coincided with the Great Depression, from 1930 to 1933, when President Hoover and his administration had more pressing priorities at home.[18]

President Hoover finally appointed Charles E. Mitchell as consul general to Liberia in September 1930. Mitchell was a member of the West Virginia Republican State Committee and was nominated for the post by the Republican National Committee. Born in Saint Michaels, Maryland, on May 30, 1870, he served as the president of the Mutual Savings and Loan in Charleston, West Virginia. He, like Francis before him, arrived in Monrovia with impeccable business and political credentials.[19]

Mitchell was a veteran of the Spanish-American War and lost a leg in combat. Mitchell used a thumbtack instead of a garter on his wooden leg, and one morning after a party pushed a tack into his good leg by mistake, which he recalled was a "most awakening experience." He took the recommendation of a State Department official and exchanged his wooden leg for one made of aluminum as a defensive measure against Liberian termites before departing the United States.[20]

Mitchell experienced unexpected delays in taking his new post in Monrovia. As a matter of American policy, he could not depart for Liberia until after the resignation of President King in December 1930. In a further postponement, the United States upgraded the consul general post in Monrovia to ambassadorial rank (envoy extraordinary and minister plenipotentiary) in January 1931. Finally, Mitchell shipped out after Senate reconfirmation and arrived in Monrovia in February 1931.[21]

Mitchell never had the opportunity to fully employ his talents in Monrovia to represent the United States effectively. The Hoover administration directed Mitchell not to present his diplomatic credentials until after Liberia took satisfactory steps to end forced labor and slavery in the country. This took several years, and the delay angered the embattled Barclay regime, further complicating the relationship between Monrovia and Washington.[22]

When Ambassador Mitchell journeyed from Liverpool to Monrovia on board the MV *Adda* in February 1931, he traveled with an African American investigative journalist named George S. Schuyler. NAACP president Arthur Spingarn recommended Schuyler to publisher George Putnam to research and write a book about slavery in Liberia. Once in Liberia, Mitchell hosted Schuyler at the consulate and helped him get access to visit the Firestone plantation, the Booker T. Washington School, and the interior of the country.[23]

Despite a bout of malaria, Schuyler completed his research and published a series of articles the summer of 1931 in the *New York Evening Post*, the *Washington Post*, and other newspapers. His articles told stories of kidnapped indigenous people, young boys sold into forced labor, young girls bought by wealthy officials, and community chiefs tortured. His articles and a later book of fiction called *Slaves Today* created a firestorm of protest and controversy in the United States. The fact that the consul general sponsored Schuyler pitted Monrovia against Mitchell.[24]

After the forced labor scandal, President Barclay served out the one year remaining in King's term and was reelected in 1931 on a reform platform. Despite his promises, the United States, Great Britain, and Germany demanded that Monrovia accept an international governing commission to take over Liberia and administer its affairs. In February 1931, under intense pressure from Washington, which continued to deny official recognition of Barclay's government, Liberia formally asked the League of Nations for assistance.[25]

The league convened a Liberian Committee with the United States as one of its participants. The League gave the committee two missions: to work out a program of assistance for Liberia and to restructure the loan agreement with Firestone. However, the league plan proved too expensive for Monrovia to accept. The City Bank of New York had cut off funds from the Firestone loan in 1930 due to the investigation, so Monrovia had accumulated a huge internal debt.[26]

By 1931 the Liberian administration could no longer make payments on the Firestone loan. The country was almost entirely dependent on income from Firestone's sale of rubber, and the price of the commodity suffered a precipitous drop during the worldwide depression ($1.40 per pound in 1925 to $0.16 per pound in 1930). On top of this, the fixed charges associated with the loan to pay service charges and U.S. advisers' salaries reached 50 percent of Liberian government revenues by 1931. After Monrovia failed to convince Firestone and the City Bank of New York to restructure the loan, the Liberian legislature voted in 1932 to suspend payments until it could renegotiate new terms.[27]

Liberia's suspension of payments on the loan prompted Harvey Firestone to ask Washington DC to dispatch a warship to force Monrovia to conform. Democratic president Franklin D. Roosevelt, who was inaugurated on March 4, 1933, showed little sympathy for Firestone. He responded to the State Department in a memorandum saying: "At all times we should remember that Firestone went into Liberia at its own financial risk, and it is not the business of the State Department to pull its financial chestnuts out of the fire as a friend of the Liberian people."[28]

Hoover's secretary of state Henry L. Stimson, a friend of President Roosevelt (who later made Stimson his secretary of war), convinced the new president to send a special U.S. mission to Monrovia. Stimson and Roosevelt told the team to negotiate a practical plan of assistance for adoption by League of Nations. The plan would pave the way for the restoration of diplomatic relations between Washington and Monrovia.[29]

Stimson sent retiring judge advocate general of the U.S. Army, Maj. Gen. Blanton Winship, to lead the mission, assisted by Ellis O. Briggs, the head of the State Department's West European Division, and Alure Gallant, a clerk. Roosevelt designated General Winship "Representative of the President of the United States on Special Mission to Liberia, with the Rank of Ambassador." They stopped en route in London to meet with Lord Robert Cecil, one of the architects of the League of Nations, for guidance on dealing with the government leadership in Monrovia. Cecil warned them that the Liberian secretary of state, "Mr. [Louis A.] Grimes[,] possesses only the most elementary knowledge of the meaning of veracity."[30]

After yellow fever inoculations, only recently developed, the threesome shipped off to Monrovia and arrived in March 1933. Winship wasted no time on diplomacy and threw himself into the task at hand. President Barclay received them on arrival, and they met with Secretary of State Louis A. Grimes several times a week for discussions. In one conference, Grimes replied to an inquiry: "Although I myself am not au courant with the intricacies of that matter, I shall inquire of my locum tenens." Despite Grimes's circumlocutions and misrepresentations, Winship and Briggs hammered out a practical plan of assistance that was "approved in principle" by the Liberian president. Winship took the agreement to Geneva, where it was accepted.[31]

In January 1934 the Liberian legislature accepted the plan, though not without citing constitutional reservations. Knowing that survival depended on the support and recognition of the United States, the Barclay government agreed on an extensive program of administrative reforms. The plan authorized President Barclay to negotiate a modification of the loan agreement with Firestone, and by March 1935 he had worked out a satisfactory agreement. The new arrangement reduced the interest rate of the loan and gave Firestone new tax exemptions, the right to operate radio and air transportation systems in Liberia, and exclusive mineral rights on the land it leased.[32]

Convinced that Monrovia was committed to reforms and preoccupied with the economic effects of the Great Depression, Roosevelt recognized the Barclay government in June 1935 and agreed to send a new envoy to Monrovia. He appointed Lester A. Walton of New York as ambassador on July 22, 1935. Lester Aglar Walton was born in Saint Louis, Missouri, on April 20, 1882, and was a 1927 graduate of Lincoln University. A journalist, entertainer, and civil rights activist, he first visited Liberia in 1933 to write newspaper articles for *The Age* and the *Herald Tribune*. He also covered the Versailles Peace Conference in 1919 and was a knowledgeable foreign correspondent. Walton was active with the National Democratic Committee at a time when most blacks still identified with the Republican Party. He proved a good choice and served in Monrovia until 1946.[33]

All sides claimed victory and saved face in the aftermath of the forced labor scandal. Yet it was Liberia that achieved its main goals of maintaining sovereignty and the flow of loan money by essentially waiting out the Western powers. The Americo-Liberians proved champions of delay and obfuscation, knowing that in most cases the United States and Europe would lose interest and give in to tiny, troublesome Liberia. Secretary of State Stimson once remarked if he had to spend as much time per acre on the British Empire as he did on Liberia, "ten secretaries of state would be needed for Scotland alone, with an additional man for the Channel Islands."[34]

Washington extended recognition to Monrovia despite troubling publicity concerning a new indigenous revolt in Liberia. Following the release of the Christy report, some of the Kru communities in the south revolted, marking the last significant rebellion of an indigenous group in Liberia. This Kru resurgence resulted in part from the slave labor scandal, since the Krus were among the main victims of Monrovia's forced recruitment practices. By 1931 long-held resentment over control by Monrovia, abuse by corrupt officials, and ill-treatment by the Frontier Force led to fighting. The Krus alleged the revolt was triggered by government retribution against Kru chiefs who had the courage to testify before the League of Nations commission.[35]

The Liberian government responded initially to the Kru revolt by dispatching Frontier Force reinforcements led by Col. T. Elwood Davis in 1931. Graham Greene referred to Davis as the "Dictator of Grand Bassa" in his book *Journey without Maps*. Davis served as a special commissioner or representative to the Kru coast, appointed by President Barclay, in addition to being the national director of Boy Scouts. The title "colonel" derived from his former service with the Liberian militia, where he earned a reputation for ruthlessness during previous rebellions on the Kru coast.[36]

Colonel Davis failed to restore order in Sasstown by show of force, and bloodshed resulted. The Sasstown Krus refused Davis's order to disarm, and thirty Frontier Force soldiers and an unknown number of Kru fighters died in the first clash. Subsequent fighting left about ten thousand Kru people homeless as they fled in terror into the jungle, where the Frontier Force could not or would not follow. The Western press wildly exaggerated the death toll among the Krus. A commission led by an American official later estimated that the casualties among the dissident communities totaled 159 killed (81 men, 49 women, and 29 children). Nonetheless, the newspaper and magazine reports were sufficient to incense public opinion in the United States and Europe.[37]

Western governments assumed that Monrovia was retaliating against the Kru chiefs who had stepped forward as witnesses for the League of Nations commission. World opinion shifted in favor of the Krus, and Western nations began once again to voice reservations concerning Monrovia's ability to govern. The League of Nations discussed establishing a mandate and giving Liberia to a neutral country like Poland to administer. France and Britain also made overtures so Liberian sovereignty was once again threatened.[38]

In response to the League proposition, President Barclay sent a delegation under a group of prominent Kru leaders to investigate and mediate the trouble. Barclay acceded to the Kru delegation's demand to recall Davis and replace him with Maj. Moses N. Grant, a Liberian Frontier Force officer acceptable to the Krus who was also a bitter enemy of Davis. This was the same Moses Grant that Charles Young had convinced to attend the officer academy and had mentored during both his tours.[39]

The rebellion collapsed in 1936, largely as a result of the diplomatic skills of President Barclay and delaying tactics Secretary of State Grimes. President Barclay correctly noted "the right of a state to maintain law and order within its jurisdiction is a right of international law." He also reminded the West that history was "full of expeditions directed by the British in Nigeria and India, France in Syria and Morocco, Belgium in the Congo, and these have been commented upon as necessary to preserve the corporate existence of a state." He argued that as a member of the League of Nations, Liberia should have the same right as these European countries. The rebels of Sasstown were forced to cut a deal with Monrovia.[40]

The renegotiation of the agreement between Firestone and Monrovia in 1935 paved the way for the return of an African American officer to the Liberian Frontier Force, though in a different capacity than under previous contracts. In February 1936 Monrovia selected Capt. William D. Nabors as a "senior instructor and military advisor" to the Liberian Frontier Force. Captain Nabors, who had served in Liberia from 1920 to 1923 under Col. Charles Young, returned to Monrovia in April 1936 to begin training the Frontier Force.[41]

Captain Nabors acquired additional military skills between his departure from Liberia in 1923 and his return thirteen years later. After recovering from chronic malaria and other health problems brought on by three years of service in Liberia, Nabors became a U.S. Civil Service employee, a member of the municipal planning board of Orange, New Jersey, and beginning in 1931, helped organize the New Jersey State Colored Militia. He served from 1931 to 1936 as a trainer and commander of A Company, First Separate Battalion, New Jersey National Guard. These supplementary accomplishments and his service as an officer made him acceptable to the Liberian government.[42]

A Liberian major continued to command the Liberian Frontier Force, contrary to the terms of the Firestone Agreement of 1926. While Captain Nabors helped train the Frontier Force at Camp Johnson in Monrovia and at two battalion headquarters in the east and west of the country, Liberian majors and captains commanded the force, a significant victory for Monrovia.

Nabors served as the senior instructor and military adviser to the Liberian Frontier Force for six years. After the invasion of Poland in September 1939, Liberia feared a German coup in Monrovia. As a result, the U.S. embassy in Monrovia turned over modern arms, machine guns, and ammunition to Captain Nabors with which to arm and train the Liberian Frontier Force. Captain Nabors continued to train and modernize the Frontier Force until 1942, when the U.S. entry into World War II called him back to National Guard service in New Jersey.[43]

After 1930, the State Department began to appoint officers under the Firestone arrangement. The Liberian government continued to object to the selection of black former noncommissioned officers, demanding qualified Regular Army officers who were graduates of West Point. With no suitable black officers available, a short-lived trial employing an experienced white officer failed. Finally, the United States and Liberia identified a mutually acceptable African American candidate to serve with the Liberian Frontier Force but under different terms than earlier years. The Liberian government maintained firm control over the Liberian Frontier Force and never relinquished command after 1927.

The most consequential event for Monrovia during this era was the League of Nations investigation into the practice of slavery and forced labor in Liberia. The Christy Commission found the Americo-Liberians guilty of exploiting the local inhabitants of the hinterland through the practice of pawning, slavery, and employing the Frontier Force to round up forced labor. Monrovia condoned the practice, and some government officials, including Liberian Vice President Yancy, directly profited. This investigation led to the fall of the administration of President King and his replacement with Edwin Barclay. It did not, however, lead to any quick or meaningful improvements in the Americo-Liberian treatment of the indigenous population.

In the midst of the League of Nations investigation, the last great indigenous revolt of the twentieth century in Liberia erupted on the Kru coast. The Kru communities around Sasstown rebelled in 1931 as a result of the slave labor scandal and years of mistreatment by the government in Monrovia. The United States and European countries sympathized with the Krus, yet were too preoccupied with the Great Depression during the period to focus any effort on the issue. The Liberian Frontier Force, under the leadership of Liberian officers, successfully quashed the revolt by 1936, bolstering Liberian control over the force.

The last American officer to serve with the Liberian Frontier Force, Captain Nabors, arrived in the wake of the Kru revolt in 1936 and stayed until 1942. However, Nabors served strictly as a trainer, subordinate to Liberian officers during his entire period of service. The regime in Monrovia maintained firm command and control of the Frontier Force in the troubled decade leading to World War II.

FIG. 36. A visit to the Firestone Tire and Rubber Company in 1943.
Left to right: Liberian Frontier Force Capt. Alford Russ, Brig. Gen. Benjamin
O. Davis Sr., Liberian consul general Walter F. Walker, John W. Thomas,
Liberian president Edwin Barclay, Harvey S. Firestone Jr., President-Elect
W. V. S. Tubman, Frederick Hibbard (State Department), B. H. Larabee.
U.S. Army Heritage and Education Center.

FIG. 37. Centennial celebration in Monrovia, 1947. *Left to right:* Col. Benjamin O. Davis Jr., Brig. Gen. Benjamin O. Davis Sr., and President W. V. S. Tubman. U.S. Army Heritage and Education Center.

FIG. 38. The Liberian Frontier Force marches in Monrovia during the Centennial Celebration, 1947. Notice the soldiers wear the same red kepi hats and march barefoot as they did when the force was formed in 1908. U.S. Army Heritage and Education Center.

9

Aftermath

Starting Over

Why are some countries able, despite their very real and
serious problems, to press ahead along the road to reconciliation,
recovery, and redevelopment while others cannot?

—ELLEN JOHNSON SIRLEAF, 2009

American involvement with Liberia or its military did not
end after the withdrawal of the last African American officers assigned to the Liberian Frontier Force under the 1912
and 1926 agreements. Liberia joined the United States and the Allies
in the fight against Germany during World War II as it had during
World War I. Liberia's strategic location on the West African coast
made it an essential ally, so soon after Pearl Harbor American military forces began arriving in Monrovia.

The American presence in Liberia during World War II was a
great deal larger than during the previous war. The U.S. Army Air
Forces took over Roberts Field, an airport established by Firestone, and quickly transformed it into one the largest and most significant in a string of transatlantic bases. Pan-American Airways
also maintained a hub in Liberia beginning in 1942 to support both
commercial and contract military traffic. More than one thousand
African American troops served in Liberia as part of the Lend-
Lease Agreement of 1942.[1]

Reflecting the importance of Liberia, President Franklin D. Roosevelt stopped at Roberts Field to refuel on his return from the

Casablanca Conference in 1943 and met with Liberian president Edwin Barclay, the same man that Col. Charles Young had known as secretary of state in 1920. Yet Barclay, who had served as the head of state since 1930, was about to pass from the political scene. The country elected William V. S. Tubman as his successor in May 1943, and he was inaugurated on January 3, 1944. Both Tubman and Barclay traveled to Washington DC in June 1944 as guests of President Roosevelt, the first African heads of state to be so honored.[2]

The United States inked several military agreements with Liberia during the war. Two defense agreements signed in 1942 and 1943 provided for American military occupation of the country, defense of Liberia in case of attack, and withdrawal of the force at the end of World War II. Washington and Monrovia also signed an agreement on the construction of a port in Monrovia in December 1943. The port agreement stipulated that the United States could use any military, naval, and air facilities in Liberia for the "protection of the strategic interests of the United States in the South Atlantic." These agreements essentially set the conditions for the United States military to stay in Liberia for many years after the war.[3]

At least one American veteran of the earlier Liberian Frontier Force training mission served in Liberia during World War II. Maj. William D. Nabors, U.S. Army, who had served with the Liberian Frontier Force from 1920 to 1923 and again from 1936 to 1942, returned in April 1943 with an all-black New Jersey National Guard engineer unit to help build the infrastructure at the newly established American air base in Monrovia. He served there through the end of the year as a liaison officer and psychological expert on the staff of the American task force in Liberia.[4]

Outside Roberts Field where Nabors worked, a migrant town of temporary huts sprang up, populated by indigenous Liberians who hoped to find employment in the large construction project. Eager to find jobs as temporary workers, they squatted near the homes and barracks of the U.S. contractors and soldiers who supervised the projects. Every night, Americans cooked meals inside their compounds and the smell of the food drifted to the rude huts of the Liberians who were waiting for work. The town came to be known to the natives as Smell No Taste and still bears that name. The name was a good metaphor for the relationship between the United States and Liberia, where a great deal of money was spent on development but little trickled down to the indigenous inhabitants.[5]

Even though Liberia allied itself closely with the United States during World War II, it delayed the decision to declare war on Germany until late in the conflict, just as in World War I. It did so for the same reason: German merchants controlled much of the Liberian economy, and Germany was Liberia's largest trading partner. Cutting ties with Germany had crippled the economy of Liberia during World War I. Although Monrovia worried the same collapse would occur in World War II, it finally declared war in January 1944, followed by a lend-lease agreement with the United States in October 1944. After declaring war, Liberia signed the Declaration by the United Nations in April 1944.[6]

Monrovia was pleased to experience growth and expansion in private economic investment in Liberia during World War II, in contrast to the previous war. Part of the reason for this development was Firestone operations, begun in 1926 and expanded in the intervening years. Rubber exports from Liberia provided one of the few sources of natural rubber for the United States and the Allies during the global conflict. Thus, Liberia benefited economically from the demand for rubber driven by war, with exports from 1940 to 1946 jumping from $2.75 million to nearly $13 million. The economy continued to improve and allowed Monrovia to pay off a great deal of its accumulated debt. Aside from Firestone, other private investment continued after the war with the 1946 concession granted to an American investment group to develop iron ore deposits in the Bomi Hill area.[7]

The United States withdrew the bulk of its armed forces from Liberia after World War II but kept a military presence in Monrovia. The United States also continued construction of the port facilities, which were not yet complete at the end of the war. Port construction by the American firm Raymond Concrete Pile Company of New York cost about $15 million, which was repaid from future port revenues. This gave Liberia an ocean-going port for the first time in its history.[8]

Liberia continued its close military and economic alignment with the United States after World War II. President Tubman, a tough, reform-minded career politician, ushered his country into an era when the spotlight turned increasingly toward Africa. As the senior leader in Africa, he positioned Liberia, a founding member of the United Nations, as a champion of African independence. While maintaining close economic and military ties to the United States, Tubman built connections to leaders in Africa and the Third World and expanded links with Europe.[9]

Two years after the war, President Tubman and Liberia celebrated one hundred years of independence in 1947. Brig. Gen. Benjamin O. Davis Sr., the first African American to reach that rank, attended the ceremony as the official representative and ambassador of U.S. president Harry S. Truman. General Davis sailed to Liberia on board the aircraft carrier USS *Palau*, flagship of a small task force sent for the centennial, departing the United States in July 1947. The heavy U.S. Navy presence was appropriate in view of the large role American fighting ships played in establishing Liberia and defending the Americo-Liberians against the indigenous locals.[10]

General Davis, who had not set foot in Liberia since he completed his military attaché tour in 1911, found the changes he observed in the country remarkable. He spent a week traveling in Liberia as the special representative of the United States with his son Col. Benjamin O. Davis Jr., who won fame commanding the black 332nd Fighter Group in Italy during World War II. The elder Davis was not totally convinced of Liberia's progress, however, and remarked, "While I enjoyed my visit, I would not care to reside there for any great length of time." Davis did not specify why, though Tubman criticized the general's speech on Centennial Day as "boasting, haughty, and in bad taste."[11]

The centennial celebration in 1947 showcased Liberia's rising prestige in Africa as well as its economic prosperity. Economic growth continued after World War II with rising revenues from rubber, iron, and timber. President Tubman took advantage of this growth and prosperity to widen his power base beyond the ruling True Whig Party. He hailed from of the coastal town of Harper in the far southeast of Liberia, the first president born outside of Monrovia. He expanded his base by enfranchising women and members of the indigenous population in 1946, while simultaneously consolidating his hold on power with the creation of enormous patronage and extensive security networks. With his security services, Tubman ruthlessly suppressed opposition parties formed by both the indigenous people and Americo-Liberian dissidents.[12]

The core of Tubman's program was his "Open Door" policy, intended to exploit Liberia's large, undeveloped hinterland. He did this through joint ventures between the government and mainly American private investors. Though this policy led to building roads and expanding development for some rural residents, it also made it easier for the government to collect taxes, recruit laborers, and draft soldiers in the interior. Moreover, it led to one of the largest land grabs in African history, where select members of the Americo-Liberian elite acquired vast tracts of the hinterland that had been previously controlled by the indigenous people.[13]

Tubman carefully cultivated ties with the United States and became a close Cold War ally. This relationship deepened as the Cold War split the world into two camps. Washington DC set up a permanent military training mission in Liberia and sent Liberian officers to the United States for professional training in the postwar era. The Liberian Frontier Force, reorganized as the Liberian National Guard Brigade in 1956 and later known as the Armed Forces of Liberia, grew in size and capability thanks to U.S. support. In 1959 Liberia signed a mutual defense pact with the United States, culminating a military assistance relationship that had begun with Lt. Benjamin O. Davis in 1910.[14]

As U.S. aid increased steadily from 1946 to 1961, Liberia received a total of $41 million in assistance, the fourth largest in sub-Saharan Africa. Between 1962 and 1980, U.S. economic and military aid to Liberia swelled to an aggregate of $278 million, the largest per capita level of aid to any country in Africa. As compensation for this aid, Liberia allowed the United States to build sophisticated communications facilities that handled diplomatic and intelligence traffic to and from Africa, monitored radio broadcasts in the region, and relayed the U.S.-funded international news program "Voice of America" throughout the continent. These facilities served a role similar to that played by cable relay and wireless stations in Monrovia earlier in the century when Davis, Young, and Green served there.[15]

All this development and aid came at a price. Through his policies, Tubman managed to alienate members of his own Americo-Liberian elite as well as the indigenous population. Moreover, Tubman's programs continued after his death in 1971 when replaced by William R. Tolbert Jr., his handpicked heir. U.S. support continued despite Monrovia's repressive policies against its people. Liberia's importance as a U.S. ally was highlighted when Jimmy Carter became the first American president to make a formal head of state visit in 1978.[16]

Carter was still president when a bloody 1980 coup led by M.Sgt. Samuel Doe toppled the Tolbert regime. Doe's Krahn people belonged to the same ethnolinguistic group as the Krus and Greboes, whose rebellions the American officers and Liberian Frontier Force put down repeatedly earlier in the century. Doe and his fellow coup members killed the twentieth and last True Whig president of Liberia, William Tolbert, on April 12, 1980, along with twenty-six of his inner circle. The coup leaders tried Tolbert's thirteen cabinet members by court-martial and executed them on a public beach in Monrovia ten days later, thus ending the uninterrupted 133-year reign of Americo-Liberians in Liberia.[17]

The coup caught the Carter administration off-guard, so it reacted cautiously at first. Yet after a policy review, President Carter approved an aid package the summer of 1980 and opened a dialog with Doe and his People's Redemption Council (PRC). As part of this package, the U.S. Army deployed a Special Forces mobile training team to Liberia for six months in 1980 to train a commando company. No VIPs or government officials attended the graduation of this unit for fear of a coup. The members of the company were quickly scattered in small detachments throughout the hinterland to eliminate any threat of trouble from these trained soldiers. The unit was seen as too well trained and a potential threat to the government, much like the Frontier Force earlier in the century.[18]

Support for Liberia increased after President Ronald Reagan took office in early 1981, with aid levels rising from about $20 million a year in 1979 to an annual level of about $80 million between 1981 and 1985. The United States expanded cooperation with the Liberian military and Monrovia sent officers to American senior staff colleges. The U.S. military accepted Liberian cadets at West Point beginning in 1986, with the first graduating in 1990. Col. Charles Young would have marveled at seeing a black Liberian receiving his diploma from the academy 101 years after his own graduation.[19]

The Reagan administration believed that Samuel Doe and the military regime could be coaxed back into the barracks and Liberia set on the path toward democracy. The United States also needed Liberia to help fight the Cold War against the Soviet Union and its African proxies. Doe responded positively to American support by closing the Libyan mission in Monrovia and reducing the size of the Soviet embassy staff. He also had several members of the PRC who had been identified as pro-Libyan tried and summarily executed for plotting a coup. As part of the expanding relationship with the United States, Doe agreed to modify the mutual defense pact to allow the new U.S. Rapid Deployment Force use of its bases and ports on twenty-four-hour notice.[20]

In 1985 President Reagan and the State Department convinced Samuel Doe to hold elections, make constitutional reforms, reverse the ban on political parties, and release political prisoners. Even after an openly fraudulent election that year which Doe probably lost, the United States continued to support his regime. With this election, President Doe became the first elected indigenous head of state in Liberia's history.[21]

Yet President Doe had little time to rest on his laurels and soon faced challenges to his rule. In November 1985 Thomas Quiwonkpa, a member of the Gio ethnic group and former comrade of Doe's from the 1980 coup, launched a countercoup. Doe's Krahn troops brutally suppressed the rebellion and went on a rampage in Nimba County, executing people from the same Gio and Mano communities that Young and Browne had defeated in 1912.[22]

Doe faced a challenge again in December 1989 when insurgents from the National Patriotic Front of Liberia (NPFL) began infiltrating quietly into Liberia from the Ivory Coast. Charles Taylor, an Americo-Liberian and former official of Doe's government, led this new insurgency. Doe's Krahn-dominated army responded to the uprising ruthlessly, burning villages and murdering Gio and

Mano civilians in Nimba County, fueling the insurgency. Washington sent U.S. Army advisers to help restore discipline and halt human rights abuses, but later withdrew them under the contention that their presence signaled support for Doe.[23]

Charles Taylor defeated Doe by 1990 with the backing of Burkina Faso and the Ivory Coast, triggering the First Liberian Civil War. Rebel forces captured Samuel Doe in September 1990. Faction leader Gen. Prince Y. Johnson had him executed but not before cutting off Doe's ear and eating it, washing it down with an American beer. As the situation on the ground worsened and the country descended into one of Africa's most brutal civil wars, the United States limited its military role to evacuating American and third-country nationals and protecting the U.S. embassy.[24]

Nigeria and other West African countries created the Economic Community of West African States Monitoring Group in 1990 to intervene and restore peace during the First Liberian Civil War. Nigeria and the monitoring group consented in 1992 to the founding of the Black Berets, a Liberian paramilitary group formed to control disorder in Monrovia. A former officer of the AFL named Brownie Samukai commanded the Black Berets, assisted by the two Liberian graduates of the U.S. Military Academy at West Point: James Madison Tukpah, who graduated in 1990, and Fombah Teh Sirleaf, who graduated in 1992. However, a West African peacekeeping force remained in the country to maintain order until African states negotiated peace in 1995, then held elections.[25]

After a sham election brought Charles Taylor to the presidency in 1997, he began to systematically run down both the country and what was left of the largely Krahn-dominated Armed Forces of Liberia (AFL). The AFL survived as just another faction fighting in the civil war until it was completely demobilized after the end of the Second Liberian Civil War. The civil war finally ended in July 2003 when Taylor, under heavy domestic and international pressure, resigned in exchange for exile in Nigeria. He was later extradited to The Hague, Netherlands, tried for crimes against humanity, found guilty, and sentenced to fifty years in prison.[26]

The election of President Ellen Johnson Sirleaf in 2005 opened a new chapter for Liberia. Sirleaf, born in 1938, has a family tree that reflects the complexities of Liberian history. Her grandfather was a Gola chief who sent his son to Monrovia to become the ward of an Americo-Liberian family, where he received an education and took the name Carney Johnson. Johnson read law, became a successful lawyer, and was the first Liberian from an indigenous group to sit in the country's national legislature. Sirleaf's mother, Martha Dunbar Johnson, was the daughter of a Kru woman and a German trader from Greenville in Sinoe County. After her father was expelled during World War I, Martha was sent as a ward and later adopted by the same prominent Americo-Liberian family in Monrovia, where she eventually married Carney Johnson.[27]

Sirleaf earned a degree in accounting at the Madison Business College in Madison, Wisconsin, an economics degree from the University of Colorado in Boulder, and a master's in public administration from Harvard. She served as assistant minister of finance in the Tolbert administration and went into exile in Kenya after the Doe coup in 1980. After returning to Liberia in 1985 to run for the Senate, Sirleaf spoke out against the Doe regime and received a sentence of ten years in prison. She served part of her sentence before she was released and moved to Washington DC to work in international banking.[28]

After returning to Liberia from exile in 2003, Sirleaf ran for president in 2005 against former soccer star George Weah, a member of the Kru ethnic group. Few believed she would win an election in an African country that traditionally insisted on male leadership. She was thought too closely associated with Americo-Liberians, too light-skinned, and too well educated to appeal to the majority of the population. Moreover, she was sixty-seven and thought by many too old to win balloting in a country so painfully dominated by young fighters and child soldiers from the civil war.[29]

Ellen Johnson Sirleaf ran for president as leader of the Unity Party, campaigning on national renewal, fundamental rights, economic prosperity, and an end to corruption and civil war. Weah and Sirleaf received the most votes of the top five candidates in the initial balloting, but neither won a clear majority, so the vote went to a runoff. In what Western observers declared was the freest and fairest election in Liberian history, Sirleaf won 60 percent of the vote in the second polling. The National Election Commission declared her the winner on November 23, 2005, and she was inaugurated the twenty-third president of Liberia on January 16, 2006.[30]

Three members of President Sirleaf's cabinet had served in the Armed Forces of Liberia or in the short-lived Black Berets during the civil war. The two former Liberian graduates of the U.S. Military Academy at West Point held key posts. James Madison Tukpah, class of 1990, served initially as national security advisor. The second, Fombah Teh Sirleaf, class of 1992, who was also the president's stepson, became the director of Liberian National Security. And finally, Sirleaf appointed Brownie Samukai as defense minister to supervise the rebuilding of Liberia's military forces.[31]

In 2004, the year before the election, the United Nations began comprehensive security sector reform in Liberia. The UN formed a new military force with a striking resemblance to the one formed with American help a century earlier. The effort aimed to completely draw down the former Armed Forces of Liberia and then vet, organize, and train a new force of approximately two thousand officers, noncommissioned officers, and soldiers. For the UN, the challenge of demobilizing an army in a post–civil war country and building another force from the ground up was unprecedented.[32]

The United States agreed to take the lead in rebuilding the Armed Forces of Liberia. The U.S. State Department contracted with DynCorp International and Pacific Architects and Engineers to undertake this challenging mission. The task was really twofold: dissolve the old army and recruit and train a new force. Both had their unique risks and challenges and proved far more comprehensive than the U.S. effort in the early 1900s. The United States pledged $210 million to the task of creating a new Liberian military, a far larger financial and political commitment than that begun in 1912 with the Liberian Frontier Force.[33]

The decommissioning of the AFL began in May 2005 and immediately encountered problems. The first phase of demobilizing 9,400 irregulars went smoothly with each man getting his severance pay. The second phase, involving the discharge of 4,273 regular members of the AFL, ran into difficulties and was only partially complete by the end of the year. A standoff occurred in January 2006 when former soldiers refused to vacate the barracks to protest the terms of their separation. Later, eight hundred decommissioned soldiers stormed the ministry of defense demanding more money, reminiscent of Frontier Force mutinies the previous century. Nevertheless, authorities completed this painful decommissioning process by the end of January 2006 so work could proceed on the new force.[34]

The United Nations Mission in Liberia (UNMIL) began accepting applications for the new Armed Forces of Liberia in early 2006. UNMIL required all recruits to be high school graduates and to pass literacy, physical fitness, and medical tests. Additionally, all had to agree to a thorough screening to make sure they were not guilty of past human rights violations. UNMIL teams of one international and one Liberian investigator traveled to each recruit's home village to verify data and get character references. With this done, the first class of 110 recruits graduated from three months of basic training in November 2006.[35]

UNMIL formed a Twenty-Third Infantry Brigade consisting of two infantry battalions, a headquarters company, an engineer company, a military police company, a training base, and a band, similar to the organization outlined by Maj. Moody Staten in 1927. Planning called for a force of 2,000, comprising 146 officers and 1,854 enlisted personnel. DynCorp handled the recruitment and basic training of the new army personnel while Pacific Architects and Engineers provided advanced individual training and supervised the construction and renovation of facilities that had been ravaged by the civil war. DynCorp and Pacific Architects and Engineers completed their work of training and construction and departed Liberia in 2009.[36]

While the basic and advanced individual training of enlisted soldiers and junior officers was straightforward, establishing senior command and staff positions in the new Armed Forces of Liberia proved more difficult. The country demobilized all the senior officers of the former AFL, so Nigeria, a West African regional power, stepped in to help with a loan of officers and training. UNMIL appointed a senior Nigerian officer to command the force temporarily and sent Nigerian officers to Liberia to help train the new force. In mid-2008, five vetted and reinstated AFL officers completed the Nigerian Armed Forces Command and Staff College and returned to Liberia to serve with the new brigade.[37]

On January 1, 2010, the United Nations handed over operational control of the Armed Forces of Liberia to President Sirleaf. To supplement earlier training, the U.S. Africa Command deployed sixty-one training personnel to Liberia to continue to assist and mentor the new force. The Armed Forces of Liberia passed its first test when it successfully deployed to the Ivory Coast border in June 2012 after armed militants killed seven UN peacekeepers and eight civilians there. And a company of the brigade sent to Mali to take part in an Economic Community of West African States mission in 2013 performed well.[38]

The temporary commander-in-chief of the Liberian Armed Forces, Nigerian major general S. A. Abdurrahman, turned over command to Liberian brigadier general Daniel D. Ziankahn on February 12, 2014, the fifty-seventh anniversary of the creation of the Armed Forces of Liberia. Col. Prince C. Johnson III assumed command of the Twenty-Third Infantry Brigade on the same day. Both Ziankahn and Johnson had graduated from the U.S. Army Command and General Staff College. This completed the transition of the Liberian Armed Forces and transferred command to Liberian officers once again.[39]

Liberia joined the United States and the Allies in the fight against Germany during World War II as it had during World War I, though this time Liberia came out of the effort economically stronger. It also signed several defense agreements during the war that set the conditions for the U.S. military to build bases and stay in Liberia many years after the war. Washington continued close economic, political, and military ties after World War II during the Cold War. Liberian presidents Tolbert and Tubman managed the U.S. relationship adroitly, winning economic and military aid despite increasingly repressive policies aimed at both Americo-Liberian opposition parties and indigenous resistance movements.

A bloody coup led by M.Sgt. Samuel Doe ended 133 years of Americo-Liberian domination in 1980. Yet the ethnic Krahn leaders of the rebellion were ill-equipped to deal with the massive task of rebuilding a ruined economy and achieving reconciliation among a deeply divided population. Charles Taylor, an Americo-Liberian, deposed Doe in turn in 1990. Even though the Liberian government was guilty of clear human rights abuses, the United States continued to support both Doe and Taylor as Cold War partners. After the Cold War ended, Liberia descended into one of Africa's bloodiest civil wars, which lasted from 1989 to 2003.

The election of President Ellen Johnson Sirleaf in 2005 ushered in a new era for Liberia. Hard on the heels of her inauguration in January 2006, candidates submitted the first applications for membership in the newly formed Armed Forces of Liberia. After careful vetting, organizing, and training, the fresh force of approximately two thousand officers, noncommissioned officers, and soldiers of the newly formed Twenty-Third Brigade stood ready for its first assignment. By the time the United Nations handed operational control of the force to Liberia in 2010, the organization of this new force was strikingly similar to the one Lt. Benjamin O. Davis had proposed and Maj. Charles Young had begun building a century earlier.

10

Conclusion

Accomplishments

> After a trek of more than three hundred miles through dense
> deserted forest, after the little villages and the communal ember,
> the great silver anklets, the masked devil between the huts,
> it was less easy to appreciate this civilization of the coast.
>
> —GRAHAM GREENE, *Journey without Maps*, 1936

Between 1910 and 1942, the United States dispatched African American officers to the West African country of Liberia to reorganize, train, and lead its constabulary forces. American military assistance, accompanied by economic support, helped the Americo-Liberian regime in Monrovia escape territorial partition by colonial Europe, defeat a series of indigenous rebellions, and eventually harness the economic potential of its resource-rich interior. In the face of great difficulties, American officers formed a Frontier Force led by Americo-Liberian officers, guaranteeing an independent minority regime in Liberia.

Yet American support perpetuated a system in which the Liberian elite, composed mainly of the descendants of emancipated American slaves, subjugated and exploited the indigenous population. Never exceeding 5 percent of the populace, 15,000 Americo-Liberians misgoverned nearly 750,000 West African ethnic inhabitants. Whenever a powerful group such as the Krus or Greboes resisted Americo-Liberian control, a U.S. Navy ship sailed in and taught them hard lessons by guns and steel. Every time the United States intervened, it propped up the minority regime and eliminated any real incentive to bring the indigenous people into the existing social order. Monrovia's failure to realize the potential of the majority population stunted the economic growth of the nation and made Liberia dependent on loans from Europe and the United States.

African American officers only partially succeeded in reorganizing the Frontier Force because of Americo-Liberian intransigence and lack of resources. The xenophobic regime in Monrovia distrusted all outsiders, especially whites but also African Americans, and resisted pressure to change its oppressive policies regarding the indigenous people. Americo-Liberians opposed all attempts to eliminate the endemic graft and patronage of the one-party system ruling Liberia. Moreover, the cash-poor Liberian government diverted American loan money to other projects it considered more important than maintaining the Frontier Force. And lastly, Monrovia was only interested in training a force that was sufficient to control the hinterland and maintain the borders yet not so effective as to be a threat to the regime.

The program undertaken in Liberia by the United States was military assistance on a shoestring budget. Although the plan began in 1910 with good intentions, it suffered from delays, false starts, and inadequate funding and never provided sufficient qualified African American officers to produce decisive results. World War I nearly destroyed the fragile economy of Liberia and set back early gains in the military aid program. Certainly, the war diverted the attention and resources of Paris, London, and Berlin at a time when Liberia was vulnerable to territorial partition. Yet it also distracted Washington when it might have lent more economic, political, and military support to the regime in Monrovia.

Seventeen African American officers served in Liberia in the three decades after 1910 under the terms of U.S. military support agreements. During this period, the United States appointed three men, Benjamin Davis, John Green, and Charles Young, the only three black Regular Army officers serving at the time, as military attachés to the American consulate in Monrovia. These officers reported to the War Department in Washington but worked under the authority of the resident U.S. consul general as military advisers on the mission in Liberia. The other fourteen were typically former African American noncommissioned officers or officers with temporary commissions who had served with black volunteer regiments. They worked under contract with the government in Monrovia, received their commissions from the president of Liberia, and served as officers in the Liberian Frontier Force.

Lt. Benjamin Davis, Tenth U.S. Cavalry, was the first American military attaché to Liberia; he served in Monrovia from 1910 to 1911, analyzing the mission and creating the basic plan to reorganize the Frontier Force. He reported many of the obstacles the American training endeavor would encounter in Liberia: Americo-Liberian resistance to change, Monrovia's mistreatment of the indigenous population, and a Liberian Frontier Force that was a menace to the people it was intended to protect. He witnessed such abuse firsthand when Frontier Force soldiers mutinied and held the Liberian secretary of war hostage for payment of back wages.

Maj. Charles Young, Ninth U.S. Cavalry, launched the military assistance mission with his first group of American officers from 1912 to 1915 under the plan outlined by Davis. Young selected a talented team of three officers to accompany him to Liberia, though the group proved too small to make a decisive impact. Still, due to his experience and prestige in the U.S. Army, as well as connections he developed with American and Liberian officials in Monrovia, Young accomplished a great deal more than anyone who followed. His superior leadership and single-minded commitment conferred an auspicious start.

Lt. John Green, Twenty-Fifth U.S. Infantry, who served as military attaché in Liberia from 1916 to 1920, achieved positive results with the scarcest resources and manpower. Green continued the work begun by Young, advising and training the Liberian Frontier Force. However, due to his arrival six months after Young's departure and leadership turmoil among the American officers commanding the force, much of the progress of previous years was lost. Because of World War I and the near collapse of the Liberian economy, Green never regained the momentum of previous years.

During his second tour in Liberia, Col. Charles Young recovered some of the progress of earlier years, expanding the capabilities of the Frontier Force with his new team of American officers. However, during an intelligence mission to Nigeria in 1922, Young died from lingering illnesses, leaving his work in Liberia incomplete. Yet even before Young's death, the U.S. War Department had made the decision not to replace him as military attaché, as U.S. dollar diplomacy in Liberia began to change.

It did not take long for Young's achievements to unravel, especially with the U.S. government shifting to postwar isolationism and minimizing government loans in favor of private business investments. Most of Young's team of officers grew disenchanted with the mission and departed shortly after his death in 1922, leaving just one officer to deal with a Liberian government intent on wresting control of the Frontier Force from American command.

After the Liberian government forced the last two assigned American officers to ship out by 1930, conditions were set for a major transition in American military and economic support. By this time Washington was tired of supporting the minority regime in Monrovia with direct assistance, and in any case the Great Depression dominated the government's attention. Moreover, the Liberian government was dissatisfied with the U.S. selection of black former noncommissioned officers and volunteer officers to command the Frontier Force, considering them unsuitable officer material. Monrovia wanted West Point–trained African American officers like Young, but none were available at the time.

Enter the American Firestone Corporation, prepared to pay off Liberia's debts and develop the economy of Liberia to the mutual advantage of Firestone and ruling elites in Monrovia.

Firestone's plan promised to shift the U.S. government's burden of responsibility for support of Liberia. After three tough years of negotiations among Firestone, Monrovia, and Washington, the Liberian legislature ratified an agreement in 1927. This led to an era of private, capitalist support for Monrovia's regime, as well as a smaller role for the U.S. government.

Liberia possessed an officer corps showing signs of military competence when Firestone stepped in, thanks to fifteen years of American leadership, mentoring, and training. Americo-Liberian junior officers had served important roles leading the Frontier Force in combat against the indigenous groups since 1915. A decade later, the best of these lieutenants had advanced to the rank of captain and had further sharpened their skills as small unit leaders.

Firestone and the State Department commenced appointing U.S. officers under the new agreement after 1930. With no qualified black Regular Army candidates available, a short-lived experiment assigning a white officer failed. In the end, Firestone and the State Department found a mutually acceptable African American aspirant who had served in Liberia before—William D. Nabors. However, Nabors served strictly as a trainer and adviser from 1936 to 1942; Americo-Liberian officers continued to command the Frontier Force.

The U.S. military assistance mission in Liberia that began in 1910 and lasted in one form or another until 1942 was unique. Americans trained constabulary forces following the invasions of Cuba, the Philippines, and Haiti in the early 1900s after occupation by troops. Only in Liberia did the United States attempt to handle such a military mission with a handful of African American officers on a modest budget. From its onset, this unusual military assistance mission was a notable though qualified success, helping Liberia defeat internal and external threats to its sovereignty and setting the conditions for the Americo-Liberian regime to stay in power.

Total success in this endeavor in Liberia as envisioned by the United States and African American officers proved unachievable, especially in the face of a corrupt regime ambivalent about the task from the start. Monrovia wanted the American officers to train a force that was just good enough to cow the indigenous groups and keep the colonial powers at bay, but not so good as to pose a threat to the regime. In the end, it was the Liberian elite who achieved their goals of avoiding partition, maintaining sovereignty, subjugating the ethnic majority, and eventually seizing control of the Frontier Force from American command.

Without U.S. intervention and the presence of American officers, France and Great Britain would have partitioned Liberia in the early 1900s. And if you had asked Davis, Green, Young, or any other African American at the time about that prospect, they would have preferred a flawed black minority regime that might be gradually improved over a colonial European government that was brutally efficient. For better or for worse, American military, economic, and political support, along with African American boots on the ground, enabled the Americo-Liberian regime to endure another half century.

The African American officers who served in Liberia endeavored to persuade the regime in Monrovia to improve its treatment of the indigenous groups. After all, these American officers commanded soldiers in the Frontier Force who were recruited from the ethnic communities. Young and other Americans tried to convince Washington to pressure Monrovia to stop mistreating and exploiting its indigenous population. It should be no surprise, considering the treatment of African Americans in the United States at the time, that the American officers in Liberia identified more with the oppressed indigenous majority than the ruling Americo-Liberian elite.

There was a period from 1916 to 1920, during the Wilson administration, when the dollar diplomacy policy aims of preserving the black republic and developing Liberia's economy shifted to one that focused more on improving of the treatment of the ethnic groups in the hinterland. This led to the deployment of white American interior commissioners, a policy more squarely aligned with Wilson's missionary diplomacy. However, these goals where never achievable in the face of Monrovia's xenophobia and resistance to change. The Americo-Liberian elite rejected this new undertaking, considering it incompatible with the original mission of preserving the regime.

Knowing the terrible events of the Liberian civil wars from 1989 and 2003, it is tempting to criticize the American course of action in Liberia a century ago and call it a policy failure. However, if the U.S. policy goal in Liberia was survival of the minority republic in the face of external encroachment from Europe and internal challenge by the indigenous groups, then Washington succeeded. There is no way of knowing whether Liberia's future would have been better in terms of lost lives, economic justice, or democracy achieved had Britain and France succeeded in partitioning the country.

It is more reasonable to ask why Washington did not heed the warnings of Charles Young and take more vigorous steps to force Monrovia to improve its treatment of Liberia's indigenous people. But Charles Young knew the answer to that question. It was the same reason Americans could not achieve racial equality at home and halt the lynching of blacks in the South. There was insufficient political will or social determination to do so in the American population. It would take nearly half a century for African Americans to realize these goals in the United States, even then, imperfectly. And it would take nearly a century and a civil war for Liberia to achieve some measure of real democracy and inclusion.

Appendix

Biographies of African Americans Who Served in Liberia,

1910–1942

John H. Anderson: born Baltimore, Maryland, September 12, 1871; attended public school, Alexandria, Virginia; became teacher, Fairfax County, Virginia, 1887; enlisted, private, Twenty-Fifth U.S. Infantry, 1890–93; enlisted, private, post teacher, saddler sergeant, sergeant major, Ninth U.S. Cavalry, 1893–98; received honorable mention, Battle of Santiago, Cuba, 1898; appointed first lieutenant, Tenth U.S. Volunteer Infantry, 1898–99; enlisted, Ninth U.S. Cavalry, 1899; appointed first lieutenant, Forty-Eighth U.S. Volunteer Infantry, Philippines, 1899–1901; enlisted, Twenty-Fourth U.S. Infantry, 1901–15; retired April 19, 1915; served as major, Liberian Frontier Force, 1917–22; died Washington DC, January 15, 1956; buried Arlington National Cemetery.

Henry Oliver Atwood: born Washington DC, May 8, 1881; attended public school, Zanesville, Ohio; attended high school, Washington DC; attended Oberlin University, Ohio; enlisted, corporal, Ninth Ohio Volunteer Infantry Battalion, Spanish-American War, 1898–99; graduated Lincoln University, Pennsylvania, 1901; completed graduate studies, Howard University; completed army officer training, Fort Des Moines, Iowa, 1917; commissioned captain, 368th Infantry Regiment, France, World War I, 1918–19; served as captain, Liberian Frontier Force, 1919–22; commissioned, U.S. Army Reserve, 1925; served as instructor, military science and tactics, Armstrong and Dunbar high schools, Washington DC, 1930s–1940s; died Washington DC, July 1969.

Wilson Ballard: born Concordia Parish, Louisiana, June 17, 1877; attended Howard University, 1897–98, and Wilberforce University, Ohio, 1898; appointed lieutenant and adjutant, Ninth Ohio Volunteer Battalion, Spanish-American War, 1898–99; graduated Wilberforce University, Ohio, 1899; appointed first lieutenant, Forty-Eighth U.S. Volunteer Infantry, Philippine War, 1899–1901; completed dental degree, Ohio State University, Ohio, 1901–4; opened dental practice, Louisville, Kentucky, 1904–12; served as major, Liberian Frontier Force, 1912–15; returned to dental practice, Louisville, Kentucky, 1915; died 15 December 1943, Louisville, Kentucky; buried Zachary Taylor National Cemetery, Louisville, Kentucky.

Allen Clyde Bean: born Davenport, Iowa, September 5, 1896; graduated Wilberforce University, Ohio, 1918; completed army officer training, Camp Dodge, Iowa, 1918; completed postgraduate courses, Wilberforce University, Ohio, 1919; served as captain, Liberian Frontier Force, 1919–22; last known residing with parents, Davenport, Iowa, 1925.

Arthur Albert Browne: born Omaha, Nebraska, January 7, 1881; enrolled as student and military cadet, Wilberforce University, Wilberforce, Ohio, 1898; appointed corporal, Ninth Ohio Volunteer Infantry Battalion, Spanish-American War, 1898–99; attended Wilberforce University, 1899–1902; completed teachers college, Howard University, Washington DC, and pharmacy school, Kansas State University, Manhattan, Kansas, after 1902; taught mathematics and natural science at a number of schools, to 1910; established private podiatry practice in Chicago, 1911–12, served as captain, Liberian Frontier Force, 1912–13, commissioned, first lieutenant, Camp Funston, Kansas, 1917; returned to medical practice, Newark, New Jersey, 1942.

Benjamin Oliver Davis Sr.: born May 28, 1880, Washington DC; attended M Street High School (Preparatory High School for Negroes), Washington DC; appointed first lieutenant, Eighth Volunteer U.S. Infantry, Spanish-American War, 1898–99 (lied about age, listed birth 1877); enlisted, private, corporal, sergeant major, Ninth U.S. Cavalry, 1899–1901; commissioned, Regular Army second lieutenant, Tenth U.S. Cavalry, February 2, 1901;

stationed in the Philippines, 1901–2; stationed at Fort Washakie, Wyoming, 1902–5; promoted to first lieutenant, Tenth U.S. Cavalry, March 30, 1905; served as professor of military science and tactics at Wilberforce University, 1905–9; stationed at Fort Ethan Allen, Vermont 1909; served as military attaché to Liberia, 1910–11; promoted to captain, December 24, 1915; promoted to lieutenant colonel, July 1, 1920; promoted to colonel, February 18, 1930; promoted to brigadier general (temporary), October 25, 1940; retired July 31, 1941; recalled to active duty as brigadier general, August 1, 1941, served throughout World War II; retired July 14, 1948, having served fifty years; assigned to the National Battlefield Monuments Commission, 1953–62; died November 26, 1970, Great Lakes Naval Base, Chicago, Illinois; buried Arlington National Cemetery.

James R. Gillespie: born Washington DC, December 25, 1865; enlisted private through master sergeant, Ninth U.S. Cavalry, Tenth U.S. Cavalry, and Twenty-Fifth U.S. Infantry; served in Indian Wars, Spanish-American War, Philippine War, 1881–1915; appointed first lieutenant, Eighth U.S. Volunteer Infantry, Cuba, 1898–99; served with the Liberia Frontier Force, 1915–17; died January 26, 1936; buried Arlington National Cemetery.

John Ernest Green: born Murfreesboro, Tennessee, April 27, 1878; attended Walden University, Tennessee, 1899; enlisted Twenty-Fourth U.S. Infantry Regiment, Alcatraz Island, California, Philippine Islands, 1899–1901; commissioned, Regular Army second lieutenant, Twenty-Fifth U.S. Infantry, Philippine Islands, 1901; stationed at Fort Reno, Oklahoma, Fort Bliss, Texas, 1902–9; served as professor of military science, Wilberforce University, Ohio, 1909–13; stationed at Schofield Barracks, Hawaii, 1913–16; served as military attaché to Liberia, 1916–19; promoted to captain, July 1, 1916; promoted to major (temporary), August 5, 1917; promoted to lieutenant colonel (temporary), July 30, 1918; appointed Knight Official of the Liberian Humane Order of African Redemption, July 25, 1919; reverted to permanent rank of captain, February 9, 1920; promoted to major, July 1, 1920; served as professor of military science, Wilberforce University, Ohio, 1920–29; promoted to lieutenant colonel, November 23, 1923; retired, November 15, 1929; died May 8, 1965; buried Golden Gate National Cemetery, San Bruno, California.

Eldridge Thornton Hawkins: born Washington DC, November 24, 1889; graduated, Armstrong Manual Training School at the M Street High School, Washington DC, 1907; served as public stenographer and legal clerk, Washington DC, until 1911; served as clerk at the U.S. consulate in Monrovia, Liberia, 1911–13; served as captain, Liberian Frontier Force, 1913–15; served as U.S. postal clerk, 1917–40s; retired, U.S. Postal Service; died February 25, 1960.

Joseph H. Martin: born Washington DC, June 20, 1885; graduated, Armstrong Training School at the M Street High School, Washington DC; commissioned first lieutenant, District of Columbia National Guard; served as lieutenant, Liberian Frontier Force, 1914–15; worked as real estate broker, Washington DC, 1920s–1930s; served as clerk, Treasury Department, Washington DC, 1940s; died June 20, 1952; buried Arlington National Cemetery.

William Durward Nabors: born Aliceville, Alabama, June 21, 1897; enlisted, Ninth U.S. Cavalry, 1912–15 (lied about age, listed birth 1891); enlisted, Tenth U.S. Cavalry, 1916–17; served in Mexican Punitive Expedition, 1916–17; officer training, Texas National Guard, Leone Springs, Texas, 1917; officer training, Fort Des Moines, Iowa, 1917; commissioned second lieutenant, 368th Infantry Regiment, France, World War I, 1917–18, resided, Cleveland, Ohio, 1919; served as captain, Liberian Frontier Force, 1919–23; served in U.S. Civil Service, 1923; served on Municipal Planning Board and New Jersey National Guard, Orange, New Jersey, 1931–36; served as captain, Liberian Frontier Force, 1936–42; commissioned captain, major, U.S. Army, 1942–47; died July 10, 1960, Orange, New Jersey; buried July 13, 1960, Beverly National Cemetery, Beverly, New Jersey.

Richard Harper Newton Jr.: born Baltimore, Maryland, August 1, 1879; enlisted Ninth U.S. Cavalry, 1900 (lied about age, listed birth August 14, 1878); served with Troop L, Ninth Cavalry in Philippine War, 1900–1902; served as lieutenant, Philippine Scouts, 1903–7; enlisted Ninth Cavalry, 1907–10; stationed with Army War College Detachment, Fort Myer, Virginia, 1911; served as printing clerk, U.S. Civil Service, Washington DC, 1911–12, served as captain, Liberian

Frontier Force, 1912–14; died of tuberculosis, Monrovia, Liberia, July 13, 1914; buried Monrovia, Liberia.

Hansen Outley: born Houston, Texas, October 22, 1898; attended two years of college; enlisted, Ninth U.S. Cavalry, 1913–17 (lied about age, listed birth October 22, 1892); served as a noncommissioned officer with the 349th Field Artillery Regiment, France, World War I, 1917–19; awarded Purple Heart and the French Croix de Guerre for wounds and bravery in combat, 1919; enlisted, Ninth U.S. Cavalry, 1919–25; served as captain, Liberian Frontier Force, 1926–30; re-enlisted as a noncommissioned officer, Ninth U.S. Cavalry, 1931–41; died June 20, 1941, Fort Riley, Kansas; buried Los Angeles National Cemetery, Los Angeles, California.

William Rountree: born Xenia, Ohio, May 30, 1885; enlisted, Ninth U.S. Cavalry and served at Fort D. A. Russell, Wyoming, 1909–15; served as lieutenant, captain, Liberian Frontier Force, 1915–18; operated pool parlor, Xenia, Ohio, 1930s; died Xenia, Ohio, April 26, 1934; buried Cherry Grove Cemetery, Xenia, Ohio.

Moody Staten: born Lincoln County, North Carolina, February 18, 1891; enlisted, Twenty-Fifth U.S. Infantry, 1912–17; officer training, Fort Des Moines, Iowa, 1917; commissioned captain, infantry, Ninety-Second Division, World War I, 1917–19; attended Cheney State Normal School (later Eastern Washington College of Education), Cheney, Washington, 1923; served as captain, major, Liberian Frontier Force, 1923–27; resided, Los Angeles, California, 1930; appointed colonel, commanding 7th Regiment, California National Guard, December 7, 1941; worked as real estate broker, Los Angeles, California, 1948; died Los Angeles, California, March 6, 1970; buried Evergreen Cemetery, Los Angeles, California.

William Henry York: born Pana, Illinois, October 5, 1888; served in Spanish-American War, Illinois National Guard, 1898–99; graduated Wilberforce University, 1912; served as lieutenant, captain, major, Liberian Frontier Force, 1914–17; enlisted, U.S. Army, 1918; commissioned, second lieutenant, 368th Infantry Regiment, France, World War I, 1918–19; resided, New Brunswick, New Jersey, 1924; died New Jersey, July 13, 1927; buried Cypress Hills National Cemetery, Brooklyn, New York.

Charles Young: born March 12, 1864, Mays Lick, Kentucky; escaped enslavement and grew up in Ripley, Ohio, 1864–84; attended United States Military Academy, 1884–89; commissioned, Regular Army second lieutenant, Ninth U.S. Cavalry, 1889; served at Fort Robinson, Nebraska and Fort Duchesne, Utah, 1889–94; served as professor of military science at Wilberforce University, Ohio, 1894–98; promoted to first lieutenant, 1896; appointed volunteer major and commander of Ninth Ohio Volunteer Infantry Battalion, Spanish-American War, 1898–99; served in Ninth U.S. Cavalry, Fort Duchesne, Utah, 1899–1901; served in Ninth U.S. Cavalry, Philippine War, 1901–2; assigned to Presidio of San Francisco, California, 1902–04; served as acting superintendent of Sequoia National Park, 1903; served as military attaché to Hispaniola (Dominican Republic and Haiti), 1904–7; served in Ninth U.S. Cavalry, Philippines and Fort D. A. Russell, Wyoming, 1907–12; served as military attaché to Liberia, 1912–15; awarded NAACP Spingarn Medal, February 22, 1916; served in Tenth U.S. Cavalry Fort Huachuca, Arizona, and Mexican Punitive Expedition, 1916–17; medically retired and promoted to colonel, 1917; recalled to active duty for service at Camp Grant, Illinois, 1919; appointed Knight Commander of the Liberian Humane Order of African Redemption, November 15, 1919; served as military attaché to Liberia 1920–22; died Lagos, Nigeria, January 8, 1922; buried Ikoyi Cemetery, Lagos, Nigeria, January 9, 1922; reinterred Arlington National Cemetery, June 1, 1923.

Notes

Abbreviations

AGO   Adjutant General's Office

Dispatch List
>Registers of Communications Received from Military Attachés and Other Intelligence Officers, RG 165, M1271, NARA

FRUS   Foreign Relations of the United States, NARA. The FRUS series is the official documentary historical record of major U.S. foreign policy decisions that have been declassified and edited for publication. The series is produced by the State Department's Office of the Historian and printed volumes are available from the Government Printing Office.

Heinl Collection
>Charles Young Papers, Nancy Heinl, Private Collection

Index to General Correspondence of AGO
>Index to General Correspondence of the Adjutant General's Officer, 1890–1917, RG 94, M698, NARA

M   Microfilm roll number

MID   Military Information Division

NAAMCC   National Afro-American Museum and Cultural Center, Wilberforce, Ohio

NARA   National Archives and Records Administration, College Park, Maryland

RDSIAL   U.S. Department of State, Records of the Department of State Relating to Internal Affairs of Liberia, 1910–1929, Roll 11, RG 59, M613.

RG   Records Group

USAHEC   U.S. Army Heritage and Education Center

1. Liberia

1. Ethiopia was free of white rule until 1935, when it was invaded and occupied by Italy until 1941.

2. Ellis, "Dynamic Factors," 256–57.

3. Ranard, *Liberians*, 2–3.

4. Nelson, *Liberia*, xxiii–xxiv; Ranard, *Liberians*, 2–9; Debra Newman Ham, ed., *The African-American Mosaic: Colonization*, www.loc.gov/exhibits/african/afam002.html. This website provides a good summary of colonization. *The African-American Mosaic: A Library of Congress Resource Guide for the Study of Black History and Culture*, edited by Debra Newman Ham, is part of a series of Library of Congress Resource Guides. The American Colonial Society donated its records to the Library of Congress at its dissolution in 1964.

5. Morison, *"Old Bruin,"* 61–76; Schufeldt, *U.S. Navy in Connection*, 3–4; Younger, "Liberia and the Last Slave Ships," 424–42; Hahn, "Experience of Land Grabbing," 72.

6. Morison, *"Old Bruin,"* 72–73; Schufeldt, *U.S. Navy in Connection*, 3–4.

7. Morison, *"Old Bruin,"* 73.

8. Morison, *"Old Bruin,"* 163–78; Schufeldt, *U.S. Navy in Connection*, 5–6.

9. Morison, *"Old Bruin,"* 173–74; Schufeldt, *U.S. Navy in Connection*, 5–6; Morgan, "Kru Wars," 4.

10. Schufeldt, *U.S. Navy in Connection*, 5–6; Ranard, *Liberians*, 3–11.

11. Akpan, "Black Imperialism," 223–24; Clegg, "A Splendid Type," 47–48; Ellis, "Dynamic Factors," 258–65; Boahen, *Africa under Colonial Domination*, 15–16.

12. Gardiner, *Conway's*, 418; *Wanganui Chronicle* (New Zealand), September 11, 1900, 1. *Rocktown* sank in Monrovia Harbor, and *Goronnamah* capsized in the Saint Paul River and sank. The Liberians were either unable or uninterested in raising them.

13. Davis, "Liberian Struggle for Authority," 241–49; Winkler, *Nexus*, 15–17.

14. Clegg, "A Splendid Type," 48; Ciment, *Another America*, 134–36.

15. Ranard, *Liberians*, 2–3.

16. Ranard, *Liberians*, 4–7; Morgan, "Kru Wars," 2–4.

17. Ranard, *Liberians*, 2–5; Mower, "Republic of Liberia," 266.

18. Ranard, *Liberians*, 3.

19. Akpan, "Black Imperialism," 224–25.

20. Ranard, *Liberians*, 10–13. Status based on skin color or "colorism" originated in the hierarchy of the Southern slave plantations.

21. Pham, *Liberia*, 52–53.

22. Pham, *Liberia*, 52–54.

23. Pham, *Liberia*, 59.

24. Sirleaf, *This Child*, 8–13; Pham, *Liberia*, 53–59.

25. Starr, *Liberra*, 188–33; Nevin, "Uncontrollable Force," 279–80.

26. Ambassador Henry White to the Secretary of State, October 4, 1907, U.S. Department of State, FRUS, 1907: Liberia, 830–32; Hurlbut, "Liberia's New Boundary," 21–22; Gershoni, *Black Colonialism*, 43; Nevin, "Uncontrollable Force," 279–80.

27. Affairs in Liberia, Message from the President of the United States, transmitting a letter of the Secretary of State submitting a report of the Commission which visited Liberia, March 25, 1909, U.S. Congressional Serial Set, 1909–1910, Document

No. 457, Senate Documents, vol. 60, 17–19; Starr, *Liberia*, 118–30; Ellis, "Dynamic Factors," 260–71.

28. Secretary of the Navy to State Department, December 17, 1908, Folder 9574-29, Box 426, RG 80, NARA; "Lark," *Sea Breezes Magazine*, June 1958; "Lark," Ship Stamp Society, September 10, 2008, www.shipstamps.co.uk/forum/viewtopic.php ?f=2&t=7770, accessed October 9, 2017. According to the Ship Stamp Society,The *Lark* was built in 1885 by Shuttleworth and Chapman, to the designs of Mr. A. H. Brown, at Erith, on the Thames, her original name being *Eros*. She was the second yacht of this name built for Baron A. de Rothschild and had a tonnage-770 with the dimensions 228 ft. x 26 ft. x 15 ft. She was a schooner-rigged vessel with two raked single pole masts, on which auxiliary sail could be set. She was placed in the hands of Summer and Payne for alterations converting her into a gunboat, intended for use primarily against smugglers and for transporting troops along the Liberian coast. The vessel left Southampton for Portsmouth early in September 1908, where she was fitted with her armament of two 6-pdr., two 3-pdr., and several machine guns. She left Southampton on October 7, 1908, manned by a British crew under Lieut. J. M. Bugge.

29. Affairs in Liberia, March 25, 1909, U.S. Congressional Serial Set, 1909–1910, Document No. 457, Senate Documents, vol. 60, 17–18; Starr, *Liberia*, 118–30; Akingbade, "Pacification of the Liberian Hinterland," 282.

30. Affairs in Liberia, March 25, 1909, U.S. Congressional Serial Set, 1909–1910, Document No. 457, Senate Documents, vol. 60, 17–18; Starr, *Liberia*, 118–30; Ellis, "Dynamic Factors," 270–71.

31. Affairs in Liberia, March 25, 1909, U.S. Congressional Serial Set, 1909–1910, Document No. 457, Senate Documents, vol. 60, 18–19; Harlan, "Booker T. Washington and the White Man's Burden," 453.

32. Starr, *Liberia*, 124–27; Ellis, "Dynamic Factors," 270–73.

33. Affairs in Liberia, March 25, 1909, U.S. Congressional Serial Set, 1909–1910, Document No. 457, Senate Documents, vol. 60, 18–19; Starr, *Liberia*, 127–28.

2. American Support

1. Mower, "Republic of Liberia," 269–71; Ciment, *Another America*, 138.

2. Mower, "Republic of Liberia," 269–71; Booker T. Washington as quoted in Ciment, *Another America*, 138. The Berlin Conference of 1884–85, also called the Congo or West Africa Conference, regulated European colonization and led to the General Act of the Berlin Conference, which formalized the rules governing the "Scramble for Africa."

3. Liberian Commission to the Secretary of State, May 22, 1908, Secretary of State to the Liberian Commission, May 23, 1908, Secretary of State to Ambassador Reid, June 13, 1908, Minister of Foreign Affairs to Ambassador Reid, July 23, 1908, FRUS, 1910: Liberia, 694–99; Affairs in Liberia, March 25, 1909, U.S. Congressional Serial Set, 1909–1910, Document No. 457, Senate Documents, vol. 60, 1–2. The British recognized the special relationship between Liberia and the United States, had its hands full with the rise of the military power of Germany, and could ill afford to alienate Washington.

4. Affairs in Liberia, March 25, 1909, U.S. Congressional Serial Set, 1909–1910, Document No. 457, Senate Documents, vol. 60, 1–2; "Our Liberian Envoys Meet President Roosevelt, Liberia" *Washington Herald*, June 11, 1908, quoted in *Liberia* 33 (November 1908): 28–30; Davis, *Guest of Honor*, 1–2; Starr, *Liberia*, 221–22; Ciment, *Another America*, 138–39. There was precedent for this, as Roosevelt had shattered convention on October 16, 1901, by inviting Booker T. Washington to dine with him in the White House.

5. "Our Liberian Envoys Meet President Roosevelt, Liberia," *Washington Herald*, June 11, 1908.

6. "Our Liberian Envoys Meet President Roosevelt, Liberia" *Washington Herald*, June 11, 1908; Campbell, *Middle Passages*, 233.

7. Affairs in Liberia, March 25, 1909, U.S. Congressional Serial Set, 1909–1910, Document No. 457, Senate Documents, vol. 60, 1–2; Secretary of State to President Roosevelt, January 18, 1909, FRUS, 1910: Liberia, 699–701; Ciment, *Another America*, 138–39.

8. Tilley, *Between Homeland and Motherland*, 45; Ciment, *Another America*, 138–39, 165.

9. Secretary of State Knox to the Minister of Foreign Affairs of Liberia, April 23, 1909, FRUS, 1910: Liberia, 708; "Roland Post Faulkner," 543–45; Harlan and Smock, *Booker T. Washington Papers, Vol. 10*, 82.

10. "Chairman Shuster Resigns," *New York Times*, April 17, 1909.

11. "Go Separately to Liberia," *New York Times*, April 22, 1909; "Commission to Liberia," *New York Age*, July 8, 1909; Harlan, "Booker T. Washington and the White Man's Burden," 455–56; Forbes, *Land of the White Helmets*, 223; Letter from Booker T. Washington to Seth Low, February 16, 1909, Booker T. Washington Society, www.btwsociety.org/library/letters/3.php.

12. "Roland Post Faulkner," 543–45; Fred R. Moore to the editor of the *New York Times*, April 19, 1909, quoted in Harlan and Smock, *Booker T. Washington Papers, Vol. 10*, 82.

13. Secretary of State Knox to the Minister of Foreign Affairs of Liberia, April 23, 1909, FRUS, 1910: Liberia, 708.

14. Affairs in Liberia, March 25, 1909, U.S. Congressional Serial Set, 1909–1910, Document No. 457, Senate Documents, vol. 60, 2–13. Annual Report of the War Department, 1910, 487–90.

15. Gatewood, "Black Americans," 556–58; Miller, *Benevolent Assimilation*, 122–23.

16. Gatewood, "Black Americans," 556–58; Dineen-Wimberly, "To Carry 'the Black Man's Burden,'" 69–74; Booker T. Washington as quoted from Dineen-Wimberly, "To Carry 'the Black Man's Burden.'"

17. Rosenberg, *Financial Missionaries*, 69–70; "Our Liberian Envoys Meet President Roosevelt," *Washington Herald*, June 11, 1908.

18. USS *Chester* Log Book, April 24–May 8, 1909, RG 24, NARA 1. *Chester* (CL-1), *Birmingham* (CL-2), and *Salem* (CL-3) were all Chester-class scout cruisers commissioned in 1908. They were used in the years before World War I for diplomatic duty and for patrolling the Caribbean, Mediterranean, and African coast. They displaced 3,750 tons, carried a crew of 63 officers and 332 enlisted, and were armed with 4 five-inch guns, 2 three-inch guns, 1 three-inch antiaircraft gun, and 2 torpedo tubes.

19. USS *Chester* Log Book, May, 8, 1909, RG 24, NARA 1; "Commission to Liberia," New York Age," 1.

20. USS *Chester* Log Book, May 13–20, 1909, RG 24, NARA 1; "Commission to Liberia," New York Age," 1.

21. USS *Chester* Log Book, May 29–July 3, 1909, RG 24, NARA 1; "Commission to Liberia," New York Age," 1.

22. Annual Report of the War Department, 1910, 487–90.

23. Affairs in Liberia, March 25, 1909, U.S. Congressional Series Set, 1909–1910, Document No. 457, Senate Documents, vol. 60, 1–37; Rosenberg, *Financial Missionaries*, 70; Meiser, "Power and Restraint," 42–43. Only the Dominican Republic receivership got formal Senate approval, while those in Honduras, Nicaragua, and Liberia were implemented by the State Department without formal congressional approval.

24. Nelson, *Liberia*, 37–39; Duignan and Gann, *United States and Africa*, 195–97.

25. U.S. House of Representatives, Improvement of the Foreign Service, 1912, 33; Rosenberg, *Financial Missionaries*, 69–70.

3. Davis

1. U.S. Department of State, Office of the Historian, Principal Officers and Chiefs of Mission, by Year, 1909, https://history.state.gov/departmenthistory/people/by -year/1909, accessed October 10, 2017; Johnson, *Negro in the New World*, 327; Fletcher, *America's First Black General*, 40; Index to General Correspondence of AGO, Roll 298, RG 94, M698, NARA. Haiti, the only other black republic, hosted the other African American Head of Mission, Minister Henry W. Furniss.

2. Index to General Correspondence of AGO, Roll 298, RG 94, M698, NARA. Captain Charles Young, the first American military attaché, was accredited to Haiti and the Dominican Republic from 1904 to 1907.

3. Fletcher, *America's First Black General*, 40; Index to General Correspondence of AGO, Roll 298, RG 94, M698, NARA.

4. Fletcher, *America's First Black General*, 40; Index to General Correspondence of AGO, Roll 298, RG 94, M698, NARA; Manby, *Citizenship Law in Africa*, 3–4.

5. Index to General Correspondence of AGO, Roll 298, M698, NARA; Fletcher, *America's First Black General*, 6–19. Davis biographer Marvin Fletcher states he was born on May 28, 1880, lying about his age to join the army without his parents' consent. The military records list his birthday as July 1, 1877. The AGO records cited above show that he was disbarred on account of age on June 27, 1889, but accepted a commission as first lieutenant in the Eighth U.S. Volunteer Infantry on July 25, 1889. Fletcher also states that Davis's father contacted someone close to President McKinley, but the president's staff said appointing a black man to West Point was not politically feasible at the time.

6. Index to General Correspondence of AGO, Roll 298, M698, NARA; Fletcher, *America's First Black General*, 19–27; Shellum, *Black Officer*, 102–5. The commissioning examination comprised a physical examination, a series of written tests (on the English language, the U.S. Constitution, international law, mathematics, geography, history, and army regulations), and oral questioning on various subjects. Davis ranked third of twelve who passed the examination that year at Fort Leavenworth, Kansas.

By enlisting in the army and taking the commissioning exam, Davis had seniority in date of rank over about two hundred of his fellow lieutenants, whom he would otherwise have been junior to had he attended West Point.

7. Consul General Lyon to Davis, November 20, 1909, 1st Endorsement War Department, November 22, 1909, 2nd Endorsement Davis, November 25, 1909, Adjutant General McCain to Davis, November 30, 1909, Benjamin O. Davis Papers, USAHEC; Index to General Correspondence of AGO, Roll 298, M698, NARA; Fletcher, *America's First Black General*, 6–27.

8. Farrow, *Dictionary of Military Terms*, 363. Infantry, cavalry, and artillery officers were considered officers of the line. Because Davis served four years on detached duty at Wilberforce from 1905 to 1909, he should have gone back to his regiment, but the necessity of having a black officer assigned to Monrovia trumped the congressional mandate.

9. "Clifton R. Wharton, Sr.," Black History Now, August 11, 2011, http://blackhistorynow.com/clifton-r-wharton-sr/, accessed October 9, 2017. The "Negro Circuit" will be discussed in detail in chapter 7 herein. Wilberforce University established the first black officer cadet training program in the country in 1884.

10. War Department Instructions to Davis, December 13, 1909, Benjamin O. Davis Papers, USAHEC; Memorandum to the Adjutant General from the Officer in Charge, MID, Maj. Arthur L. Wagner, September 28, 1897, Article 639-6, Army War College Department Correspondence, RG 165, NARA; Votaw, "U.S. Military Attachés, 1885–1919," 235–41. The War Department instructions to Davis listed the following countries with military attachés in 1909: England, France, Germany, Russia, Mexico, Italy, Austria-Hungary, Japan, China, Venezuela, Argentina, Peru, Ecuador, Columbia, Brazil, Chile, Cuba, and Liberia.

11. Votaw, "U.S. Military Attachés, 1885–1919," 1–6.

12. Adjutant General McCain to Davis, November 30, 1909, Major Todd to Davis, December 13, 1909, Benjamin O. Davis Papers, USAHEC; Index of General Correspondence of AGO, Roll 298, M698, NARA; Fletcher, *Black Soldier and Officer*, 93.

13. Votaw, "U.S. Military Attachés, 1885–1919," 66.

14. Index to General Correspondence of AGO, Roll 298, M698, NARA; Fletcher, *Black Soldier and Officer*, 93.

15. War Department to Davis, January 14, 1910, Consul General Lyon to Davis, January 26, 1910, Davis to Adjutant General, March 21, 1910, Benjamin O. Davis Papers, USAHEC.

16. Booker T. Washington to Henry Cabot Lodge, April 10, 1910, Booker T. Washington to James J. Dossen, April 10, 1910, in Harlan and Smock, *Booker T. Washington Papers, Vol. 10*, 317–18; Acting Secretary of the Navy to Secretary of State , March 17, 1910, Secretary of State to Assistant Secretary of the Navy, March 19, 1910, Folder 9574-33, Box 426, RG 80, NARA 1. Lyon was stateside on home leave and spent a great deal of time in Washington meeting with government officials and traveling the United States in support of the commission recommendations to aid Liberia. He visited the Tuskegee Institute in October, and his efforts to aid Liberia received favorable coverage in black newspapers. Lyon and Emmett Scott, the only black member of the

Liberian commission, supported Booker T. Washington's efforts to throw his weight behind the effort to assist Liberia.

17. USS *Birmingham* Log Book, April 4–13, 1910, RG 24, NARA; Fletcher to the Secretary of the Navy, April 12, 1910, RG 80, NARA. Dossen and King were appointed "Special Commissioners, to settle the Grebo Uprising in Maryland County," as noted in Fletcher's correspondence.

18. USS *Birmingham* Log Book, April 13–May 5, 1910, RG 24, NARA. Since *Lark* still boasted many accommodations of a luxury yacht, Liberian government official were sometimes criticized for using her on junkets.

19. USS *Birmingham* Log Book, April 14–17, 1910, RG 24, NARA. One sailor drowned on the spot, and the second went missing, washing ashore later.

20. Secretary of State Knox to Ernest Lyon, Consul General Monrovia, June 14, 1910, Charles Young Collection, NAAMCC; Dispatch List, Liberia, Davis, 1909–11, NARA; Fletcher, *America's First Black General*, 40–41.

21. Acting Secretary of the Navy to Secretary of State (forwarding text of telegram), May 10, 1910, Fletcher to the Secretary of the Navy, April 30, 1910, Folder 9574-33, Box 426, RG 80, NARA.

22. Acting Secretary of the Navy to Secretary of State (forwarding text of telegram), May 10, 1910, Fletcher to the Secretary of the Navy, April 30, 1910, Folder 9574-33, Box 426, RG 80, NARA.

23. USS *Des Moines* Log Book, May 4–6, 1910, RG 24, NARA.

24. USS *Des Moines* Log Book, May 6–9, 1910, USS *Birmingham* Log Book, May 6–9, 1910, RG 24, NARA.

25. USS *Birmingham* Log Book, May 9–11, 1910, RG 24, NARA; Acting Secretary of the Navy to Secretary of State (forwarding text of telegram), May 10, 1910, Folder 9574-33, Box 426, RG 80, NARA; Dispatch List, Liberia, Davis, 1909–11, NARA.

26. Dispatch List, Liberia, Davis, 1909–11, NARA; Fletcher, *America's First Black General*, 40–42.

27. Commander Luby to the Secretary of the Navy, May 23, 1910, Special Commissioners to the Civilized Greboes, May 17, 1910, King Gyude to the Special Commissioners, April 23, 1910, Commander Luby to the Special Commissioners, May 19, 1910, Folder 9574-48, Box 426, RG 80, NARA. The U.S. officers who accompanied Luby included Lt. C. P. Burt, Lt. N. E. Nichols, Passed Assistant Paymaster N. W. Grant, and Midshipman E. H. Williams (Williams was promoted to ensign on July 7, 1910, off Cape Palmas).

28. USS *Des Moines* Log Book, May 19, 1910, RG 24, NARA; Special Commissioners to Commander Luby, May 21, 1910, Commander Luby to Special Commissioners, May 21, 1910, Folder 9574-48, Box 426, RG 80, NARA.

29. Commander Luby to the Secretary of the Navy, May 29, 1910, Folder 9574-50, Box 426, RG 80, NARA. Luby noted that yellow fever had broken out in Freetown, Sierra Leone, so he would have to steam to Dakar, Senegal, to resupply with coal.

30. Commander Luby to the Secretary of the Navy, June 9, 1910, Folder 9574-51, Box 426, RG 80, NARA.

31. Commander Luby to the Secretary of the Navy, June 9, 1910, Folder 9574-51, June 12, 1910, Folder 9574-52, July 5, 1910, Folder 9574-57, Box 426, RG 80, NARA; USS *Des Moines* Log Book, June 5–30, 1910, RG 24, NARA. Luby did not resupply in Freetown, Sierra Leone, because of yellow fever there.

32. Commander Luby to the Secretary of the Navy, June 9, 1910, Folder 9574-51, June 12, 1910, Folder 9574-52, July 5, 1910, Folder 9574-57, Box 426, RG 80, USS *Des Moines* Log Book, June 5–30, 1910, RG 24, NARA. Ens. E. H. Williams went ashore to collect intelligence at Cape Mount, Marshall, Grand Bassa, Grand Cess, Sinoe, and Cape Palmas. Williams and Grant were not formally assigned on the ship's manifest as intelligence officers but had this as an additional duty.

33. Commander Luby to the Secretary of the Navy, July 5, 1910, Folder 9574-57, July 24, 1910, Folder 9574-61, Box 426, RG 80, NARA; USS *Des Moines* Log Book, July 2–21, 1910, RG 24, NARA.

34. Commander Luby to the Secretary of the Navy, July 5, 1910, Folder 9574-57, , July 24, 1910, Folder 9574-58, July 30, 1910, Folder 9574-61, Box 426, RG 80, NARA. The French army doctor serving with the Frontier Forces was Dr. Jourdan, and the U.S. Navy surgeon was D. G. Sutton.

35. Commander Luby to the Secretary of the Navy, August 13, 1910, Midshipman G. C. Barnes to Commander Luby, August 29, 1910, Folder 9574-60, Box 426, RG 80, NARA. Those left behind in the hospital with blackwater fever included Ens. E. H. Williams, Cabin Steward G. W. Griffith, and Fireman 2nd Class J. S. Watland. Two others were also left behind: Chief Carpenter's Mate William Hayes with diabetes and Seaman T. R. McLaughlan for a fractured hip from the breaking of a lewis bolt while a mooring line was being hauled in.

36. Midshipman G. C. Barnes to Commander Luby, August 29, 1910, Luby to the Secretary of the Navy, August 13, 1910, Folder 9574-60, Box 426, RG 80, NARA. General Padmore provided Luby with a final summary of the major engagements against the Greboes. The Liberians attacked and defeated the Greboes on June 27 at Sokoki, suffering five killed and thirteen wounded. They attacked and then retreated from Nitelu on July 15 with five killed and forty-three wounded. Nitelu was later taken, burned, and garrisoned by the Frontier Forces with three wounded. A force subsequently attacked a fortified place called Kyake and built a garrison there; five other Grebo towns were taken. Luby steamed south to Cape Palmas to verify the Liberian account of affairs and was back in Monrovia a few days later.

37. Booker T. Washington to Ernest Lyon, June 11, 1910, in Harlan and Smock, *Booker T. Washington Papers, Vol. 10*, 336; Commander Luby to the Secretary of the Navy, September 12, 1910, Folder 9574-63, Box 426, RG 80, NARA. The *New York Age* noted on June 16, 1910 that there had been complaints that Lyon had been too active in religious matters in Liberia. He had been a minister in the Methodist Episcopal Church for nineteen years before his appointment.

38. USS *Des Moines* Log Book, September 1–30, 1910, RG 24, NARA; Secretary of the Navy to Commander Luby, September 17, 1910, Folder 9574-61, Box 426, RG 80, NARA.

39. USS *Des Moines* Log Book, September 1–30, 1910, RG 24, NARA; Secretary of the Navy to Commander Luby, September 17, 1910, Folder 9574-61, Box 426, RG 80,

NARA. While in Gibraltar, Des Moines was ordered to Lisbon, Portugal from October 7 to November 18 1910 in reaction to a republican uprising.

40. Lieutenant Davis, "Laws: Organization of the Military Forces," November 8, 1910, Folder 5797-5, Charles Young Collection, NAAMCC.

41. Lieutenant Davis, "Laws: Organization of the Military Forces," November 8, 1910, Folder 5797-5, Charles Young Collection, NAAMCC.

42. Fletcher, *America's First Black General*, 40–42.

43. Lieutenant Davis to War Department, January 23, 1911, Benjamin O. Davis Papers, USAHEC. "Blackwater fever pathology," *Encyclopedia Britannica*, www.britannica.com /science/blackwater-fever, accessed October 10, 2017. Blackwater fever, or malarial hemoglobinuria, is one of the less common and most dangerous complications of malaria, and it occurs almost exclusively with infection from the parasite Plasmodium falciparum.

44. Lieutenant Davis, "The Military Forces of Liberia," October 12, 1911, Charles Young Collection, NAAMCC; Fletcher, *America's First Black General*, 42–43.

45. Nevin, "Uncontrollable Force," 276.

46. Nevin, "Uncontrollable Force," 284.

47. Nevin, "Uncontrollable Force," 282–83. In many ways, the ethnic groups of Liberia perceived the Americo-Liberians as just another group to be fought, resisted, and overcome if possible.

48. Nevin, "Uncontrollable Force," 276.

49. USS *Des Moines* Log Book, December 10, 1910–January 2, 1911, RG 24, NARA.

50. USS *Des Moines* Log Book, December 3, 1910–January 4, 1911, RG 24, NARA.

51. USS *Des Moines* Log Book, December 19, 1910, January 8, 1911, RG 24, NARA; "Cruiser Commander Dies," *New York Times*, January 11, 1911. Luby was born in Ireland on June 25, 1858, appointed a midshipman in the navy on June 25, 1876, promoted to commander in 1907, and assumed command of the Des Moines on April 1, 1910, just before the mission to Liberia.

52. Commander Luby to the Secretary of the Navy, May 23, 1910, Folder 9574-48, Box 426, RG 80, NARA.

53. Lieutenant Davis to Secretary of State Johnson, February 13, 1911, Benjamin O. Davis Papers, USAHEC; American Minister Crum to the Secretary of State, April 17, 1911, FRUS, 1912: Liberia, 662; Fletcher, *America's First Black General*, 42–43.

54. Secretary of State Johnson to Davis, April 5, 1911, Benjamin O. Davis Papers, USAHEC; Dispatch List, Liberia, Davis, 1909–11, NARA; Liberian Secretary of State Johnson to Consul General Crum, April 17, 1911, RDSIAL, 2; Fletcher, *America's First Black General*, 42–43.

55. Lieutenant Davis to the Chief, Second Section, War Department General Staff, January 23, 1911, Adjutant General McCain to Davis, August 12, 1911, Benjamin O. Davis Papers, USAHEC; Dispatch List, Liberia, Davis, 1909–11, NARA; Fletcher, *America's First Black General*, 43–44.

56. Dispatch List, Liberia, Davis, 1909–11, NARA.

57. Lieutenant Davis, "Military Forces of Liberia," October 12, 1911, Charles Young Collection, NAAMCC.

58. Lieutenant Davis to Capt. Matthew E. Hanna, General Staff, War Department, December 21, 1911, Benjamin O. Davis Papers, USAHEC; Dispatch List, Liberia, Davis, 1909–11, NARA; Fletcher, *Black Soldier and Officer*, 94.

59. Lieutenant Davis to Capt. Matthew E. Hanna, General Staff, War Department, December 21, 1911, Benjamin O. Davis Papers, USAHEC; Clegg, "A Splendid Type," 56.

60. Reed Paige Clark to Booker T. Washington, November 10, 1911, Charles Young Collection, NAAMCC.

61. Reed Paige Clark to Booker T. Washington, November 10, 1911, Charles Young Collection, NAAMCC. It is unclear whether this was Stewart's personal opinion or that of the Liberian government. Stewart and Young later became very close friends.

62. Captain Young to Booker T. Washington, November 24, 1911, Charles Young Collection, NAAMCC.

63. Ninth Regimental Return, December 1911, NARA; Index to Records of the War College Division and Related General Staff Offices, Charles Young, NARA.

4. Young: Rescuing Liberia

1. Shellum, *Black Cadet*, 3–35.

2. Shellum, *Black Officer*, xix–xxi.

3. Shellum, *Black Officer*, 159–81. Young was fluent in German, Spanish, and French. He mastered Haitian Creole soon after assuming his post in Port-au-Prince and authored an English-Creole dictionary that he sent to the War Department.

4. Young, *Military Morale*, 4. Publishing a book was one way for a Regular Army officer to prove his ability and improve his chances for promotion.

5. Young, *Military Morale*, 259–60.

6. Lewis, *W. E. B. Du Bois: Biography of a Race*, 176.

7. American Minister Crum to Secretary of State, May 2, 1912, FRUS, 1912: Liberia, 665; Charles Young Lease, July 1, 1912, Charles Young Collection, NAAMCC. Daniel Edward Howard was the sixteenth president of Liberia, serving from 1912 to 1920. He was born in Buchanan, Grand Bassa County, elected for his first term in 1911, assumed office January 1, 1912, and served two terms from 1912 to 1920.

8. Padgett, "Ministers to Liberia," 83; Gatewood, "William D. Crum." In 1906 Secretary of State Elihu Root reorganized the consular service, instituting an entrance examination and raising annual salaries, ranging from $2,000 to $12,000, to attract a higher quality diplomatic corps. William Demos Crum served from August 25, 1910, to September 17, 1912. In September Minister Crum became so gravely ill with blackwater fever that he sailed back to Charleston, where he died three months later.

9. Padgett, "Ministers to Liberia," 83, 91; U.S. Passport Application, Richard C. Bundy, December 2, 1916, Special Diplomatic Passport Applications, 1916–1925, NARA, via U.S. Passport Applications, 1795–1925 database, Ancestry.com, accessed October 10, 2017; Kilroy, *For Race and Country*, 84; Schneller, *Breaking the Color Barrier*, 60–61. In 1897 Congressman W. B. Shattuc, a former Union cavalry officer and representative of the First Ohio District, appointed Richard C. Bundy to the U.S. Naval Academy at Annapolis. Shattuc was pressured to withdraw Bundy's name by fellow congressmen but refused. Bundy failed the entrance exam on September 1, 1897.

10. Padgett, "Ministers to Liberia," 83; Clegg, "A Splendid Type," 56; Booker T. Washington to William D. Crum, August 26, 1911, Booker T. Washington to Daniel T. Howard, August 26, 1911, in Harlan and Smock, *Booker T. Washington Papers, Vol. 11*, 297–99.

11. Major Young to the American Minister, October 9, 1912, FRUS, 1912: Liberia, 665–67; Padgett, "Ministers to Liberia," 83; Clegg, "A Splendid Type," 56.

12. McCants-Stewart to Starr, May, 11, 1915, Frederick Starr Papers, Howard University Library, Washington DC. Frederick Starr was born in Auburn, New York, on September 2, 1858; graduated with a BA and PhD from Lafayette College in Easton, Pennsylvania; founded the Anthropology Department at the University of Chicago; and traveled extensively to the Congo, Liberia, and Japan (from biographic summary in Frederick Starr Papers). Young later made his extensive collection of African artifacts available to Starr for a display at the Chicago Field Museum. Thomas McCants-Stewart was born in Charleston, South Carolina, one of the first black students to enroll in the University of South Carolina, and graduated with BS and LLB degrees in 1875. Stewarts practiced law in South Carolina before moving to New York in 1880 and Liberia in 1883, where he served as a professor at Liberia College. After living in the United States and London for a time, he was appointed associate justice to the Liberian Supreme Court in 1911. He was removed from the court in 1914 as a result of his criticism of President Howard and moved to London. He died in Saint Thomas, Virgin Islands, in 1923. Wynes, "T. McCants Stewart," 311–17; Albert Broussard, "Stewart, T. McCants (1853–1923)," www.blackpast.org/aah/stewart-t-mccants-1853-1923, accessed October 16, 2017.

13. Selected Appointments, Commission, and Personnel Branch of the Adjutant General's Office Records for Charles Young, RG 94, NARA. Company grade officers are those in the ranks of second lieutenant, first lieutenant, and captain who served in company or troop level positions. Field grade officers, or those in the rank of major and above, served in command or staff positions at higher levels.

14. Affairs in Liberia, March 25, 1909, U.S. Congressional Serial Set, 1909–1910, Document No. 457, Senate Documents, vol. 60, 34–35; Clegg, "A Splendid Type," 55–56.

15. Acting Secretary of War to the American Minister, February 13, 1912, FRUS, 1912: Liberia, 664.

16. Edward Lee Baker to the State Department, November 28, 1911, RDSIAL, 7; War Department to Captain Young, January 15, 1912, RDSIAL, 13.

17. Passport Application, Wilson Ballard, March 23, 1912, Passport Applications, January 2, 1906–March 31, 1925, NARA, via U.S. Passport Applications, 1795–1925 database, Ancestry.com, accessed October 10, 2017; Wilberforce University Annual Catalogue, 1898, 35–36, Charles Young Collection, NAAMCC; Powell, "Roster 9th Ohio Volunteers," 2; Yenser, *Who's Who*, 38.

18. Passport Application, Arthur A. Browne, March 23, 1912, Passport Applications, January 2, 1906–March 31, 1925, Roll 155, NARA; Wilberforce University Annual Catalogue, 1898, 35–36, Charles Young Collection, NAAMCC; Powell, "Roster 9th Ohio Volunteers," 6; Clegg, "A Splendid Type," 55. Booker T. Washington voiced these doubts about the suitability of Browne in a letter he never sent to Reed Paige Clark (March 25, 1912, Con. 916, Booker T. Washington Papers, Library of

Congress). The spelling of Browne's last name is spelled most often Browne but occasionally Brown.

19. Passport Application, Richard H. Newton, Jr., March 23, 1912, Passport Applications, January 2, 1906–March 31, 1925, NARA, via U.S. Passport Applications, 1795–1925 database, Ancestry.com, accessed October 10, 2017; Newton's enlistment papers, Richard H. Newton Jr. Papers, Bertha Rhodes Collection; Wilberforce University Annual Catalogue, 1898, 35–36, Charles Young Collection, NAAMCC; Powell, "Roster 9th Ohio Volunteers," 6.

20. Acting Secretary of State Wilson to American Minister, Monrovia, March 7, 1912, FRUS, 1912: Liberia, 662; Clegg, "A Splendid Type," 56.

21. Letters from Samuel B. Pearson to Young, May 15, 1912, and August 6, 1913, Charles Young Collection, NAAMCC; undated photo of Charles and Ada Young with Samuel Pearson, Charles Young Collection, NAAMCC (fig. 15).

22. Minister Crum to Secretary of State, May 2, 1912, RDSIAL, 21; Major Young to the American Minister, October 9, 1912, FRUS, 1912: Liberia, 666.

23. Major Young to the American Minister, October 9, 1912, FRUS, 1912: Liberia, 665–67; Gatewood, "William D. Crum," 319–20.

24. Major Young to the American Minister, October 9, 1912, FRUS, 1912: Liberia, 665–67; Message of the President (of Liberia) to the Legislature, December 19, 1912, FRUS, 1912: Liberia, 649–52.

25. Affairs in Liberia, March 25, 1909, U.S. Congressional Serial Set, 1909–1910, Document No. 457, Senate Documents, vol. 60, 11–16.

26. American Minister Crum to Secretary of State, May 9, 1912, American Minister Crum to Secretary of State, May 16, 1912, FRUS, 1912: Liberia, 658.

27. American Minister Crum to Secretary of State, January 8, 1912, FRUS, 1912: Liberia, 652–53; Message of the President (of Liberia) to the Legislature, December 12, 1912, FRUS, 1912: Liberia, 649–52. Colonel William D. Lomax was the officer who commanded contingents of the Frontier Force during the Grebo rebellion in 1910.

28. American Minister Crum to Secretary of State, January 8, 1912, FRUS, 1912: Liberia, 652–53; Message of the President (of Liberia) to the Legislature, December 12, 1912, FRUS, 1912: Liberia, 649–52.

29. Message of the President (of Liberia) to the Legislature, December 17, 1913; Chargé Bundy to Secretary of State, October 12, 1912 and November 7, 1912, FRUS, 1913: Liberia, 654–59.

30. Chargé Bundy to Secretary of State, November 7, 1912, FRUS, 1913: Liberia, 660.

31. Chargé Bundy to Secretary of State, November 11, 1912, FRUS, 1913: Liberia, 659–62.

32. Chargé Bundy to Secretary of State, November 11, 1912, FRUS, 1913: Liberia, 662; Ross, *Out of Africa*, 60. Ross and Young maintained a friendship throughout their stay in Liberia.

33. Chargé Bundy to Secretary of State, November 12 and December 26, 1912, FRUS, 1913: Liberia, 662; Ross, *Out of Africa*, 60.

34. Chargé Bundy to Secretary of State, December 26, 1912, January 10, 1913, January 14, 1913, FRUS, 1913: Liberia, 662–65.

35. Chargé Bundy to the Secretary of State, January 13, 1913, April 30, 1913, FRUS, 1913: Liberia, 666–80.

36. President Howard to Young, November 23, 1912, RDSIAL, 55.

37. Major Young to President Howard, November 24, 1912, Charles Young Collection, NAAMCC. In November Young sent a cable to the War Department requesting a pair of Colt revolvers for himself. Since Young was not a member of the LFF, he was not issued a weapon by the Liberian government. Index to Records of the War College Division, 7468-1, November 9, 1912, NARA.

38. "Diary of the Browne Relief Expedition," Charles Young Collection, NAAMCC; Major Young to Howard, November 24, 1912, Charles Young Collection, NAAMCC; Notes on Young's Report, Heinl Collection. There are several versions of Young's "Browne Relief Expedition." I chose to use the leather-bound original version written by Young that he carried with him on the mission, now held in the Charles Young Collection at the NAAMCC.

39. "Diary of the Browne Relief Expedition," Charles Young Collection, NAAMCC; Notes on Young's Report, Heinl Collection; Liebenow, Liberia, 26–27.

40. "Diary of the Browne Relief Expedition," Charles Young Collection, NAAMCC; Notes on Young's Report, Heinl Collection.

41. "Diary of the Browne Relief Expedition," Charles Young Collection, NAAMCC; Notes on Young's Report, Heinl Collection. It is unclear whether the Mano people practiced cannibalism at the time, but Graham Greene noted during his visit to Mano country in 1935 that "ritual cannibalism practiced on strangers has never been entirely stamped out." Greene, Journey without Maps, 164.

42. "Diary of the Browne Relief Expedition," Charles Young Collection, NAAMCC; Notes on Young's Report, Heinl Collection; Greene, Colonel Charles Young, 86–87. In his report Young describes the Muslim Mandingoes mistakenly as the "black Jews of Africa."

43. "Diary of the Browne Relief Expedition," Charles Young Collection, NAAMCC; Notes on Young's Report, Heinl Collection; Greene, Colonel Charles Young, 86–87.

44. "Diary of the Browne Relief Expedition," Charles Young Collection, NAAMCC; Kilroy, For Race and Country, 87.

45. "Diary of the Browne Relief Expedition," Charles Young Collection, NAAMCC; Fletcher, Black Soldier and Officer, 95; Ford, "Pacification under Pressure," 48–50.

46. "Diary of the Browne Relief Expedition," Charles Young Collection, NAAMCC; Ford, "Pacification under Pressure," 48–50.

47. Major Young to the Secretary, War College Division, General Staff, January 19, 1913, RDSIAL, 46; The Crisis, November 1915, 65; New York Age, October 18, 1915, 8.

48. Major Young to the Secretary, War College Division, General Staff, January 19, 1913, RDSIAL, 46; The Crisis, November 1915, 65; New York Age, October 18, 1915, 8.

49. Taft, "Fourth Annual Message," December 3, 1912.

50. Major Young to the Secretary, War College Division, General Staff, January 19, 1913, RDSIAL, 46.

51. Major Young to the Secretary, War College Division, General Staff, January 19, 1913, RDSIAL, 46.

52. Major Young to Washington, January 25, 1913, Harlan and Smock, *Booker T. Washington Papers*, Vol. 12, 109–10.

53. Chargé Bundy to Secretary of State, April 14, 1913, RDSIAL, 42–44; Greene, *Colonel Charles Young*, 90–91.

54. Chargé Bundy to Secretary of State, May 15, 1913, FRUS, 1913: Liberia, 681–82; U.S. Department of State Register, 1912 (Washington DC: GPO, 1912), 12; Terrell, "History of the High School," 265.

55. Chargé Bundy to Secretary of State, March 27, 1913, RDSIAL, 36–38; Major Young to Washington, January 25, 1913, in Harlan and Smock, *Booker T. Washington Papers*, Vol. 12, 109–10.

56. Wulah, *Forgotten Liberian*, 35–36. The Gbandis and Kpelles, both of the Mende-Fu ethnic cluster, lived in the highland and savannah region wedged between Liberia, the French colony of Guinea, and the British colony of Sierra Leone. The Kpella people lived on both sides of the Liberian and Guinean borders, and their lives revolved around on the secret societies of Poro (male) and Sande (female), as well as their medicine men. The Gbandis shared the Poro secret society, as well as a reverence for medicine men. Both the Kpellas and the Gbandis resisted acculturation by the Americo-Liberians, and their rebellion continued three years before the Liberian Frontier Force managed to bring it to an end.

57. Dispatch List, Liberia, Young, 1913, NARA; Kilroy, *For Race and Country*, 88.

58. Chargé Bundy to Ada Young, May 31, 1913, Charles Young Collection, NAM MSS 22, no. 5, Box 3, NAAMCC. Ada had accompanied Charles during the first part of his assignment but returned to the United States because of her health and to accommodate the education of their children.

59. *Liberia Times*, October 15 and 30, 1913, 2–3, Charles Young Collection, NAAMCC; Bundy to the Secretary of State, September 27, 1913, FRUS, 1913: Liberia, 684–85.

60. *Liberia Times*, October 15 and 30, 1913, 2–3, Charles Young Collection, NAAMCC; Bundy to the Secretary of State, September 27, 1913, FRUS, 1913: Liberia, 684–85.

61. Chargé Bundy to Secretary of State, July 7, 1913, FRUS, 1913: Liberia, 682–83.

62. *Liberia Times*, September 30, 1913, Charles Young Collection, NAAMCC.

63. Dispatch List, Liberia, Young, 1913, NARA; Kilroy, *For Race and Country*, 88.

64. Rosenberg, *Financial Missionaries*, 79–80; Mark Benbow, e-mail to the author, June 20, 2015.

65. Booker T. Washington to Reed Page Clark, May 23, 1913, Harlan and Smock, *Booker T. Washington Papers*, Vol. 12, 183.

66. Booker T. Washington to Reed Page Clark, May 23, 1913, Harlan and Smock, *Booker T. Washington Papers*, Vol. 12, 183; Padgett, "Ministers to Liberia," 85.

67. Padgett, "Ministers to Liberia," 85; Kleber, *Kentucky Encyclopedia*, 136; George Washington Buckner, Interview.

68. Major Young to War Department, April 20, 1914, RDSIAL, 110–51.

69. Major Young to War Department, April 20, 1914, RDSIAL, 111–12. One of these young officers in training, Moses Grant, wrote a heartfelt letter to Young in early 1914. In it he explained his reasons for hesitating to attend the academy and join the Liberian officer corps. He explained: "My Government does not well appreci-

ate the services of one who will try to be honest and faithful in the discharge of his duties, and who as a soldier will expose his life to danger for his country's sake." He complained that the government never awarded positions of responsibility to indigenous people or Americo-Liberians without political connections. In spite of this, Grant entered the academy and embarked on a career as an officer at the urging of Major Young. Moses N. Grant to Major Young, February 22, 1914, Charles Young Collection, NAAMCC.

70. Major Young to War Department, April 20, 1914, RDSIAL, 112–20.

71. Major Young to War Department, April 20, 1914, RDSIAL, 121–42.

72. Major Young to War Department, April 20, 1914, RDSIAL, 120–37.

73. Major Young to War Department, April 20, 1914, RDSIAL, 143.

74. Young recounted the speech as follows: "Mr. President, ladies and gentlemen: The good book says: 'be ye bretheren'. (repeated three times). Live in peace. All of the Foreign Representatives here stand for peace. When the edifice of peace is completed at the Hague I think the top-most and most important stone of the structure will be Liberia's. Why?–Because Liberia has not trampled upon the rights of any man. I call upon you all to drink to the peace of the world and to the Prince of Peace." Major Young to War Department, April 20, 1914, RDSIAL, 143–44.

75. Major Young to War Department, April 20, 1914, RDSIAL, 144–45.

76. American Minister Buckner to Secretary of State, April 27, 1914, RDSIAL, 106–7.

77. American Minister Buckner to Secretary of State, June 17, 1914, RDSIAL, 152–53.

78. Major Young to Buckner, October 8, 1914, Charles Young Collection, NAAMCC.

79. Major Young to Bundy, September 26, 1915, Charles Young Collection, NAAMCC; Chargé Bundy to Secretary of State, May 15, 1913, Charles Young Collection, NAAMCC; Secretary of State to Woodson, October 6, 1913, RDSIAL, 71; Woodson to Secretary of State October 16, 1913, RDSIAL, 75.

80. Terrell, "History of the High School," 265.

81. Major Young to Bundy, October 27, 1913, RDSIAL, 92.

82. Major Young to Bundy, September 26, 1915, Charles Young Collection, NAAMCC; Ballard to Hawkins, November 30, 1914; Charles Young Collection, NAAMCC; Buckner to Secretary of State, July 15, 1914, Richard H. Newton Jr. Papers, Bertha Rhodes Collection. Pulmonary tuberculosis is an infectious disease caused by a bacteria and is spread through the air when people who have active tuberculosis in their lungs cough, spit, speak, or sneeze.

83. "Pledges by the Cape Palmas Greboes on Restoration to their Town Sites," "Programme of the Engagement on the President's Visit to Maryland County with Reference to the Restoration of the Cape Palmas Greboes," Frederick Starr Collection, Howard University Library, Washington DC.

84. Chargé Bundy to Secretary of State, June 8, 1915, RDSIAL, 156–63.

85. Chargé Bundy to Secretary of State, June 8, 1915, RDSIAL, 156–63; Young to Bundy, September 26, 1915, Ballard to Hawkins, November 30, 1914, Ballard to Young, May 26 and June 2, 1915, Ballard to Martin, May 26, 1915, Charles Young Collection, NAAMCC; Buckner to Secretary of State, July 15, 1914, Richard H. Newton Jr. Papers, Bertha Rhodes Collection.

86. Major Young to Bundy, September 26, 1915, Charles Young Collection, NAAMCC; Dunn, Beyland, and Burrows, *Historical Dictionary of Liberia*, 196; Clegg, "A Splendid Type," 69.

87. Agreement between the United Kingdom and Liberia respecting the boundary between Sierra Leone and Liberia from the River Makona or Moa in the north to the River Magowi in the south, London, June 19/26, 1917, Treaty Series 1917, No. 9, http://treaties.fco.gov.uk/docs/pdf/1917/ts0009.pdf, accessed on October 16, 2017; Bundy to Young, July 21, 1916, Charles Young Collection, NAAMCC; *The Crisis*, November 1915, 65; *New York Age*, October 18, 1915, 8.

88. Major Young to Maj. Charles Crawford, Liberian Dispatches, December 31, 1914, RG 165, NARA.

89. Padgett, "Ministers to Liberia," 85; Kleber, *Kentucky Encyclopedia*, 136.

90. Bundy to Secretary of State Diplomatic Note 119, September 29, 1915, Charles Young Collection, NAAMCC.

91. Major Young to Bundy, September 26, 1915, Charles Young Collection, NAAMCC.

92. Major Young to York, September 26, 1915, Charles Young Collection, NAAMCC.

93. Major Young to Col. Delamere Skerrett, July 26, 1915, Delamere Skerrett Papers, U.S. Military Academy Library Special Collections; Young to Col. Alexander Piper, July 26, 1915, Alexander R. Piper Papers, U.S. Military Academy Library Special Collections. Young's records show that he paid a mapmaker named A. R. Mills between June and September 1914 to draft a map of Liberia, Vouchers June 30 and September 30, 1914, for A. R. Mills, Charles Young Collection, NAM MSS 21, no. 26, Box 1, NAAMCC.

94. Letter to Major Young from the Adjutant General, January 7, 1916, Charles Young Collection, NAAMCC; Chargé Richard Bundy to Secretary of State, December 17, 1915, FRUS, 1915: Liberia, 226–27.

95. *Boston Journal*, February 26, 1916; Spingarn Award Program, February 22, 1916, Charles Young Collection, NAAMCC.

96. Fletcher, *Black Soldier and Officer*, 95.

97. From a draft written with ideas on a book about Africa, penned sometime after his first tour in Liberia (1912–15), Charles Young Collection, NAAMCC.

5. York, Green, Anderson

1. Chargé Bundy to Secretary of State, September 28, 1915, FRUS, 1915: Liberia, 627; Hahn, "Experience of Land Grabbing," 73. State Robert Lansing issued a warning to the British ambassador if the ship remained "in Liberian water more than twenty-four hours" the U.S. would be concerned about British neutrality. FRUS, 1915: Liberia, 630.

2. Chargé Bundy to Secretary of State, December 17, 1915, FRUS, 1915: Liberia, 626–27; Executive Order by President Howard, October 26, 1915, Charles Young Collection, NAAMCC; Schmokel, "The German Factor," 37. According to Schmokel, the RLS (Republic of Liberia Ship) *President Daniel E. Howard* was a trading schooner formerly owned by the German Woermann firm that had been purchased by the Liberian government. There are other sources that indicate the ship might have been the former RLS *Lark* rechristened RLS *President Daniel E. Howard*. The only drawing we have of the RLS *Lark* shows it with two masts, so it fits the description of the RLS

President Howard. Both were referred to in descriptions as two-masted schooners, so they may have been the same ship.

3. President Howard to Major York, October 28, 1915, Charles Young Collection, NAAMCC.

4. USS *Chester* Log Book, November 8–9, 1915, RG 24, NARA.

5. USS *Chester* Log Book, November 9–10, 1915, RG 24, NARA. The other commission members included B. J. Davis, a Kru, J. F. Cooper, an Americo-Liberian, and four Kru servants.

6. USS *Chester* Log Book, November 11–12, 1915, RG 24, NARA.

7. USS *Chester* Log Book, November 11–12, 1915, RG 24, NARA.

8. USS *Chester* Log Book, November 13–21, 1915, RG 24, NARA.

9. USS *Chester* Log Book, November 18–December 5, 1915, RG 24, NARA. *Chester* departed for Freetown, Sierra Leone on December 5 to resupply its coal bunkers.

10. Chargé Bundy to Secretary of State, November 28 and December 1, 1915, FRUS, 1915: Liberia, 631–32.

11. USS *Chester* Log Book, December 15–17, 1915, RG 24, NARA; Chargé Bundy to Secretary of State, December 18, 1915, FRUS, 1915: Liberia, 633–34.

12. USS *Chester* Log Book, December 18–22, 1915, RG 24, NARA.

13. USS *Chester* Log Book, December 23, 1915 to January 19, 1916 RG 24, NARA. The full list of passengers transported from Sinoe to Monrovia included J. F. Cooper (Liberian), B. W. Payne, Liberian secretary of the interior, B. J. Davis (Liberian), Judge A. W. Witherspoon (Liberian), Major York (American), Mrs. Suchow (American), Joe Pippins (Kru), Peter Pin (Kru), and C. D. Davis (Kru). *Chester* lingered several weeks in Monrovia before steaming north to Dakar, Senegal, for replenishment on January 19, 1916.

14. Secretary of the Navy Daniels to Secretary of State, February 17, 1916, FRUS, 1916: Liberia, 455. These were model 1912 weapons, modern bolt-action magazine-fed carbines that could fire quickly and accurately.

15. Padgett, "Ministers to Liberia," 86–87; Tindall, *Emergence*, 144; Berg, *Wilson*, 409; Rountree to Young, November 6, 1916, Charles Young Collection, NAAMCC.

16. Minister James Curtis to Secretary of State, January 12 and February 7, 1916, FRUS, 1916: Liberia, 452–54; Schubert and Schubert, *On the Trail*, 110. Gillespie served in the Ninth Cavalry, Tenth Cavalry, and Twenty-Fourth Infantry.

17. Rountree to Young, November 6, 1916, Charles Young Collection, NAAMCC.

18. Rountree to Young, November 6, 1916, Charles Young Collection, NAAMCC.

19. USS *Chester* Log Book, March 17–19, 1916, RG 24, NARA.

20. USS *Chester* Log Book, March 19–24, 1916, RG 24, NARA.

21. USS *Chester* Log Book, March 19–24, 1916, RG 24, NARA.

22. Minister Curtis to Secretary of State, June 13, 1916, FRUS, 1916: Liberia, 456; Second Lieutenant Whisnant to the Commander, LFF, October 22, 1916, Charles Young Collection, NAAMCC.

23. Minister Curtis to Secretary of State, June 13, 1916, FRUS, 1916: Liberia, 456; Second Lieutenant Whisnant to the Commander, LFF, October 22, 1916, Charles Young Collection, NAAMCC.

24. Minister Curtis to Secretary of State, June 13, 1916, FRUS, 1916: Liberia, 456.

25. Dunn, Beyland, and Burrowes, *Historical Dictionary of Liberia*, 196; Clegg, "A Splendid Type," 69; Sundiata, *Brothers and Strangers*, 71.

26. Register of Enlistments in the U.S. Army, 1798–1915, 1899, RG 94, M233, NARA; Returns from Regular Army Infantry Regiments, 1821–1916, Twenty-Fourth Infantry, April 1899, RG 94, M665, NARA. Allensworth, one of four black chaplains in the Regular Army at the time, was keen to find African Americans qualified to become officers in an army expanding after the Spanish-American War.

27. Returns from Regular Army Infantry Regiments, 1821–1916, Twenty-Fifth Infantry, July 1901, RG 94, M665, NARA; Heitman, *Historical Register*, 473; Coffman, *The Regulars*, 49. Green's commission was backdated to February 2, 1901.

28. Returns from Regular Army Infantry Regiments, 1821–1916, Twenty-Fifth Infantry, July 1901, RG 94, M665, NARA; Heitman, *Historical Register*, 473. The army promoted Green to captain based on his qualifications and seniority two months after landfall in Monrovia on July 1, 1916.

29. Heitman, *Historical Register*, 626; Coffman, *The Old Army*, 222–29.

30. Gillespie to President Howard, September 6, 1916, Charles Young Collection, NAAMCC.

31. York to President Howard, September 25, 1916, Charles Young Collection, NAAMCC; Bundy to Young, July 21, 1916, Charles Young Collection, NAAMCC.

32. Second Lieutenant Whisnant to the Commander, LFF, October 22, 1916, Bundy to Young, July 21, 1916, Charles Young Collection, NAAMCC. Whisnant cited his own role as well as the initiative and bravery of Lt. Thomas E. Carr, Lt. Calvin R. Henson, Lt. James A. Holder, Lt. I. A. Tunning, Lt. Jallah Bah, and Lt. Wobayama Karwi; Henson was wounded and Tunning killed in action. Bundy mentioned the death of Tunning in a letter to Charles Young, lamenting, "I was very sorry to hear of this as he [Tunning] gave promise of being an efficient officer, and the LFF is sorely in need of good men." The effectiveness of the Americo-Liberian lieutenants during the battles against the Krus indicated the American officer academy, training, and mentorship were making headway.

33. Second Lieutenant Whisnant to the Commander, LFF, October 22, 1916, Charles Young Collection, NAAMCC. York did not play an active part in the April fighting and in June spent much of his time ferrying food and ammunition to his men and evacuating the wounded on board RLS *President Howard*.

34. Minister Curtis to Secretary of State, February 1, 1917, RDSIAL, 334–35.

35. Minister Curtis to Secretary of State, March 22, 1917, RDSIAL, 416–17; William H. York to W. E. B. Du Bois, April 8, 1924, W. E. B. Du Bois Papers, University of Massachusetts, Amherst.

36. Minister Curtis to Secretary of State, March 22, 1917, RDSIAL, 416–17; William H. York to W. E. B. Du Bois, April 8, 1924, W. E. B. Du Bois Papers, University of Massachusetts, Amherst.

37. Minister Curtis to Secretary of State, March 23 and April 19, 1917, Capt. John E. Green to Chargé Bundy, December 5, 1917, RDSIAL, 418–24, 449–53.

38. Secretary of State to Minister Curtis, April 4, 1917, FRUS, 1917: Liberia, 877–84.

39. Rosenberg, *Financial Missionaries*, 86. The white interior commissioners are discussed in detail in chapter 6 herein.

40. Major Green to Chargé Bundy December 5, 1917, RDSIAL, 449–53.

41. Ford, "Pacification under Pressure," 51–55.

42. Ford, "Pacification under Pressure," 51–55.

43. Secretary of State to Minister Curtis, April 4, 1917, Minister Curtis to Secretary of State, October 3, 1917, FRUS, 1917: Liberia, 877–87.

44. Minister Curtis to Secretary of State, August 13, 1917, FRUS, 1917: Liberia, 884–86.

45. U.S. Army Register of Enlistments, 1798–1914, RG 94, M233, NARA; John H. Anderson to Mr. Cooke, State Department, March 8, 1917, RDSIAL, 332–33.

46. John H. Anderson to Mr. Cooke, State Department, March 8, 1917, RDSIAL, 332–33; Hampton Normal and Agricultural Institute, *Southern Workman* 46, no. 1 (January 1917), 421.

47. John H. Anderson to Mr. Cooke, State Department, March 8, 1917, RDSIAL, 332–33; Hampton Normal and Agricultural Institute, *Southern Workman* 46, no. 1 (January 1917), 421.

48. Minister Curtis to Secretary of State, February 19, 1917, Chargé Bundy to Secretary of State, May 16, 1818, RDSIAL, 322–23, 481–83.

49. Minister Curtis to Secretary of State, February 19, 1917, Chargé Bundy to Secretary of State, May 16, 1818, RDSIAL, 322–23, 481–83.

50. Minister Ernest Lyon to Secretary of State, November 20, 1917, FRUS, 1917: Liberia, 895–96.

51. Helen Curtis Obituary, *Brooklyn Eagle*, May 24, 1942; U.S. Department of State Register, 1926, 109; *New York Age*, November 1, 1817, 1.

52. Helen Curtis Obituary, *Brooklyn Eagle*, May 24, 1942; U.S. Department of State Register, 1926, 109; *New York Age*, November 1, 1817, 1. After the war, Helen Curtis returned to Liberia to do missionary work and teach in Monrovia for nearly a decade.

53. Chargé Bundy to Young, July 21, 1916, Charles Young Collection, NAAMCC.

54. Chargé Bundy to Secretary of State, February 9, 1918, RDSIAL, 468–272.

55. Grant, *U-Boat Hunters*, 103–6; Johnson, *Bitter Canaan*, 125; Schmokel, "The German Factor," 37. While neutral, Liberia had closed both the French and German communications sites in Monrovia. After declaring war on Germany, Monrovia allowed the French to resume operations. President Howard refused to destroy the cable stations, but offered to close them down. This did satisfy the German submarine captain. But according to German sources, the Liberians provided sketches of the exact location of the cable stations in order to minimize civilian damage.

56. Grant, *U-Boat Hunters*, 103–6; Johnson, *Bitter Canaan*, 125. The British Royal submarine E-39 succeeded in sinking U-154 the following month off the coast of Spain on its return voyage to Germany.

57. Chargé Bundy to Secretary of State, February 9, 1918, RDSIAL, 484–89 II; USS *Raleigh* Log Book, May 7–8, 1919, RG 24, NARA.

58. "Lieutenant Colonel Green Rose From Ranks," *New York Amsterdam News*, December 25, 1929. Green was promoted to major on July 1, 1920, and to lieutenant colonel November 3, 1923, in the Regular Army.

59. Consular Reports of Marriage, 1910–1949, RG 59, NARA; Ernestine Green, interview by Anthony Powell, John E. Green Papers, Anthony Powell Collection.

60. Major Anderson to Mr. Cooke, September 19, 1918, RDSIAL, 509–11.

61. Extract From Annual Message of His Excellency, The President of Liberia, 1918, RDSIAL, 657.

62. Rosenberg, *Financial Missionaries*, 97.

63. Rosenberg, *Financial Missionaries*, 92.

64. Chargé Bundy to Acting Secretary of State, June 9, 1919, FRUS, 1919, vol. 2: Liberia, 528–30.

65. Acting Secretary of State to Secretary of the Navy, March 8, 1919, RG 80, NARA; USS *Chattanooga* Log Book, April 11–21, 1919, RG 24, NARA.

66. Chargé Bundy to Acting Secretary of State, June 9, 1919, FRUS, 1919, vol. 2: Liberia, 528–30.

67. Chargé Bundy to Acting Secretary of State, June 9, 1919, FRUS, 1919, vol. 2: Liberia, 528–30.

68. Chargé Bundy to Acting Secretary of State, June 9, 1919, FRUS, 1919, vol. 2: Liberia, 528–30.

69. Major Anderson to Mr. Cooke, September 19, 1918, RDSIAL, 509–11; Wulah, *Forgotten Liberian*, 24–25, 32–49.

70. Major Anderson to Mr. Cooke, September 19, 1918, RDSIAL, 509–11; Wulah, *Forgotten Liberian*, 35–49.

71. Leopold, "Brief History of the Loma," 20.

72. Wulah, *Forgotten Liberian*, 35–49.

73. Chargé Bundy to Acting Secretary of State, June 9, 1919, FRUS, 1919, vol. 2: Liberia, 528–30.

74. Scott, *Scott's Official History*, 82–91.

75. Colonel Young to Mitchell, Commissioner General to the Republic of Liberia, March 27, 1919, Charles Young Collection, NAAMCC. The list of candidates Young rejected included John Watson, Antony Osborne, Charles Carver, William Payne, Horace Bivens (application withdrawn), Benjamin A. Anderson, D. P. Greene, John R. Green, Samuel F. Sewell, Elmer C. Smith, Robert Johnson, and W. A. Vrooman. Young noted that if he were forced to choose from the list, he would have chosen John R. Greene and W. A. Vrooman in spite of their age.

76. Colonel Young to Mitchell, Commissioner General to the Republic of Liberia, March 27, 1919, Charles Young Collection, NAAMCC.

77. Republic of Liberia certificate, Knight Official of the Liberian Humane Order of African Redemption, John E. Green Papers, Anthony Powell Collection; Dispatch List, Liberia, Green, 1919, NARA; U.S. Passport Applications, 1795–1925, NARA, via U.S. Passport Applications, 1795–1925 database, Ancestry.com, accessed October 10, 2017; .

6. Young: Final Post

1. Brigadier General M. Churchill to Chief, Personnel Branch, Operations Division, War Department, October 21, 1919, War Department Records, RG 165, NARA; Greene, *Colonel Charles Young*, 176.

2. Name Index to Correspondence of the MID, 1917–41, RG 165 Files 2345-742 and 2345-743, M1194, Roll 261, NARA.

3. "Report of an Examining Board in the Case of Lt. Colonel Charles Young," July 7, 1917, Heinl Collection. According to the report, Young had high blood pressure measured at 220 to 230 mm Hg systolic and 140 to 150 mm HG diastolic. Nancy Gordon Heinl copied this report from Young's service record, which was subsequently destroyed by fire in 1973 at the National Personnel Records Center in Saint Louis, Missouri.

4. Spingarn to Young, November 1, 1917, Young to Spingarn, November 5, 1917, Spingarn to Young, November 8, 1917, Ovington to Young, January 9, 1918, Charles Young Collection, NAAMCC.

5. Lewis, *W. E. B. Du Bois: The Fight for Equality*, 3, 100; Young to NAACP Board of Directors, July 4, 1918, MS 312, W. E. B. Du Bois Papers, University of Massachusetts, Amherst.

6. Ethel G. Prioleau to Ada Young, undated, Charles Young Collection, NAAMCC. Ethel's husband, Capt. George W. Prioleau, was a black chaplain in the army and served with Young in the Tenth Cavalry.

7. Ada Young Diary, January 1, 1923, Young Collection, NAAMCC; Kilroy, *For Race and Country*, 144–46.

8. Telegram from Secretary of State Lansing to American Consulate, Monrovia, January 3, 1920, RDSIAL, 551–53; Kilroy, *For Race and Country*, 144–46.

9. Dispatch List, Liberia, Young, 1920, NARA.

10. Republic of Liberia certificate, Knight Commander of the Liberian Humane Order of African Redemption, Charles Young Collection, NAAMCC.

11. Post Report Monrovia, July 24, 1926, Heinl Collection. Nancy Heinl wrote the file location for this entry as Archives State Dec. File RG 59 124.82/15 Box 1905.

12. Charles to Ada Young, March 8, 1920, Charles Young Collection, NAAMCC; Dunn, Beyan, and Burrowes, *Historical Dictionary of Liberia*, 151–52. The French had occupied and then acquired by treaty a sizable piece of land in the same area in Liberia in 1892.

13. Charles to Ada Young, March 8, 1920, Charles Young Collection, NAAMCC.

14. Wilberforce University Annual Catalogue, 1898, 35–36, Charles to Ada Young, March 8, 1920, Charles Young Collection, NAAMCC.

15. *Lincoln University Class Book, 1901*, 35; Powell, "Roster 9th Ohio Volunteers," 6; Passport Application, Henry Oliver Atwood, December 31, 1919, Passport Applications, 1795–1925, NARA, via U.S. Passport Applications, 1795–1925 database, Ancestry. com, accessed October 10, 2017; Charles to Ada Young, March 8, 1920, Charles Young Collection, NAAMCC; Schneller, *Breaking the Color Barrier*, 79.

16. *Lincoln University Class Book, 1901*, 35; Ada to Charles Young, March 8, 1920, Charles Young Collection, NAAMCC; Schneller, *Breaking the Color Barrier*, 79.

17. Returns from Regular Army Cavalry Regiments, 1866–1916, Ninth Cavalry, December 1912, RG 94, M665, NARA; U.S. Army Register of Enlistments, 1798–1914, RG 94, M233, NARA; *Pittsburgh Courier*, December 19, 1942, 12; Scott, *Scott's Official History*, appendix A; Motley, *Invisible Soldier*, 12. Colonel Howard Donovan Queen attended the course taught by Young at Fort Huachuca and wrote about it in Mot-

ley's book. Nabors attended Young's Fort Huachuca training school for black officers and was among fifteen who passed the officers' exam. But the army did not recognize these commissions and made the fifteen officers attend the Fort Des Moines officers' course.

18. Iowa, State Census Collection, 1836–1925, 1925, Iowa Historical Society, United States Federal Census, 1910, NARA, Passport Application, Allen Clyde Bean, September 5, 1896, Passport Applications, 1795–1925, NARA, via U.S. Passport Applications, 1795–1925 database, Ancestry.com, accessed October 10, 2017; *Wilberforce Bulletin*, April 1917, 55th Annual Report to the Trustees of Wilberforce University, June 20, 1918, Wilberforce University Annual Catalogue, 1918–1919, Charles Young Collection, NAAMCC.

19. State Department History Office List of Chiefs of Mission for Liberia, Joseph L. Johnson, https://history.state.gov/departmenthistory/people/johnson-joseph-lowery, accessed October 17, 2017; Padgett, "Ministers to Liberia," 87; Hampton Normal and Agricultural Institute, *Southern Workman* 47, no. 1 (January 1918); U.S. Department of State Register, 1926, 109.

20. Cooper, *Woodrow Wilson*, 529–35.

21. Padgett, "Ministers to Liberia," 87; Charles to Ada Young, March 8, 1920, Charles Young Collection, NAAMCC.

22. "H. F. Worley—A True Renaissance Man," *U.S. Customs Today*, September 2000.

23. Charles to Ada Young, March 8, 1920, Charles Young Collection, NAAMCC; Dunn, Beyan, and Burrowes, *Historical Dictionary of Liberia*, 168–69, 189.

24. Ranard, *Liberians*, 13; Coger, "American District Commissioners," 29. The True Whig Party ruled Liberia from 1878 to 1980.

25. Cooper to Secretary Interior, January 16, 1920, Charles Young Collection, NAAMCC.

26. Cooper to Secretary Interior, January 16, 1920, Charles Young Collection, NAAMCC.

27. *Monrovia Weekly Review*, July 17, 1920, Charles Young Collection, NAAMCC.

28. Colonel Young to W. E. B. Du Bois, July 20, 1920, Charles Young Collection, NAAMCC.

29. Rosenberg, *Financial Missionaries*, 125; James Weldon Johnson, "The Truth about Haiti: An NAACP Investigation," *The Crisis*, September 1920, 217–24.

30. Coger, "American District Commissioners," 24–34.

31. *Engineering News Record* 82, no. 6, 310; Georgia, World War I Service Cards, 1917–1919, via U.S. Passport Applications, 1795–1925 database, Ancestry.com, accessed October 10, 2017. Mitchell returned to the United States in June 1918, enlisted in the U.S. Army, and attended Engineer Officer Training at Camp Humphreys, Virginia, but was discharged on October 31, 1918 as the war was ending.

32. USS *Chatanooga* Log Book, April 11-21, 1919, RG 24, NARA.

33. Coger, "American District Commissioners," 30–31.

34. Coger, "American District Commissioners," 30.

35. Coger, "American District Commissioners," 33.

36. Coger, "American District Commissioners," 33.

37. Coger, "American District Commissioners," 34.

38. Worley and Contee, "The Worley Report on the Pan-African Congress of 1919," 140–43; *The Crisis*, December 1920, 56; Contee, "Du Bois, the NAACP, and the Pan African Congress of 1919," 25.

39. USS *Chattanooga* Log Book, June 1–8, 1920, NARA; Coger, "American District Commissioners," 32.

40. Colonel Young to Bundy, November 8, 1920, Charles Young Collection, NAAMCC.

41. Colonel Young to Dr. Robert Russa Moton, January 22, 1921, Charles Young Collection, NAAMCC.

42. Colonel Young to Dr. Robert Russa Moton, January 22, 1921, Charles Young Collection, NAAMCC; Dispatch List, Liberia, Young, 1921, NARA.

43. Colonel Young to Dr. Robert Russa Moton, January 22, 1921, Charles Young Collection, NAAMCC.

44. "An Exposé of the Present Liberian Situation," Thomas McCants-Stewart, undated, Charles Young Collection, NAAMCC.

45. Minister in Liberia (Johnson) to the Acting Secretary of State, January 8, 1921, FRUS, 1921, vol. 2: Liberia, 363; The Secretary of State to President Harding, January 4, 1922, FRUS, 1922, vol. 2: Liberia, 606–11; Acting Secretary of State to Minister in Liberia (Hood), February 21, 1922, FRUS, 1922, vol. 2: Liberia, 612.

46. Secretary of State to Secretary of the Navy, November 5, 1921, Commanding Officer, USS *Denver* to Chief of Naval Operations, January 9, 1922, RG 80, NARA 1. The Liberian commission comprised President C. D. E. King, Associate Justice of the Supreme Court F. E. R. Johnson, former secretary of the treasury John L. Morris, commission secretary Gabriel Dennis, and the president's valet Sangba.

47. Captain Kautz to Chief of Naval Operations, January 9, 1922, RG 80, NARA 1. Capt. Austin Kautz, who later became the naval attaché to Germany, died in 1927 after a prolonged attack of hiccups following an operation for an ulcer of the stomach.

48. Rosenberg, *Financial Missionaries*, 97–119.

49. Secretary of State to President Harding, January 4, 1922, FRUS, 1922, vol. 2: Liberia, 606–11; Acting Secretary of State to Minister in Liberia (Hood), February 21, 1922, FRUS, 1922, vol. 2: Liberia, 612; Secretary of State to Minister in Liberia (Hood), May 21, 1922, FRUS, 1922, vol. 2: Liberia, 617; Secretary of State to Minister in Liberia (Hood), December 8, 1922, FRUS, 1922, vol. 2: Liberia, 632–33.

50. Garvey, *Selected Writings and Speeches*, 1–7; Ciment, *Another America*, 146.

51. King, "An Open Letter," April 13, 1921, MS 312, W. E. B. Du Bois Papers, University of Massachusetts, Amherst; Ciment, *Another America*, 154–56.

52. Colonel Young to Charles Cuney, May 15, 1920, in Hill, *Marcus Garvey*; Wilberforce University Annual Catalogue, 1898, Charles Young Collection, NAAMCC; Greene, *Colonel Charles Young*, 178–79.

53. Colonel Young to Charles Cuney, May 15, 1920, in Hill, *Marcus Garvey*.

54. Dispatch List, Liberia, Young, 1921, NARA; "The Universal Negro Improvement Association in the Liberian Legislature," *Liberian Patriot*, May 21, 1921, 4; Heinl, "Colonel Charles Young," 173–74.

55. Dispatch List, Liberia, Young, 1921, NARA; Young, "Garveyism: The Constitution of the UNIA," August 29, 1921, in Hill, *Marcus Garvey*, 78–79.

56. Young, "Garveyism: The Constitution of the UNIA," August 29, 1921, in Hill, *Marcus Garvey*, 78–79.

57. Young, "Garveyism: The Constitution of the UNIA," August 29, 1921, in Hill, *Marcus Garvey*, 78–79.

58. "Official Disapproval of Marcus Garvey's Political Propaganda," *African World*, July 30, 1921, 251.

59. Dispatch List, Liberia, Young, 1921, NARA. Of the seventeen, five concerned UNIA, four contributed to the *Liberia Monograph*, three enclosed maps, two addressed the political situation, and one each reported on Germany, aviation, and the Liberian Frontier Force.

60. American Minister Johnson to Secretary of State, December 28, 1921, and January 22, 1922, Heinl Collection; Dispatch List, Liberia, Young, 1921–22, NARA.

61. Dispatch List, Liberia, Young, 1921, NARA; Bidwell, *History of the Military*, 151–59.

62. Sherman Miles to Young, June 10, 1921, Charles Young Collection, NAAMCC; "Liberia Combat Factor" Monograph Subsection, MID, War Department, September 1920, Charles Young Collection, NAAMCC. The two War Department monographs in the NAAMCC are valuable artifacts and important sources of historical information. They were carried by Col. Charles Young on his second tour to Liberia as a military attaché and accompanied him when he died on a confidential mission to Nigeria in 1922. The monographs on Liberia and Nigeria represent early attempts by the War Department to create a series of geographic handbooks and country studies on the military and political affairs of the countries of the world. These two volumes may be the only known monographs from the 1920s to have survived.

63. Charles to Ada Young, November 11, 1921, Charles Young Collection, NAAMCC.

64. Geographic Index to Correspondence of the MID, Liberia, 1921, RG 165, M1474, NARA; American Minister Johnson to Secretary of State, December 28, 1921 and January 22, 1922, Heinl Collection; Dispatch List, Liberia, Young, 1921–22, NARA.

65. Dispatch List, Liberia, Young, 1920–21, NARA; Charles to Ada Young, December 6, 1920, October 18, 1921, November 11, 1921, Charles Young Collection, NAAMCC.

66. American Minister Johnson to Secretary of State, December 28, 1921, and January 22, 1922, Heinl Collection. Henry Atwood, who did not formally work at the legation, did arrive shortly before Young's death in Nigeria.

67. Young, "African Journey," Charles Young Collection, NAAMCC.

68. Young, "African Journey," Charles Young Collection, NAAMCC; Maynard H. Jackson, "An African Elegy," *Associated Negro Press*, October 13, 1922, Moorland-Spingarn Collection. Inside the front cover of Young's journal is the Washington DC address of H. O. Atwood (1315 T. St. NW) and the names and addresses of two individuals in Duala, Cameroon, named D. B. Onipede and M. S. Gabbidon Hayes.

69. Young, "African Journey," Charles Young Collection, NAAMCC.

70. Young, "African Journey," Charles Young Collection, NAAMCC.

71. Young, "African Journey," Charles Young Collection, NAAMCC.

72. Young, "African Journey," Charles Young Collection, NAAMCC; Receipt from Dr. Mccaulay's Dispensary to Col. Charles Young, December 15, 1921, Charles Young Collection, NAAMCC.

73. Sawyer to Ada Young, August 25, 1922, Charles Young Collection, NAAMCC.

74. Sawyer to Ada Young, August 25, 1922, Charles Young Collection, NAAMCC.

75. Telegraph, Young to British Bank of West Africa, Monrovia, December 26, 1921, Charles Young Collection, NAAMCC; Johnson to Secretary of State, December 28, 1921, and January 22, 1922, Heinl Collection; Kilroy, *For Race and Country*, 153.

76. Cable from Johnson to Secretary of State on December 28 and reply on December 31, 1921, Heinl Collection.

77. Death Certificate signed by Dr. William Walker, MD, January 9, 1921; Sawyer to Ada Young, August 25, 1922, Charles Young Collection, NAAMCC.

78. Sawyer to Ada Young, August 25, 1922, Charles Young Collection, NAAMCC; photos of the funeral ceremony, Charles Young Collection, NAAMCC; Cables from Johnson to Secretary of State, December 28, 1921, January 10 and January 22, 1922, Heinl Collection; Kilroy, *For Race and Country*, 153.

79. Photos of the funeral ceremony, Charles Young Collection, NAAMCC (fig. 32); Cables from Johnson to Secretary of State, December 28, 1921, January 10 and January 22, 1922, Heinl Collection; Kilroy, *For Race and Country*, 153.

7. Nabors, Staten, Outley

1. Name Index to Correspondence of the MID, 1917–41, File 2613-11, April 28, 1921, Charles Young File, M1194, NARA; Bidwell, *History of the Military*, 254–57. Because of spending cuts, Belgium, Czechoslovakia, Ecuador, Egypt, Holland, Hungary, Liberia, Sweden, and Switzerland lost U.S. military attaché positions. On the other hand, the MID planned to open new offices in China and Iran, leaving a total of twenty-four offices in operation by June 1922.

2. Secretary of War James Cooper to Maj. John Anderson, May 8, 1922, RDSIAL, 643–46; Maj. John Anderson to Secretary of State, February 17, 1923.

3. Consul General Solomon Hood to Secretary of State, May 8, 1923, RDSIAL, 699–701; New York Passenger Lists, 1820–1957, T517, Roll 3113, NARA, via U.S. Passport Applications, 1795–1925 database, Ancestry.com, accessed October 10, 2017; *New York Times*, February 16, 1922.

4. Consul General Solomon Hood to Secretary of State, May 8, 1923, RDSIAL, 702; New York Passenger Lists, 1820–1957, T517, Roll 3113, NARA, via U.S. Passport Applications, 1795–1925 database, Ancestry.com, accessed October 10, 2017; *New York Times*, February 16, 1922.

5. Memorandum on the Liberian Frontier Force, Facts Furnished by Major Anderson, July 21, 1922, RDSIAL, 810–17.

6. General Receiver H. M. Worley to Consul General Solomon Hood, March 18, 1922, RDSIAL, 638–39.

7. Auditor of Liberia S. de la Rue to the Liberian Secretary of State via the U.S. Consulate General, March 20, 1922, RDSIAL, 629–30.

8. Padgett, "Ministers to Liberia," 87–88; *The Crisis*, Horizon Section compiled by Madeline G. Allison, January 1922, 118.

9. A. D. Brewer to Director, United States Veterans Bureau, June 7, 1922, RDSIAL, 632; Department of State Telegram to American Legation, Monrovia, June 6, 1923, RDSIAL, 686.

10. Passport Application, Moody Staten, U.S. Passport Applications, 1795–1925, Roll 2313, NARA, via U.S. Passport Applications, 1795–1925 database, Ancestry.com, accessed October 10, 2017; Wynn, *Negro Who's Who*, 59.

11. Passport Application, Moody Staten, U.S. Passport Applications, 1795–1925, Roll 2313, NARA, via U.S. Passport Applications, 1795–1925 database, Ancestry.com, accessed October 10, 2017; Wynn, *Negro Who's Who*, 59.

12. Receiver de la Rue to Castle, Department of State, Division of Western European Affairs, July 10, 1924, RDSIAL, 804–6.

13. Rosenberg, *Financial Missionaries*, 98–119.

14. Rosenberg, *Financial Missionaries*, 98–119.

15. FRUS, 1925, vol. 2: Liberia, 367–418.

16. FRUS, 1925, vol. 2: Liberia, 367–418.

17. King to Du Bois, June 30, 1924, Du Bois to King, July 29, 1924, W. E. B. Du Bois Papers, University of Massachusetts, Amherst.

18. Du Bois, "Liberia, the League," 1; Hood to Du Bois, November 16, 1925, W. E. B. Du Bois Papers, University of Massachusetts, Amherst.

19. FRUS, 1925, vol. 2: Liberia, 367–495; FRUS, 1926, vol. 2: Liberia, 503–97.

20. Hood to Du Bois, January 20, 1926, March 11, 1926, W. E. B. Du Bois Papers, University of Massachusetts, Amherst.

21. Castle to Secretary of State, January 12, 1926, FRUS, 1926, vol. 2: Liberia, 503–5.

22. Secretary of State to President Coolidge, July 14, 1927, FRUS, 1927, vol. 3: Liberia, 152–56.

23. Chargé Wharton to Seretary of State, February 12, 1926, FRUS, 1926, vol. 2: Liberia, 521–22.

24. Draft Loan Agreement, FRUS, 1925, vol. 2: Liberia, 471.

25. Major Staten to Consul General Solomon Hood, January 19, 1925, RDSIAL, 824–26.

26. Secretary of War to Secretary of State, July 6 and September 23, 1925, RDSIAL, 827–42. The recommended names included Daniel T. Taylor, Charles H. Barbour, Abraham Morse, William B. Crawford, Frank L. Francis, Walter B. Williams, John Williams, and John Wynn.

27. Secretary of State to Liberian Consul General Ernest Lyon, December 8, 1925, RDSIAL, 923–24; "Master Sergeant Hansen Outley," *Message Magazine* 7, no. 9 (October 1941), 2.

28. Chargé Reed Paige Clark to Secretary of State, December 3, 1926, RDSIAL, 1026–31.

29. Annual Report of the Liberian Frontier Force, 1925–26, by Maj. Moody Staten, Commanding, September 29, 1926, RDSIAL, 1108–24.

30. Annual Report of the Liberian Frontier Force, 1925–26, by Maj. Moody Staten, Commanding, September 29, 1926, RDSIAL, 1108–24.

31. Annual Report of the Liberian Frontier Force, 1925–26, by Maj. Moody Staten, Commanding, September 29, 1926, RDSIAL, 1108–24.

32. Annual Report of the Liberian Frontier Force, 1925–26, by Maj. Moody Staten, Commanding, September 29, 1926, RDSIAL, 1108–24.

33. Chargé Reed Paige Clark to Secretary of State, December 3, 1926, RDSIAL, 1026–31.

34. Chargé C. E. Macy to the Secretary of State, August 10, 1927, RDSIAL, 1144–46.

35. *The Afro-American* (Baltimore MD), July 16, 1927, 15; *The Afro-American* (Baltimore MD), April 9, 1927, 4. This was shown with the arrest of Bishop W. Sampson Brooks of Baltimore, Maryland. Bishop Brooks had been in Sierra Leone for a religious conference when he heard his wife in Liberia was ill. Brooks tried to join his sick wife and was arrested in March 1927 upon arrival in Monrovia on a charge of debt filed by a disgruntled missionary.

36. Chargé Wharton to the Secretary of State, April 29, 1927, RDSIAL, 1035–36.

37. Chargé C. E. Macy to Secretary of State, August, 2, 1927, RDSIAL, 1067–68.

38. Secretary of War James W. Cooper to Maj. Moody Staten, May 26, 1927, RDSIAL, 1071.

39. Chargé C. E. Macy to the Secretary of State, July, 27, 1927, RDSIAL, 1074–77.

40. Chargé Reed Paige Clark to Secretary of State, December 3, 1926, Chargé C. E. Macy to the Secretary of State, July, 27, 1927, RDSIAL, 1026–1031, 1074–77.

41. Chargé C. E. Macy to the Secretary of State, August 4, 1927, RDSIAL, 1126–33.

42. Report of Inspection, Maj. Moody Staten, March 19, 1927, RDSIAL, 1084–1104.

43. Chargé C. E. Macy to the Secretary of State, July, 27, 1927, RDSIAL, 1074–77.

44. Chargé C. E. Macy to the Secretary of State, August 10, 1927, RDSIAL, 1144–46.

45. Douglas R. Heidenreich, "A Citizen of Fine Spirit," *William Mitchell Magazine* 18, no. 2 (Fall 2000), http://open.mitchellhamline.edu/facsch/109, accessed on October 18, 2017.

46. Consul General W. T. Francis to the Secretary of State, January 30, 1928, Capt. Hansen Outley to Secretary of War, July 1, 1927, RDSIAL, 1167–70, 1082–83.

47. Consul General W. T. Francis to the Secretary of State, January 30, 1928, June 9, 1928, RDSIAL, 1167–70, 1241–44.

48. Consul General W. T. Francis to the Secretary of State, January 30, 1928, June 9, 1928, RDSIAL, 1241–44.

49. Consul General W. T. Francis to the Secretary of State, June 9, 1928, October 31, 1928, RDSIAL, 1241–44, 1276–79.

50. Consul General W. T. Francis to the Secretary of State, May 18, 1928, RDSIAL, 1238–40.

51. Consul General W. T. Francis to the Secretary of State, May 18, 1928, RDSIAL, 1238–40.

52. Consul General W. T. Francis to the Secretary of State, May 18, 1928, RDSIAL, 1238–40.

53. Consul General W. T. Francis to the Secretary of State, November 19, 1928, RDSIAL, 1287–92.

54. Consul General W. T. Francis to the Secretary of State, November 19, 1928, RDSIAL, 1287–92.

55. Consul General W. T. Francis to the Secretary of State, November 19, 1928, RDSIAL, 1287–92.

56. Special Order No. 59, War Department, Office of the Liberian Frontier Force, November 14, 1928, RDSIAL, 1296.

57. Special Order No. 59, War Department, Office of the Liberian Frontier Force, November 14, 1928, RDSIAL, 1296.

58. Douglas R. Heidenreich, "A Citizen of Fine Spirit," *William Mitchell Magazine* 18, no. 2 (Fall 2000), http://open.mitchellhamline.edu/facsch/109.

59. Secretary Wharton to the Secretary of State, June 28, 1929, FRUS, 1929, vol. 3: Liberia, 285.

60. http://blackhistorynow.com/clifton-r-wharton-sr/. The "Negro Circuit" remained a fact of life for black diplomats until the end of World War II, after the desegregation of the Armed Forces, when President Harry Truman in 1949 appointed Wharton the diplomatic consul to Lisbon, Portugal, and President Dwight Eisenhower in 1958 appointed Wharton the Ambassador to Romania.

61. Chargé Carter to the Secretary of State, February 13, 1930, FRUS, 1930, vol. 3: Liberia, 454.

62. Chargé Carter to the Secretary of State, February 13, 1930, FRUS, 1930, vol. 3: Liberia, 454; New York Passenger Lists, 1897–1957, T715, Roll 4849, 13 October 1930. Carter was recalled due to drinking problems in June 1930 and replaced by Claude H. Hall. Samuel Reber Jr. replaced Hall in August 1930.

8. Firestone

1. Acting Secretary of State to Chargé Carter, January 13, 1930, FRUS, 1930, vol. 3: Liberia, 451–52.

2. Secretary of State to President of the United States, November 20, 1929, RDSIAL, 1492–95; Secretary of State to the Chargé Wharton, November 23, 1929, FRUS, 1930, vol. 3: Liberia, 449–50.

3. Lewis to Chargé Carter, November 20, 1929, RDSIAL, 1490–91; *The Afro-American* (Baltimore MD), June 28, 1930; *Daily Sentinel* (Rome NY), July 22, 1930.

4. Chargé Hall to the Secretary of State, July 2, 1930, FRUS, 1930, vol. 3: Liberia, 458.

5. *New York Post*, March 31, 1936, 13; Memorandum by Mr. Ellis O. Briggs of the Division of Western European Affairs, June 18, 1932, FRUS, 1932, vol. 2: Liberia, 740–41. Lewis resigned effective July 15, 1932, but departed before that because he called on Briggs at the State Department on June 16, 1932.

6. Irele, *Oxford Encyclopedia*, 301; Burrowes, *Power and Press Freedom*, 156.

7. Irele, *Oxford Encyclopedia*, 301; Burrowes, *Power and Press Freedom*, 156.

8. Report of the International Commission of Inquiry into the Existence of Slavery and Forced Labor in the Republic of Liberia, 5; Buell, "Liberian Paradox," 161.

9. Report of the International Commission of Inquiry into the Existence of Slavery and Forced Labor in the Republic of Liberia, 5; Johnson, "Seasons in Hell," 5, 214, 249, 275. Johnson was a native Virginian who later moved to Chicago to study the migration of blacks to the North. Johnson experienced combat in World War I and later moved to New York City and became a promoter of the Harlem Renaissance.

10. Report of the International Commission of Inquiry into the Existence of Slavery and Forced Labor in the Republic of Liberia, 133–34; Buell, "Liberian Paradox," 161–77.

11. Report of the International Commission of Inquiry into the Existence of Slavery and Forced Labor in the Republic of Liberia, 133–34; Buell, "Liberian Paradox," 161–77.

12. Nelson, *Liberia*, 44.

13. Chargé Reber to the Secretary of State, December 3, 1930, FRUS, 1930, vol. 3: Liberia, 378.

14. Secretary of State to Minister (Francis), June 5, 1929, FRUS, 1929, vol. 3: Liberia, 274–75.

15. Secretary of State to Minister (Francis), June 5, 1929, FRUS, 1929, vol. 3: Liberia, 274–75.

16. Colonel Young to Col. Delamere Skerrett, July 26, 1915, Chargé Bundy to Acting Secretary of State, June 9, 1919, FRUS 1919, Liberia, 528–30; "Diary of the Browne Relief Expedition," Charles Young Collection, NAAMCC.

17. Report of the International Commission of Inquiry into the Existence of Slavery and Forced Labor in the Republic of Liberia, 134.

18. Third Secretary of Legation in Liberia (Wharton) to the Secretary of State, June 28, 1929, FRUS 1929, vol. 3: Liberia, 285; Chargé in Liberia (Carter) to the Secretary of State, June 4, 1930, FRUS 1930, vol. 3: Liberia, 329; Chargé in Liberia (Hall) to the Secretary of State, June 25, 1930, FRUS 1930, vol. 3: Liberia, 333; Chargé in Liberia (Reber) to the Secretary of State, September 8, 1930, FRUS 1930, vol. 3: Liberia, 348;. After the death of Francis, a series of acting consul generals ran the mission in Monrovia for short periods. No fewer than four men led the American consulate between July 1929 and February 1931: Clifton R. Wharton, Henry Carter, Claude H. Hall Jr., and Samuel Reber Jr. Even though Wharton was a black career diplomat, Carter, Hall, and Reber were white Foreign Service officers who could never be as effective as a black political appointee. The Americo-Liberian elite had a great deal of respect for African American political appointees who enjoyed the backing and confidence of the president of the United States. However, this esteem did not convey to career diplomats.

19. Briggs, *Proud Servant*, 68.

20. Briggs, *Proud Servant*, 68.

21. Plischke, *U.S. Department of State*, 319.

22. Plischke, *U.S. Department of State*, 319. The Liberian government requested Mitchell's recall in February 1933. Mitchell left Monrovia a month later, having accomplished little in two years.

23. Williams, *George S. Schuyler*, 54–56.

24. Williams, *George S. Schuyler*, 54–56.

25. Mower, "Republic of Liberia," 290–92.

26. Mower, "Republic of Liberia," 290–93.

27. Mower, "Republic of Liberia," 290; Du Bois, "Liberia, the League," 3; Dunn, Beyan, and Burrowes, *Historical Dictionary of Liberia*, 134–35.

28. Waters, *Historical Dictionary of United States–Africa Relations*, 104. I could not find the original State Department memorandum, but the exact quote is repeated verbatim in many sources.

29. Briggs, *Proud Servant*, 70–73.

30. Briggs, *Proud Servant*, 63–80. The Western Europe desk at the State Department had the Liberia portfolio because all the other African countries were colonized by European powers, and Liberia shared borders with British and French colonies. Briggs, a career diplomat and later ambassador (seven times), devoted a chapter to this mission in this superbly written and entertaining book.

31. Briggs, *Proud Servant*, 73–79.

32. Briggs, *Proud Servant*, 80; Mower, "Republic of Liberia," 294–95; Hahn, "Experience of Land Grabbing," 75. Monrovia hired two economic specialists from Poland and later announced a three-year plan and hired eight more consultants, most of whom were American.

33. Mower, "Republic of Liberia," 294–95; "Biographical/Historical Information," Lester Walton Papers, 1905–1977, New York Public Library, http://archives.nypl.org/scm/20633, accessed on October 17, 2017.

34. Mower, "Republic of Liberia," 294–95, Briggs, *Proud Servant*, 63.

35. Minister Mitchell to Secretary of State, December 9, 1931, FRUS, 1931, vol. 2: Liberia, 696; Davis, "Liberian Struggle for Authority," 260–61.

36. Minister Mitchell to Secretary of State, December 9, 1931, FRUS, 1931, vol. 2: Liberia, 696; Davis, "Liberian Struggle for Authority," 260–61; Greene, *Journey without Maps*, 192–204. Sources often identify Davis as an American officer and commander of the Frontier Force, but he was neither. Davis had served as an enlisted soldier and medical orderly in the U.S. Army before immigrating to Liberia and becoming a Liberian citizen. He was never an officer in the Frontier Force, which was commanded by a Liberian major at the time.

37. Minister Mitchell to Secretary of State, December 9, 1931, FRUS, 1931, vol. 2: Liberia, 696; Davis, "Liberian Struggle for Authority," 260.

38. Davis, "Liberian Struggle for Authority," 261.

39. Minister Mitchell to Acting Secretary of State, April 20, 1932, FRUS, 1932, vol. 2: Liberia, 713–14; Davis, "Liberian Struggle for Authority," 261.

40. Wulah, *Forgotten Liberian*, 256–66.

41. *New York Age*, February 15, 1936, 2; *New York Post*, April 23, 1936, 6.

42. *Pittsburgh Courier*, December 19, 1942, 12; Leonard Luzky, "History of the 1st Battalion, 372nd Infantry (Rifle) New Jersey National Guard," Newark Military, http://newarkmilitary.com/units/372natguard.php, accessed October 17, 2017.

43. Minister in Liberia (Walton) to the Secretary of State, April 22, 1939, Secretary of State to the Minister in Liberia (Walton), October 12, 1939, FRUS, 1939, vol. 4: Liberia, 567–69, 612–13.

9. Aftermath

1. Mower, "Republic of Liberia," 298–99; Patton, "Liberia and Containment Policy," 48.

2. Mower, "Republic of Liberia," 298–99.

3. Mower, "Republic of Liberia," 299.

4. "Soldier and Diplomat," *Carolina Times*, December 19, 1942, 2; Chargé Hibbard to Secretary of State, October 28, 1942, FRUS, 1942, vol. 4: Liberia, 415–16; *Fort Benning Bayonet*, November 4, 1943, 5.

5. Truth and Reconciliation Commission of Liberia, Final Report, 74.

6. Mower, "Republic of Liberia," 299.

7. Mower, "Republic of Liberia," 301.

8. Mower, "Republic of Liberia," 303–4.

9. Kramer, "Liberia," 4.

10. Fletcher, *America's First Black General*, 153–56. Davis had become the first African American general with his promotion to brigadier general on October 25, 1941.

11. Fletcher, *America's First Black General*, 153–56.

12. Kramer, "Liberia," 4.

13. Kramer, "Liberia," 4.

14. Kramer, "Liberia," 4–5; Robinson, "Where the State," 209.

15. Kramer, "Liberia," 4–5; Foster et al., *House with Two Rooms*, 288.

16. Kramer, "Liberia," 5. Roosevelt's visit in 1943 was a not an official state visit.

17. Foster et al., *House with Two Rooms*, 55–56.

18. Kramer, "Liberia," 5; Foster et al., *House with Two Rooms*, 288; Axel Krigsman, e-mail to author, July 29, 2015.

19. Kramer, "Liberia," 5; Foster et al., *House with Two Rooms*, 288; *Register of Graduates and Former Cadets, 2010*, 5–15; Axel Krigsman, e-mail to author, July 29, 2015. James Madison Tukpah graduated in 1990 and Fombah Teh Sirleaf graduated in 1992. A West Point faculty member remembered that Tukpah had feared returning to his country because of the civil war. He worried that one faction or the other would incarcerate him upon his return.

20. Kramer, "Liberia," 5; Foster et al., *House with Two Rooms*, 288.

21. Kramer, "Liberia," 6; Foster et al., *House with Two Rooms*, 289.

22. Kramer, "Liberia," 7; Foster et al., *House with Two Rooms*, 289.

23. Kramer, "Liberia," 7–8; Foster et al., *House with Two Rooms*, 290.

24. Foster et al., *House with Two Rooms*, 290. The interrogation and torture were caught on film in grizzly detail.

25. Williams, *Liberia*, 164; *Register of Graduates and Former Cadets, 2010*, 5–15.

26. Foster et al., *House with Two Rooms*, 56–58.

27. Sirleaf, *This Child*, 8–13, 35–40, 57–62, 155–59, 221–27.

28. Sirleaf, *This Child*, 8–13, 35–40, 57–62, 155–59.

29. Sirleaf, *This Child*, 245–46. This was not the first time Sirleaf ran for president. After initially supporting Charles Taylor's bloody rebellion against Samuel Doe in 1990, she ran against Taylor in 1997. When Sirleaf continued to oppose Taylor after the election she was charged with treason, threatened with arrest, and forced into exile.

30. Sirleaf, *This Child*, 244–69. President Sirleaf ran successfully for reelection in 2011.

31. *Register of Graduates and Former Cadets, 2010*, 5–15; Johnny Dwyer, "Strained Relations," October 28, 2010, http://content.time.com/time/world/article/0,8599 ,2028194,00.html, accessed October 17, 2017. James Madison Tukpah, who gradu-

ated with the class of 1990, served initially as national security advisor but was dismissed from his post in 2006 for failure to perform his duties and allegations of graft.

32. Briggs, "Civilian and Enlisted," 5.

33. Briggs, "Civilian and Enlisted," 5; Malan, *Security Sector Reform in Liberia*, X.

34. Accra Peace Agreement, Implementation History of Military Reform, https://peaceaccords.nd.edu/accord/accra-peace-agreement, accessed December 11, 2013.

35. Accra Peace Agreement, Implementation History of Military Reform, https://peaceaccords.nd.edu/accord/accra-peace-agreement, accessed December 11, 2013; McFate, "I Built an African Army."

36. Accra Peace Agreement, Implementation History of Military Reform, https://peaceaccords.nd.edu/accord/accra-peace-agreement, accessed December 11, 2013; McFate, "I Built an African Army"; Malan, *Security Sector Reform in Liberia*, 36–37.

37. Accra Peace Agreement, Implementation History of Military Reform, https://peaceaccords.nd.edu/accord/accra-peace-agreement, accessed December 11, 2013; McFate, "I Built an African Army"; Malan, *Security Sector Reform in Liberia*, 37.

38. Accra Peace Agreement, Implementation History of Military Reform, https://peaceaccords.nd.edu/accord/accra-peace-agreement, accessed on December 11, 2013; Mae Azango, "Liberia: On Their Own—Liberia Trains Armed Forces Without Foreign Input, Post DYNCORP," December 4, 2013, online at http://allafrica.com/stories/201312050840.html, accessed October 17, 2017; Twenty-Sixth Progress Report of the Secretary-General on the United Nations Mission in Liberia, 10; "Liberia: New Army Chief Inducted," *New Dawn* (Monrovia), February 12, 2014. Prince C. Johnson III is the son of Prince Johnson, who was Charles Taylor's first AFL chief of staff.

39. Accra Peace Agreement, Implementation History of Military Reform, https://peaceaccords.nd.edu/accord/accra-peace-agreement, accessed December 11, 2013; Azango, "Liberia: On Their Own"; Twenty-Sixth Progress Report of the Secretary-General on the United Nations Mission in Liberia, 10; "Liberia: New Army Chief Inducted," *New Dawn* (Monrovia), February 12, 2014.

Bibliography

Manuscripts and Archives

Anthony Powell, Private Collection
  John E. Green Papers.
Bertha Rhodes, Private Collection, Baltimore MD
  Richard H. Newton Jr. Papers.
Keith Rountree, Private Collection, Atlanta GA
  William Rountree Papers.
Library of Congress, Washington DC
  Booker T. Washington Papers
Marcus Garvey Papers and UNIA Project, Los Angeles, California
  Marcus Garvey Papers.
Moorland-Spingarn Collection, Howard University, Washington DC
  Charles Young Papers.
  Frederick Starr Papers.
Nancy Heinl, Private Collection, Washington DC
  Charles Young Papers.
National Afro-American Museum and Cultural Center, Wilberforce OH (NAAMCC)
  Benjamin O. Davis Papers.
  Charles Young Collection.
  John E. Green Papers.
National Archives and Records Administration, Washington DC (NARA)
  Annual Reports of the War Department.
  Congressional Documents.
  Foreign Relations of the United States (FRUS).
  General and Special Indexes to General Correspondence of the Secretary of the
    Navy, 1897–1926, RG 80, M1052.
  General Records of the Navy Department, General Correspondence, 1897–
    1915, RG 80.

Geographic Index to Correspondence of the MID of the War Department General Staff, 1917-41 RG 165, M1474.

Index to General Correspondence of the Adjutant General's Officer, 1890–1917, RG 94, M698 (Index to General Correspondence of AGO).

Index to Records of the War College Division and Related General Staff Offices, 1903–1914, RG 165, M912. (Index to Records of the War College Division).

Log Books of U.S. Navy Ships, Records of the Bureau of Naval Personnel, 1798–2007, RG 24.

Military Intelligence Division (MID) of the War Department General Staff, 1917–41, RG 165, M1194.

Name Index to Correspondence of the MID, 1917-41, RG 165, M1194.

Office of Naval Intelligence, Naval Attaché Reports, 1886–1939, RG 38.

Records of the War Department, Correspondence of the Secretary of War, Liberia.

Registers of Communications Received from Military Attachés and Other Intelligence Officers, 1889–1941, RG 165, M1271 (Dispatch List).

Register of Enlistments in the U.S. Army, 1798–1915, RG 94, M233.

Registers of the Department of State.

Returns from Regular Army Cavalry Regiments, 1866–1916, RG 391, M744.

Returns from Regular Army Infantry Regiments, 1821–1916, RG 94, M665.

Selected Documents Relating to Blacks Nominated for Appointment to the United States Military Academy During the 19th Century, 1870–1887. RG 94, M1002.

United States Congressional Serial Set, Issue 5659, 1910.

U.S. Department of State, Office of the Historian, Principal Officers and Chiefs of Mission, RG 59.

U.S. Department of State, Records of the Department of State Relating to Internal Affairs of Liberia, 1910–1929, Roll 11, RG 59, M613 (RDSIAL).

U.S. Department of State, Records of the Department of State Relating to Political Relations Between Liberia and Other States, 1919–1929, RG 59, M613.

U.S. Passport Applications, 1795–1905, RG 59, M1379.

U.S. Passport Applications, January 2, 1906–March 31, 1925, RG 59, M1490.

U.S. Army Heritage and Educational Center

Benjamin O. Davis, Sr. Papers

Special Collections, U.S. Military Academy Library, West Point NY

Joseph D. Leitch Papers.

Alexander R. Piper Papers.

Delamere Skerrett Papers.

Charles Young Papers.

W. E. B. Du Bois Papers, University of Massachusetts, Amherst

W. E. B. Du Bois Papers.

Published Works

Accra Peace Agreement. United Nations Security Council. August 29, 2003. Accessed at University of Notre Dame Kroc Institute for International Peace Studies Peace Accords Matrix, https://peaceaccords.nd.edu/accord/accra-peace-agreement.

Akingbade, Harrison. "The Pacification of the Liberian Hinterland." *Journal of Negro History* 79, no. 3 (Summer 1994): 277–96.

Akpan, M. B. "Black Imperialism: Americo-Liberian Rule over the African Peoples of Liberia, 1941–1964." *Canadian Journal of African Studies* 1, no. 2 (1973): 217–36.

Appiah, Anthony, and Henry Louis Gates. *Africana: The Encyclopedia of the African and African American Experience.* Oxford University Press, 2005.

Association of Graduates. *Register of Graduates and Former Cadets of the United States Military Academy.* West Point NY: Association of Graduates, 2000.

Association of Graduates. U.S. Military Academy Annual Reports. West Point: Association of Graduates Library, West Point.

Berg, A. Scott. *Wilson.* New York: G. P. Putnam's Sons, 2013.

Bidwell, Bruce W. *History of the Military Intelligence Division, Department of the Army General Staff: 1775–1941.* Frederick MD: University Publications of America, 1986.

Boahen, A. Adu. *Africa under Colonial Domination, 1880–1935, Volume 7.* London: James Currey, 1990.

Boot, Max. *The Savage Wars of Peace: Small Wars and the Rise of American Power.* New York: Basic Books, 2002.

Briggs, Ellis. *Proud Servant: Memoirs of a Career Diplomat.* Kent OH: Kent State University Press, 1998.

Briggs, Liza E. A. "Civilian and Enlisted Perspectives on the Armed Forces of Liberia: A Qualitative Research Study Report." U.S. Africa Command Directorate of Intelligence and Knowledge Development Social Science Research Center (October 2010).

Broussard, Albert. *African American Odyssey: The Stewarts, 1853–1963.* Lawrence: University Press of Kansas, 1998.

Broadstone, M. A. *History of Greene County Ohio.* Indianapolis: B. F. Bowen, 1918.

Buckley, Gail. *American Patriots: The Story of Blacks in the Military from the Revolution to Desert Storm.* New York: Random House, 2001.

Buell, Raymond L. "The Liberian Paradox." *Virginia Quarterly Review,* Spring 1931: 161–77.

Burrowes, Carl Patrick. *Power and Press Freedom in Liberia: 1830–1970.* Trenton NJ: Africa World Press, 2004.

Butcher, Tim. *Chasing the Devil: A Journey Through Sub-Saharan Africa in the Footsteps of Graham Greene.* New York: Atlas, 2010.

———. "Graham Greene: Our Man in Liberia," *History Today* 60, no. 10 (October 2010).

Campbell, James T. *Middle Passages: African American Journeys to Africa, 1787–2005.* New York: Penguin Books, 2006.

Chase, Hal S. "Struggle of Equality: Fort Des Moines Training Camp for Colored Officers, 1917." *Phylon* 39, no. 4 (1978): 297–310.

Ciment, James. *Another America: The Story of Liberia and the Former Slaves Who Ruled It.* New York: Hill and Wang, 2013.

Cirillo, Vincent J. *Bullets and Bacilli: The Spanish-American War and Military Medicine.* New Brunswick NJ: Rutgers University Press, 2004.

Clegg, Claude A. "A Splendid Type of Colored American: Charles Young and the Reorganization of the Liberian Frontier Force." *International Journal of African Historical Studies* 29, no. 1 (1996): 47–70.

Coffman, Edward M. *The Old Army: Portrait of the American Army in Peacetime, 1784–1898*. New York: Oxford University Press, 1986.

———. *The Regulars: The American Army, 1898–1941*. Cambridge MA: Belknap Press of Harvard University, 2004.

Coger, Dalvan M. "American District Commissioners on the Liberian Frontier." *Liberian Studies Journal* 10, no. 2 (1984): 24–38.

Conrad, Joseph. *Heart of Darkness*. 1902. Reprint, New York: Norton, 1963.

Contee, Clarence G. "Du Bois, the NAACP, and the Pan-African Congress of 1919." *Journal of Negro History* 57, no. 1 (January 1972): 13–28.

Cooper, John Milton, Jr. *Woodrow Wilson: A Biography*. New York: Alfred A. Knopf, 2009.

Davis, Deborah. *Guest of Honor: Booker T. Washington, Theodore Roosevelt, and the White House Dinner That Shocked the Nation*. New York: Simon and Schuster, 2013.

Davis, Ronald W. "The Liberian Struggle for Authority on the Kru Coast." *International Journal of African Historical Studies* 8, no. 2 (1975): 222–65.

Dineen-Wimberly, Ingrid. "To Carry 'the Black Man's Burden': T. Thomas Fortune's Vision of African American Colonization of the Philippines in 1902 and 1903." *International Journal of Business and Social Science* 5, no. 10 (November 2014): 69–74.

Du Bois, W. E. B. "Liberia, the League, and the United States." *Foreign Affairs* 11, no. 4 (July 1933): 682–95.

———. *The Souls of Black Folk*. Chicago: A. C. McClurg, 1903.

Duignan, Peter, and L. H. Gann. *The United States and Africa: A History*. Cambridge: Cambridge University Press, 1985.

Dunn, D. Elwood. *The Annual Messages of the Presidents of Liberia, 1848–2010*. Berlin: Walter de Gruyter, 2011.

Dunn, D. Elwood, Amos J. Beyan, and Carl P. Burrowes. *Historical Dictionary of Liberia*. Second Edition. Lanham MD: Scarecrow Press, 2001.

Ellis, George W. "Dynamic Factors in the Liberian Situation." *Journal of Race Development* 1, no. 3 (January 1911): 255–76. Charles Young had a copy of this in his library, now at the NAAMCC, page numbered 1–24, so there was one other separate printing.

Farrow, Edward S. *A Dictionary of Military Terms*. New York: Thomas Y. Crowell, 1918.

Fletcher, Marvin E. *American's First Black General: Benjamin O. Davis, Sr., 1880–1970*. Lawrence: University of Kansas Press, 1989.

———. *The Black Soldier and Officer in the United States Army*. Columbia: University of Missouri Press, 1974.

———. "The Black Volunteers in the Spanish-American War." *Military Affairs* 38, no. 2 (April, 1974): 48–53.

Forbes, Edgar Allen. *The Land of the White Helmets*. New York: Fleming H. Revell, 1910.

Ford, Martin. "Pacification under Pressure: The Political Economy of Liberian Intervention in Nimba, 1912–1918." *Liberian Studies Journal* 14, no. 2 (1989): 44–63.

Foster, Dulce, Dianne Heins, Mark Kalla, Michelle Garnett McKenzie, James O'Neal, Rosalyn Park, Robin Phillips, Jennifer Prestholdt, Ahmed K. Sirleaf II, and Laura A. Young. *A House with Two Rooms: Final Report of the Truth and Reconciliation Commission of Liberia Diaspora Project*. Saint Paul MN: DRI Press, 2009.

Gardiner, Robert. *Conway's All the World's Fighting Ships, 1860–1905*. Annapolis MD: Naval Institute Press, 1979.

Garvey, Marcus. *Selected Writings and Speeches of Marcus Garvey*. Edited by Bob Blaisdell. Dover DE: Dover Publications, 2004.

Gatewood, Willard B., Jr. *Aristocrats of Color: The Black Elite, 1880–1920*. Fayetteville AR: University of Arkansas Press, 2000.

———. *Smoked Yankees and the Struggle for Empire*. Chicago: University of Illinois Press, 1971.

———. "Black Americans and the Quest for Empire, 1898–1903." *Journal of Southern History* 38, no. 4 (November 1972): 545–66.

———. "William D. Crum: A Negro in Politics." *Journal of Negro History* 53, no. 4 (October 1968): 301–20.

Gershoni, Yekutiel. *Black Colonialism: the Americo-Liberian Scramble for the Hinterland*. London: Westview Press, 1985.

Gerber, David A. *Black Ohio and the Color Line*. Chicago: University of Illinois Press, 1976.

Grant, Robert McQueen. *U-Boat Hunters: Code Breakers, Divers and the Defeat of the U-Boats, 1914–1918*. Cornwall, UK: Periscope Publishing, 2003.

Greene, Graham. *Journey without Maps*. 1936. Reprint, London: Vintage, 2002.

Greene, Robert E. *Colonel Charles Young: Soldier and Diplomat*. Washington DC: R. E. Greene, 1985.

———. *Early Life of Colonel Charles Young: 1864–1889*. Washington DC: Department of History, Howard University, 1973.

Hahn, Niels. "The Experience of Land Grabbing in Liberia." In *Handbook of Land and Water Grabs in Africa*, edited by Tony Allan, Martin Keulertz, Suvi Sojamo, and Jeroen Warner. London: Routledge, 2013.

Harlan, Louis R. "Booker T. Washington and the White Man's Burden." *The American Historical Review* 71, no. 2 (January 1966): 441–67.

———. *Booker T. Washington, Volume 2: The Wizard Of Tuskegee, 1901–1915*. London: Oxford University Press, 1983.

Harlan, Louis R., and Raymond W. Smock. *The Booker T. Washington Papers, Volume 10: 1909–11*. Urbana IL: University of Illinois Press, 1981.

———. *The Booker T. Washington Papers, Volume 11: 1911–12*. Urbana IL: University of Illinois Press, 1981.

———. *The Booker T. Washington Papers, Volume 12: 1912–14*. Urbana IL: University of Illinois Press, 1983.

Heinl, Nancy G. "Colonel Charles Young: Pointman." *Army Magazine*, March 1977: 173–74.

Heitman, Francis B. *Historical Register and Dictionary of the U.S. Army*, Volume 1 and 2. Washington DC: U.S. Government Printing Office, 1903.

Hill, Robert A., ed. *The Marcus Garvey and Universal Negro Improvement Association Papers, Vol. 9*. Los Angeles: University of California Press, 1995. Available at http://mep.blackmesatech.com/mep/, accessed October 10, 2017.

Hurlbut, George C. "Liberia's New Boundary" *American Geographical Society* 40, no 1 (1908) 21–22.

Hurley, Vic. *Jungle Patrol: The Story of the Philippine Constabulary*. E. P. Dutton, 1938.

Irele, F. Abiola, and Biodun Jeyifo. *The Oxford Encyclopedia of African Thought, Volume 1*. New York: Oxford University Press, 2010.

Johnson, Charles, Jr. *African American Soldiers in the National Guard: Recruitment and Deployment During Peacetime and War*. Westport CT: Greenwood Press, 1992.

Johnson, Charles S. *Bitter Canaan: The Story of the Negro Republic*. New Brunswick NJ: Transaction Books, 1987.

Johnson, Harry H. *The Negro in the New World*. London: Methuen, 1910.

Johnson, Phillip James. "Seasons in Hell: Charles S. Johnson and the 1930 Liberian Labor Crisis." PhD diss., Louisiana State University, 2004. LSU Doctoral Dissertations 3905. http://digitalcommons.lsu.edu/gradschool_dissertations/3905.

Justesen, Benjamin R. "African-American Consuls Abroad, 1897–1909." *Foreign Service Journal*, September 2004: 72–76.

Karnow, Stanley. *In Our Image: America's Empire in the Philippines*. New York: Random House, 1989.

Kilroy, David P. *For Race and Country: The Life and Career of Colonel Charles Young*. Westport CT: Praeger, 2003.

Kleber, John E., Lowell H. Harrison, and Thomas Dionysius Clark. *The Kentucky Encyclopedia*. Lexington: University Press of Kentucky, 1992.

Kramer, Reed. "Liberia: A Casualty of the Cold War's End." *CSIS Africa Notes* 174 (July 1995).

Kromah, Alhaji G. V. "Capital Inflow and Sovereignty: Performance of Firestone in Liberia, 1926–1977." Alhaji Kromah Page. July 4, 2008. http://alhajikromahpage .org/alhajifirestone.htm.

Leopold, Robert S. "Brief History of the Loma People." *Liberran Studies Journal* 31, no. 2 (2006): 5–30.

Levitt, Jeremy I. *The Evolution of Deadly Conflict in Liberia*. Durham NC: Carolina Academic Press, 2005.

Lewis, David L. *W. E. B. Du Bois: Biography of a Race, 1868–1919*. New York: Henry Holt, 1993.

———. *W. E. B. Du Bois: The Fight for Equality and the American Century, 1919–1963*. New York: Henry Holt, 2000.

"The Liberian Commission." *Liberia* 33 (November 1908), 18–21.

Liebenow, J. Gus. *Liberia: The Quest for Democracy*. Bloomington: Indiana University Press, 1987.

Lincoln University Class Book, 1901. Lincoln PA: Lincoln University, 1901.

———. *Guardians of Empire: The U.S. Army and the Pacific, 1902–1940*.

Malan, Mark. *Security Sector Reform in Liberia: Mixed Results From Humble Beginnings.* Carlisle PA: Strategic Studies Institute, 2008.

Manby, Bronwen. *Citizenship Law in Africa: A Comparative Study.* New York: Open Society Institute, 2010.

Martin, Tony. *Race First: The Ideological and Organizational Struggles of Marcus Garvey and the UNIA.* Westport CN: Greenwood Press, 1976.

M'Bayo, Tamba E. "W. E. B. Du Bois, Marcus Garvey, and Pan-Africanism in Liberia, 1919–1924." *Historian* 66, no. 1 (2004): 19–44.

McFate, Sean. "I Built an African Army." *Foreign Policy,* January 7, 2010. http://foreignpolicy.com/2010/01/07/ i-built-an-african-army-2/.

Meiser, Jeffrey W. "Power and Restraint: Liberal Foreign Policy Theory and America's Rise, 1904–1912." Johns Hopkins University, 1910. Prepared for delivery at the 2010 Annual Conference of the American Political Science Association, Washington DC.

Melady, Thomas P. *Profiles of African Leaders.* New York: Macmillan, 1961.

Meredith, Martin. *The Fate of Africa.* New York: Public Affairs, 2005.

Miller, Stuart C. *Benevolent Assimilation: The American Conquest of the Philippines: 1899-1903.* Yale University Press, 1982.

Morgan, Anthony, Jr. "Kru Wars: Southeastern Revolt in 19th to Early 20th Century Liberia." nyenpan18.blogspot.com, January 6, 2011. http://mnyenpan18.blogspot .com/2011/01/kru-wars-southeastern-revolt-in-19th-to.html. Accessed October 8, 2017.

Morison, Samuel Eliot. *"Old Bruin": Commodore Matthew Calbraith Perry.* Boston: Little, Brown, 1967.

Moses, Wilson J. *The Golden Age of Black Nationalism.* Oxford, UK: Oxford University Press, 1988.

Motley, Mary P. *The Invisible Soldier: The Experience of the Black Soldier, World War II.* Detroit MI: Wayne State University Press, 1975.

Mower, J. H. "The Republic of Liberia." *Journal of Negro History* 32, no. 3 (July, 1947): 265–303.

Nelson, Harold D. *Liberia: A Country Study.* Third ed. Washington DC: U.S. Government Printing Office, 1985.

Nevin, Timothy D. "The Uncontrollable Force: A Brief History of the Liberian Frontier Force: 1908–1944." *International Journal of African Historical Studies* 44, no. 2 (2011): 275–97.

"Our Liberian Envoys Meet President Roosevelt." *Liberia* 33 (November 1908), 28–32.

Padgett, James A. "Ministers to Liberia and their Diplomacy." *Journal of Negro History* 22, no. 1 (January 1937): 50–92.

Patton, Adell. "Liberia and Containment Policy against Colonial Take-over: Public Health and Sanitation Reform, 1912–1953," *Liberian Studies Journal,* 2005: 40–65.

Pendleton, Leila A. *A Narrative of the Negro.* Chapel Hill: University of North Carolina, 1999.

Pham, John-Peter. *Liberia: Portrait of a Failed State.* New York: Reed Press, 2004.

Plischke, Elmer. *U.S. Department of State: A Reference History.* Westport CT: Greenwood Publishing Group, 1999.

Powell, Anthony. "Roster 9th Ohio Volunteers, Spanish-American War–1898/99." Portraits in Black. 2001. Accessed June 15, 2014. www.portaitsinblack.com.

Rainey, Timothy. "Buffalo Soldiers in Africa: The Liberian Frontier Force and the United States Army, 1912–1927." PhD diss., Johns Hopkins University, 2001.

Ranard, Donald A., ed. *Liberians: An Introduction to their History and Culture*. Washington DC: Center for Applied Linguistics, 2005.

Register of Graduates and Former Cadets, 2010. West Point NY: Association of Graduates, 2010.

Report of the International Commission of Inquiry into the Existence of Slavery and Forced Labor in the Republic of Liberia. September 8, 1930. Washington DC: U.S. Government Printing Office, 1931.

Robinson, Colin D. "Where The State Is Not Strong Enough: What Can Army Reconstruction Tell Us about Change Necessary to the OEDC DAC SSR Principles?" PhD diss., Cranfield University, 2015.

"Roland Post Faulkner." *Journal of the American Statistical Association* 35, no. 211 (September 1940): 543–45.

Rosenberg, Emily S. *Financial Missionaries to the World: the Politics and Culture of Dollar Diplomacy, 1900–1930*. Durham NC: Duke University Press, 2003.

——. "The Invisible Protectorate: The United States, Liberia, and the Evolution of Neocolonialism, 1909–40." *Diplomatic History* (1985): 191–214.

Ross, Emory. *Out of Africa*. New York: Friendship Press, 1936.

Schmokel, Wolf W. "The German Factor in Liberia's Foreign Relations." *Liberian Studies Journal* 7, no. 1 (1976): 37.

Schneller, Robert J., Jr. *Breaking the Color Barrier: The U.S. Naval Academy's First Black Midshipman and the Struggle for Racial Equality*. New York: New York University Press, 2005.

Schubert, Irene, and Frank N. Schubert. *On the Trail of the Buffalo Soldier II*. Lanham MD: Scarecrow Press, 2004.

Schufeldt, Robert W. *The U.S. Navy in Connection with the Foundation, Growth, and Prosperity of the Republic of Liberia*. Washington DC: John L. Ginck, 1877.

Scott, Emmett J. *Scott's Official History of the American Negro in the World War*. Emmett J. Scott, 1919.

Shellum, Brian G. *Black Cadet in a White Bastion: Charles Young at West Point*. Nebraska: University of Nebraska Press, 2006.

——. *Black Officer in a Buffalo Soldier Regiment: The Military Career of Charles Young*. Nebraska: University of Nebraska Press, 2010.

Sirleaf, Ellen Johnson. *This Child Will Be Great*. New York: Harper Collins, 2009.

Starr, Frederick. *Liberia: Description, History, Problems*. Chicago: Self-published, 1913.

Sundiata, Ibrahim. *Brothers and Strangers: Black Zion, Black Slavery, 1914–1940*. Durham NC: Duke University Press, 2003.

Taft, William Howard. "Fourth Annual Message," December 3, 1912. The American Presidency Project, edited by Gerhard Peters and John T. Woolley. www.presidency.ucsb.edu/ws/?pid=29553.

Terrell, Mary C. "History of the High School for Negroes in Washington." *Journal of Negro History* 2, no. 3 (July 1917): 252–66.

Tilley, Alvin B., Jr. *Between Homeland and Motherland: Africa, U.S. Foreign Policy, and Black Leadership in America.* Ithaca NY: Cornell University Press, 2011.

Tindall, George B. *The Emergence of the New South, 1913–1925.* Baton Rouge: Louisiana State University Press, 1967.

Truth and Reconciliation Commission of Liberia. Final Report. December 4, 2009. www.usip.org/publications/truth-commission-liberia.

Twenty-Sixth Progress Report of the Secretary-General on the United Nations Mission in Liberia. United Nations Security Council. August 12, 2013.

U.S. Congressional Serial Set, 1909–1910. Senate Documents, Document No. 457, Volume 60. Washington DC: GPO, 1910.

U.S. Department of State. Foreign Relations of the United States Diplomatic Papers, 1932. Volume 2: The British Commonwealth, Europe, Near East and Africa. Washington DC: GPO, 1932.

———. Foreign Relations of the United States Diplomatic Papers, 1939. Volume 4: The Near East and Africa. Washington DC: GPO, 1939.

———. Papers relating to the Foreign Relations of the United States with the Annual Message of the President Transmitted to Congress December 3, 1907. Part 2. Washington DC: GPO, 1907.

———. Papers relating to the Foreign Relations of the United States with the Annual Message of the President Transmitted to Congress December 7, 1909. Washington DC: GPO, 1909.

———. Papers relating to the Foreign Relations of the United States with the Annual Message of the President Transmitted to Congress December 6, 1910. Washington DC: GPO, 1910.

———. Papers relating to the Foreign Relations of the United States with the Annual Message of the President Transmitted to Congress December 7, 1911. Washington DC: GPO, 1911.

———. Papers relating to the Foreign Relations of the United States with the Annual Message of the President Transmitted to Congress December 3, 1912. Washington DC: GPO, 1912.

———. Papers relating to the Foreign Relations of the United States with the Address of the President to Congress December 2, 1913. Washington DC: GPO, 1913

———. Papers relating to the Foreign Relations of the United States with the Address of the President to Congress December 8, 1914. Washington DC: GPO, 1914.

———. Papers relating to the Foreign Relations of the United States, 1914. Supplement, The World War. Washington DC: GPO, 1914.

———. Papers relating to the Foreign Relations of the United States with the Address of the President to Congress December 7, 1915. Washington DC: GPO, 1915.

———. Papers relating to the Foreign Relations of the United States with the Address of the President to Congress December 5, 1916. Washington DC: GPO, 1916.

———. Papers relating to the Foreign Relations of the United States with the Address of the President to Congress December 4, 1917. Washington DC: GPO, 1917.

———. Papers relating to the Foreign Relations of the United States, 1918. Washington DC: GPO, 1919.

———. Papers relating to the Foreign Relations of the United States, 1919. Volume 2. Washington DC: GPO, 1919.

———. Papers relating to the Foreign Relations of the United States, 1921. Volume 2. Washington DC: GPO, 1921.

———. Papers relating to the Foreign Relations of the United States, 1922. Volume 2. Washington DC: GPO, 1922.

———. Papers relating to the Foreign Relations of the United States, 1925. Volume 2. Washington DC: GPO, 1925.

———. Papers relating to the Foreign Relations of the United States, 1926. Volume 2. Washington DC: GPO, 1926.

———. Papers relating to the Foreign Relations of the United States, 1927. Volume 3. Washington DC: GPO, 1927.

———. Papers relating to the Foreign Relations of the United States, 1929. Volume 3. Washington DC: GPO, 1929.

———. Papers relating to the Foreign Relations of the United States, 1930. Volume 3. Washington DC: GPO, 1930.

———. Papers relating to the Foreign Relations of the United States, 1931. Volume 2. Washington DC: GPO, 1931.

———. Register of the Department of State, 1912. Washington DC: GPO, 1912.

———. Register of the Department of State, 1926. Washington DC: GPO, 1926.

U.S. House of Representatives. Improvement of the Foreign Service: Hearings before the Committee on Foreign Affairs of the House of Representatives in H.R. 20044. Washington DC: GPO, 1912.

Van der Kraaij, F. P. M. *The Open Door Policy of Liberia*. Bremen, DE: Selbstverlag des Ubersee-Museum Bremen, 1983.

Vesser, Cyrus. *A World Safe for Capitalism: Dollar Diplomacy and America's Rise to Global Power*. New York: Columbia University Press, 2007.

Votaw, John F. "United States Military Attachés, 1885–1919: The American Army Matures in the International Arena." PhD diss., Temple University, 1991.

Wallis, Braithwaite. "A Tour in the Liberian Hinterland." *Geographic Journal* 35, no. 3 (March 1910): 285–95.

Washington, Booker T. *Up from Slavery*. Whitefish MT: Kessinger Press, 2004.

Waters, Robert A., Jr. *Historical Dictionary of United States–Africa Relations*. Lanham MD: Scarecrow Press, 2009.

Weigley, Russell F. *History of the United States Army*. New York: Macmillan, 1967.

Wilberforce University Annual Catalogue, 1898. Wilberforce OH: Wilberforce University, 1898.

Wilberforce University Annual Catalogue, 1918–19. Wilberforce OH: Wilberforce University, 1919.

Williams, Gabriel I. H. *Liberia: The Heart of Darkness, Accounts of Liberia's Civil War and Its Destabilizing Effects in West Africa*. Victoria, Canada: Trafford, 2002.

Williams, Oscar R. *George S. Schuyler: Portrait of a Black Conservative.* Knoxville: University of Tennessee Press, 2007.

Winkler, Jonathan R. *Nexus: Strategic Communications and American Security in World War I.* Cambridge MA: Harvard Historical Studies, 2008.

Wolters, Raymond. *Du Bois and His Rivals.* Columbia: University of Missouri Press, 2004.

Worley, H. F., and C. G. Contee. "The Worley Report on the Pan-African Congress of 1919." *Journal of Negro History* 55, no. 2 (April 1970): 140–43.

Wulah, Teah. *The Forgotten Liberian: History of Indigenous Tribes.* Bloomington IN: Author House, 2005.

Wynes, Charles E. "T. McCants Stewart: Peripatetic Black South Carolinian." *South Carolina Historical Magazine* 80 no. 4 (October 1979): 311–17.

Wynn, Commodore, ed. *Negro Who's Who in California.* Los Angeles: Negro Who's Who in California, 1948.

Yellin, Eric S. *Racism in the Nation's Service: Government Workers and the Color Line in Woodrow Wilson's America.* Chapel Hill: University of North Carolina Press, 2013.

Yenser, Thomas, ed. *Who's Who in Colored America.* Brooklyn NY: Thomas Yenser, 1944.

Young, Charles. *Military Morale of Nations and Races.* Kansas City MO: Franklin Hudson Publishing, 1912.

Young, James C. *Liberia Rediscovered.* Garden City NY: Doubleday, Doran, 1934.

Younger, Karen F. "Liberia and the Last Slave Ships." *Civil War History* 54, no. 4 (December 2008): 424–42.

Index

CPSIA information can be obtained
at www.ICGtesting.com
Printed in the USA
LVHW04s0231260818
588133LV00005B/402/P